GOD'S COP

Anderton admits to having a demanding, possessive mistress who dominates his life for 18 hours of every working day. Her name is Duty. Even though she is not always attractive and comforting, she has to be obeyed, without equivocation. She has heart, but no sentiment. And it was she, 'that stern mistress of the soul', who compelled him to call, in May 1986, for the suspension of his popular and distinguished deputy chief constable, John Stalker, and to have him permanently removed from what was to become known as the 'shoot to kill' inquiry into Northern Ireland's Royal Ulster Constabulary. 'But it was the blackest day of my life,' Anderton insists, explaining that he was under the influence of an uncompromising force that allowed him to make no concessions.

About the Author

Michael Prince was born in 1939 in the
Midlands. After school, he became a journalist
on his local paper. Following National Service,
he joined the *Daily Herald* in Manchester and
was soon transferred to London. Since then, he
has worked extensively throughout the world for
many national newspapers, including the *Daily
Mail*, the *Daily Telegraph* and *Time/Life*, New
York.

Michael Prince has always had a great interest in
politics – he was a speechwriter for various
government ministers for a number of years. He
now lives in Dorset with his wife and their son.

GOD'S COP

— THE BIOGRAPHY OF —
JAMES ANDERTON

MICHAEL PRINCE

NEW ENGLISH LIBRARY
Hodder and Stoughton

For Julie and Mark

Copyright © 1986 by Michael Prince

First published in Great Britain in 1988 by Frederick Muller, an imprint of Century Hutchinson Ltd

First published by New English Library paperbacks 1989

British Library C.I.P.

Prince, Michael, *1939–*
 God's cop: the biography of
 James Anderton.
 1. Great Britain. Police. Anderton,
 C. James (Cyril James), *1932–*
 Biographies
 I. Title
 363.2'092'4

ISBN 0-450-49362-8

Photoset by Centracet, Cambridge. Printed and bound in Great Britain for Hodder and Stoughton paperbacks, a division of Hodder and Stoughton Ltd., Mill Road, Dunton Green, Sevenoaks, Kent TN13 2YA (Editorial Office: 47 Bedford Square, London WC1B 3DP) by R. Clay Ltd., Bungay, Suffolk.

Contents

An Explanation and Some Acknowledgements

On Monday, 2 February 1987, I received the telephone call that was to shape this book.

'I read your article in the *Sunday Express* [it appeared on 25 January] about James Anderton,' said a male caller with a distinctly northern accent. 'I thought you were very fair. So did he. I've made my own enquiries about you. It seems you can be trusted. Are you interested in writing a much bigger story about Anderton?'

'That depends on what the story is,' I said. 'But first, who are *you*?'

Instead of answering my question, he said, 'All that matters is I know how to reach you.'

I had been contemplating a biography of James Anderton – surely the world's most enigmatic and controversial policeman – since I started literary negotiations with George Oldfield, the late assistant chief constable of West Yorkshire, leader of the Yorkshire Ripper hunt, who died before we could take the venture further. What I did not know on 2 February 1987 was that the mysterious caller knew all about my relationship with Oldfield.

The outcome of that conversation was a meeting in a Manchester pub. My new-found contact was to become one of four inside informants, reminiscent of Watergate's 'Deep Throat', who were brave to the point of foolhardy in the way they helped me, without financial reward, to uncover and piece together a series of intricate plots – sinister cases of subterfuge that I would never have believed possible before the revelations already made known to me by Oldfield.

At that initial meeting in Manchester was someone I had known for 13 years; he was to become my second 'Deep Throat'. The other two were to be introduced to me later; they were specialists in matters of military intelligence and were to assist me in untangling the web of intrigue into which Anderton and his deputy, John Stalker, had unwittingly become ensnared during the 'shoot to kill' inquiry in Northern Ireland, dubbed the Stalker Affair.

Every so often I would receive a call. Sometimes information would be given over the telephone, but very rarely. Usually I would be told, 'I have someone you ought to meet. When can you be in Manchester next?' Occasionally meetings would take place in London, as in the case of a former Customs investigator.

They trusted me not to tape-record conversations, but took the precaution of arranging each rendezvous in a noisy place, so that even if I did not act in good faith, I could do little damage.

Whenever they contacted me, they would use only their initials: 'It's MF . . . FH . . . CW . . . PH . . .' They know who they are and I cannot thank them enough.

The star of this book is, of course, James Anderton and I am deeply indebted to him for sparing me the time to interview him at length in his office at Chester House, the headquarters of the Greater Manchester police. In fact, it was his frankness and 'superstar' quality that convinced me this book had to be written.

I shall never forget his words to me in reply to a rather delicate question, especially when put to a chief constable with a reputation for being the toughest in Europe: 'You've asked the question and I cannot tell a lie. Yes, I've cried. . . . '

I must also single out John Stalker who, while busily writing his own autobiography, devoted most of a day to me at his smallholding home in Warburton, Cheshire.

Much of the tedious side of my research was made all the more tolerable by the smiling help of the *Manchester Evening News* library staff and employees of the Wigan Record Office, which comes under the jurisdiction of the Wigan Metropolitan Borough Council.

Neither must I forget the many policemen and ex-policemen, friends of Anderton and enemies of Anderton, who have contributed so much towards my book, well aware that their experiences would, by necessity, be locked in anonymity.

Paul Sidey and Kathy Gale, my editors, and Chris Green, my long-suffering agent, know already how grateful I am for their faith and support in this project, and it would be remiss of me not to make public my sincere appreciation.

But most of my thanks must go to James Anderton for being the man he is and, therefore, so worthy a subject for a full-length focus.

In fairness to Mr Anderton and to avoid any misunderstanding, I must emphasise that this is not an official biography. At no time during the compilation of this manuscript did Mr Anderton ever breach his agreement with the Home Office or the Greater Manchester Police Authority. In a letter to me, he was explicit that it would be inappropriate for him 'to collaborate in the fullest sense'. Indeed, my interview with him was completed before Mr Anderton gave his undertaking to the Home Office to try to avoid controversy. The first approach to me by my informants was not inspired by Anderton and he was never aware of the clandestine working arrangements which I have already outlined.

This is my book, not Anderton's. If it has a virtue, it is its independence.

Part One

1

Ripper Madness

The mutilated body of Vera Millward was found in the car-park of Manchester Royal Infirmary during the early hours of Tuesday 17 May, 1978. Alive, the 42-year-old prostitute had not been a pretty sight. Dead, she made even hardened police officers retch.

At first, it was thought that she must have been run over in the car-park by a vehicle and propped up against the perimeter fence by the driver, who then panicked and drove off. She was still in the slumped sitting position when discovered, her head crushed and her tawdry clothes dyed scarlet with her own wasted body fluids.

A doctor from the hospital's casualty department pronounced her dead, but it was not until he undid her overcoat that the full horror became apparent and the accident theory was abandoned. As the coat parted, so Vera's intestines spilled on to the ground, unveiling a madman's mutilation.

Around the same time, the chief constable of Greater Manchester, Cyril James Anderton, would have been tucking into a traditional breakfast of grapefruit and fried eggs and bacon, served to him in bed on a tray by his wife, Joan. Breakfast in bed at 7.00 am precisely had become a feature of Anderton's daily ritual.

By 8.15, his chauffeur-driven Jaguar was always parked outside the house in rural Sale. During the 15-minute drive to Manchester through a commuter belt that could become painfully congested, Anderton would recline in the back of his official car, often meditating and reciting his prayers. The driver knew better than to try to make conversation at a time when his boss was mulling over the day ahead with his Maker. Morning prayers-on-wheels were as much a custom as breakfast in bed.

By the time Anderton reached his office at 8.30, the murder at the infirmary was destined to dominate the day. Detective Chief Superintendent Jack Ridgeway, the head of Manchester CID, had taken charge of the investigation and was at the scene of the crime with his team, including the forensic scientists. Just a few yards from the body was a flowerbed which, after dark, made a regular makeshift mattress for the street whores who worked Manchester's south side, an area of the city Anderton knew well. The Victorian buildings of Moss Side had decayed into slums during the Fifties and Sixties; this had been Anderton's beat when he first joined the Force in 1953. The brothels, the pimps, the child prostitutes – boys as well as girls – the pornography and drug-trafficking had all made an indelible impression on him, partly explaining his moral crusade on vice from day one of his reign as chief constable, which had begun two years previously.

It did not take long for Vera Millward to be identified; she was already known to the police. Not married, she was the mother of two children. She had a relatively stable relationship with a Jamaican-born immigrant whom she regarded as her common-law husband. He told Ridgeway that Vera had been expecting a regular client to call on her at home 'for business' late on the Monday night. When the 'punter failed to show' she had gone touting on the streets, looking for 'kerb trade'.

The time of death was pinpointed by a witness who had entered the hospital around 1.15 am on the Tuesday. He had heard screams – 'maybe three' – and a woman's cry for help, which he believed came from a distant corner of the car-park. He had taken a few steps in the direction of the noise, but had stopped and turned back when he heard nothing further.

The moment Ridgeway set eyes on the victim, he was instantly reminded of a similar crime the previous autumn. On 10 October 1977, the rotting remains of another prostitute, Jean Jordan, had been found among tangled undergrowth on overgrown wasteland next to the Southern Cemetery and some neatly cultivated allotments. She had been clubbed eleven times on the head with a hammer and hacked to pieces with a knife and a sliver of glass. One wound curved all the way from her right knee to her left shoulder. The murder had been committed on the night of 1 October, the body remaining undetected for 10 days.

Jean Jordan had been the Yorkshire Ripper's sixth victim. Was Vera Millward the ninth? Ridgeway was convinced that the answer was yes and he gave his reasons personally to Anderton later the same day.

After the Jordan murder the previous October, Ridgeway was given permission by Anderton to join forces with George Oldfield, the ailing assistant chief constable of West Yorkshire, who was leading the Ripper hunt. Oldfield responded by putting at Ridgeway's disposal a disused schoolroom in Baildon, high on the moors above Shipley and Bingley. Ridgeway took with him 30 hand-picked detectives and in a further public demonstration of goodwill, Oldfield agreed to double Ridgeway's manpower by loaning 30 of his own officers to the Manchester CID chief.

However, by the end of February 1978, Ridgeway was on his way back to Manchester with his defeated team, declaring, 'We have just about exhausted the inquiry. It has drawn a blank.'

But after the discovery in May that year of Vera Millward's body, Ridgeway decided that it was time to cross the Pennines yet again with his travelling circus. Anderton told Ridgeway simply, 'You must do what you

5

have to do. You have my backing . . . and blessing . . . all the way.' Anderton's encouragement for cross-pollination of effort between the Lancashire and Yorkshire forces was hardly surprising. Although he had been in the hot seat for barely two years, he was already campaigning vociferously in political circles for a national crime-busting cabinet. He described crime as 'the fastest growing enterprise in the world'. Co-operation between regional forces and the lubrication of the machinery of communication and intelligence were ideals close to his heart.

Oldfield was not so enthusiastic. Although on the surface, as a public relations exercise, he appeared to welcome his Manchester colleagues, deep down he resented their intrusion. Detectives close to him even sensed a resentment of the Ripper himself for having slipped across the county border to kill.

'It had become very personal with George,' one of them explained. 'It had developed into a game of chess, a battle of brains. Chess players don't appreciate interference from spectators. That's how George had become. After the second murder in Manchester, I honestly think George feared that the Ripper might be based in Lancashire, outside his jurisdiction, and that the investigation could be taken away from him. He was becoming very paranoid and secretly distrusted both Ridgeway and Anderton. Especially Anderton, because of his overt ambition and his academic cleverness. He felt intellectually inferior to Anderton and openly derided him as an example of the "new breed of bookworm coppers", insinuating that he [Anderton] was full of knowledge and empty of experience. In a strange way, Oldfield felt flattered that the Ripper had picked on him to duel with. It was as if the Ripper was saying, "You're the best. You're the one I have to beat to prove myself the champ." That's the way George saw it and we allowed him to delude himself. What else could we do? It didn't make any difference. We all get our juice from different sources.'

Late one night towards the end of May, one of the Manchester detectives telephoned Oldfield at home. It was immediately obvious to the Lancashire officer that Oldfield had been drinking heavily. His speech was slurred and he quickly became abrasive. After a brief introduction this is how the conversation is remembered by the officer who made the call:

Detective: 'I should like to make an appointment to see you in private, sir.'

Oldfield: 'What about?'

Detective: 'The Ripper case.'

Oldfield: 'Why can't you go through Ridgeway? You're responsible to him, aren't you?'

Detective: 'We can't do that.'

Oldfield: '*We?*'

Detective: 'There's two of us, sir. This is a very delicate matter.'

Oldfield: 'If you've got a complaint against a senior officer, I don't want to hear it.'

That put the Manchester detective on the spot. After a pause, he continued in a manner that left the matter hanging.

Detective: 'I assure you, sir, that we do not wish to make allegations against Chief Superintendent Ridgeway.'

Oldfield: 'If you're wasting my time, I'll have your nuts!'

Detective: 'This is not a frivolous matter, sir.'

Oldfield: 'I'll be the judge of that. Come to my office tomorrow evening, around seven. I'll give you five minutes. Not a second more.'

By 'my office' he meant a room at Leeds police headquarters, from where the nationwide Ripper investigation was being co-ordinated. Oldfield was working 16 hours a day and it was showing. He was living on drink, cigarettes,

tablets, his nerves (and other people's) and hope – just
about in that order. The prayers he left to Anderton.

The two Manchester detectives reported to the Ripper
incident room a couple of minutes before 7.00 pm on the
next day. They had both had a couple of pints 'across the
road' to stoke up their courage. The incident room was
bristling with activity, impatient telephones and expletives
fragmenting the taut atmosphere.

Oldfield was the caricature of an overworked provincial
cop with his shirt-sleeves rolled up, collar-button undone,
tie-knot askew, belly hanging out, and a necklace of
sweat-beads strung across his forehead. He came through
the incident room with a swagger, hitching up his trousers,
indicating with a finger that he wished – no, he ordered –
the two officers to follow him to an office which he had
made his own.

Already on his desk was a cup of tepid tea, half of
which had been slopped into the saucer. Oldfield flopped
into his chair and began rummaging in a lower righthand
drawer. 'Sit down,' he said, without looking up; there
were two chairs on the opposite side of the desk. From
the drawer, he took a half-bottle of whisky, from which
the label had been removed. He poured a liberal amount
into his tea and stirred. Before drinking, he took two
tablets from separate bottles and swallowed them with the
whisky-laced beverage. Then he added more scotch to the
tea, stirred again with his finger, and sat back.

'Well? Remember what I said? Five minutes, no more.'

The detectives had their heads bowed, their sweaty
hands fidgeting in their laps. The one who had made the
appointment took the initiative. The dialogue reproduced
here is a reconstruction by the Manchester men.

'There's a rumour circulating in the Manchester force.'

'What's that to do with me?'

'It's connected . . . to the case.'

'I'm not interested in rumour.'

8

'I still think you ought to hear it, sir . . . now we're here.'

'Very well. Brief, mind you!'

This was the moment the two junior detectives had been dreading.

The story that came out was probably the most absurd ever to be presented to an investigating officer and is more of indictment of those telling it than the man it was supposed to incriminate – James Anderton. The story is historic for its unparalleled malevolence, but it established the extraordinary extremes to which some people have been prepared to go, even risking their own careers, in their efforts to discredit Anderton, something he has maintained since he became a chief constable. In a nutshell, they were suggesting that Anderton, the Methodist lay preacher, should be treated as a suspect. Their evidence? Simply that physically he resembled the man they were looking for, he was a hardliner against pornography and vice, and he was probably the most atypical policeman in the history of law enforcement, of whom they, and many others, were vindictively covetous.

Oldfield was crouched over his desk, fists clenched, the focus of his watery eyes unnerving the dapper, younger men. 'You're taking the piss! You're either taking the piss or you're fucking insane! The pair of you! I'll have you both back on the beat for this. Here I am, with not one minute of my day to spare, not even for my family – and I've wasted five of them on you two, listening to this cock-an'-bull story. I'll never forgive you. Never!'

'Please, sir, will you just hear us out?'

More than a year later, Oldfield explained to me how he felt at the moment he listened to the diatribe against Anderton, who commanded the largest British police force outside London, with almost 7,000 officers under him, covering an area of some 500 square miles and responsible for the protection of a population of nearly three million. After the Metropolitan police commissioner at Scotland Yard, Anderton was the most powerful police-man in the land.

'It was like being asked to believe that Sir Winston Churchill was really Adolf Hitler. I didn't know much about the officers, except that they had impeccable police pedigrees. I was angry because I smelt a set-up, but I couldn't figure it out. I was well aware that I was becoming a butt of a lot of ridicule and criticism, especially from the Manchester mob, but I couldn't see the purpose of their scheme, unless it was to encourage me to make a prick of myself.'

His initial instinct was to suspect Ridgeway, erro-neously, of being the architect of the plot, if indeed there was one. Although the public relations propaganda poured honey on their 'harmonious professional relation-ship', the truth was rather different. Oldfield's 'generous' donation of 30 men was nothing of the sort. There was a machiavellian motive for this loan. Bluntly, Oldfield wanted to keep an eye on Ridgeway; what better way than to have 30 spies in the enemy camp? Oldfield was not far off retirement. The Yorkshire Ripper case was becoming the biggest manhunt in British criminal history. Detectives had questioned almost 150,000 possible sus-pects. Some 20,000 statements had been taken, typed, signed, fed into the system and filed, and 25,000 warrants issued for the search of property. Money invested in the investigation was approaching three million pounds.

As with the Moors Murders case, it had touched an exposed public nerve. Northern towns were genuinely in the grip of fear. Women were afraid to venture out at night. Self-imposed curfews had become a restrictive feature in Yorkshire life, a county at war. A war that, for Oldfield, went far beyond the Ripper borders. The drums of the Roses War were beating in Oldfield's defective heart. The prospect of being beaten to the Yorkshire Ripper by a detective from Lancashire was a new demon that had come to haunt him. Was Ridgeway trying to entice him into making a spectacle of himself, so that he (Oldfield) might be removed from the case? The assistant chief constable of West Yorkshire began to wonder. Against that, if he refused to hear in full the detectives' narrative, he could later find himself retiring in disgrace, instead of the glory for which he hungered, accused of masterminding a police cover-up that would dwarf even the Watergate scandal.

He opted for compromise. The detectives would be allowed to make their case, but Oldfield reserved the right not to record in writing or on tape the allegations; neither would he intimate whether he intended to act.

The haranguing that followed described a 'religious bigot obsessed with fighting promiscuity and the evils of the flesh', who blew his top about pornographers and pimps being 'garbage in the sea of life, not content until nearly everyone is floating like trash in the same filthy waters'. Anderton apparently made no secret of praying in his office for the strength to 'smite the devil from the streets'. Out poured emotive and totally unsubstantiated phrases like, 'Mad mullah' and 'raving nutter' and, when referring to the Greater Manchester police headquarters, 'it's a nuthouse'. Lie after lie was told about Anderton's private life and habits in an effort to incriminate him.

At last the other Manchester detective spoke. He had been rehearsing his lines for days and this is what he recalls saying about Anderton in relation to the crackdown on street vice, 'His language is so strident. It's all fire and brimstone, hell and damnation, cutting out the cancerous cells of society; all that sort of wild-eyed stuff. Normal policemen don't talk that way. He's scary.' He went on to describe Anderton's days on the beat in the red-light district of Moss Side, where the street-girls 'laughed at him: some to his face, others behind his back. Everyone on his manor knew him as Bible Jim.'

'Finished?' Oldfield asked.

The answer was communicated without words.

11

Oldfield replied that what he had just heard was not evidence but mischievous prejudice and unscrupulous vilification, based purely on conjecture and lurid imagination. 'By the same token, you could point the finger at any other local religious fanatic,' said Oldfield, which seemed to the detectives, at the time, to be an admission by the West Yorkshire deputy that he considered Anderton, at the very least, to be a rather irregular police mandarin. If nothing else, this baleful chicanery, aimed at character assassination, demonstrates how Anderton had already, in just two years, polarised his Force and made enemies – though probably more friends – through the ranks.

At the end of the interview, Oldfield warned the two men that they would face disciplinary action if ever they repeated their 'treacherous' theory, without hard evidence to back it up. The officers departed convinced that they had made fools of themselves and that Oldfield would immediately report them to Ridgeway. They were wrong.

There was considerable press speculation that the Yorkshire Ripper might be a policeman. Of course, we all now know that he was Bradford lorry driver Peter Sutcliffe. But at the time he did seem to have an uncanny knack of avoiding police patrols and was always one step ahead of the pursuing pack. Even Doris Stokes, the late medium who often helped the police with high-profile cases, believed that this disciple of Jack the Ripper had 'the vibrations of someone close to law enforcement,' though privately Oldfield dismissed her mystic messages as 'mumbo-jumbo'.

In this connection there had, however, been a number of developments, unknown to the Manchester team. As Oldfield was to tell me, 'Every night I had men and women working undercover in the red-light districts of Bradford and Leeds. Their duty was to record the registration number of all kerb-crawling cars. The names and addresses of the car-owners were obtained from the licensing headquarters in Swansea and this information was pumped into the system. When names kept recurring, then we started to take a closer look. Only a week before those two Manchester lads came to see me, I'd been handed a report from one of my own senior officers which gave me something to think about.'

A large number of cars noted kerb-crawling in the vice districts of the industrial towns and cities of Yorkshire during the first three months of 1978 were the private vehicles of policemen. An examination of the duty rosters established that very few of those men had been working when they were logged loitering on wheels among the labyrinthine flesh markets. In the early hours of one Saturday morning that February, a car had been observed on three separate occasions kerb-crawling in the infamous Chapeltown suburb of Leeds. On 25 June the previous year, Chapeltown was the location of the Ripper's fifth lethal strike: sixteen-year-old Jayne MacDonald.

Later, it was discovered that the suspicious car belonged to an officer stationed at Manchester's police headquarters. Discreet enquiries had also established that this man had carried out duties on a number of occasions for the Chief Constable's department, although not officially a part of its retinue.

'It's important to bear in mind this background when considering what action I took,' Oldfield pleaded his case. 'You must respect the circumstances. Everything in life has to be considered in context.'

After several days' soul-searching, Oldfield assigned two of his most trusted men to go to Manchester for a fortnight to place James Anderton under the microscope. 'If ever you tell anyone what you're doing, I'll disown you,' he warned them, true to form. 'It's our secret. Nobody else must ever know, unless something comes of it.'

The first question from one of them was, naturally enough, 'What are we looking for?'

Oldfield had given careful thought to his answer to this inevitable question. 'It's best that I should give you no guidelines. As far as you're concerned, you're not looking for anything specific. Just try to follow him wherever he goes, particularly at night, and then you give me a blow-by-blow account. It's a straighforward surveillance job, but if you overstep your brief, don't cry to me for a lifeline.'

By the following year, Oldfield had lost the respect of virtually every member of his demoralised force. But at the time of this covert mission on Anderton, he still commanded considerable loyalty from the majority of those who were responsible for policing West Yorkshire.

The two men Oldfield despatched to Manchester he trusted implicitly and they did not let him down. They did the business with unswerving professionalism. Anderton did not step from his Manchester lair without being stalked. They even spied on him through binoculars while he was at home. One part of the operation was entrusted to a London-based private detective; the more extreme dirty tricks they preferred to sub-contract, lengthening the chain of command, putting distance between them and the frontline. The hired man's function was to bug Anderton's home telephone, the rest of his house, including the bedroom, and his official police car. This was done.

What remains obscure is who funded the sub-contracting, which must have been expensive. If it came from the Ripper inquiry budget, then this is indeed an even bigger scandal than the one I am chronicling. Only four people could possibly have known the answer: Oldfield, one or both of the undercover detectives deployed in Manchester, and/or the private eye. Realistically, it is unlikely that the identity of the paymaster was disclosed to the private investigator. For such people, ignorance has its appeal. He is now in exile on an island in the Far East. Oldfield is dead and his two subordinates have families and futures to safeguard.

Irrefutable, however, is the fact that two weeks after leaving for Manchester, Oldfield's factotums were back in Leeds, their undertaking fulfilled. Wisely, Oldfield refused to see them at headquarters. Instead, they met for a meal in Leeds at the Griffin, a small commercial hotel in the city centre. There, late at night, a bulky brown package was handed to the assistant chief constable.

One of them was about to say something pertinent, only to be silenced by a head-shake from Oldfield, who took the parcel home with him, and that is where it stayed. It was not until the Sunday that he examined the contents. The surveillance reports revealed nothing more than a very busy police chief going about his hectic daily schedule with a passion for punctiliousness and perfection. The tape-recordings were of a more personal nature. Oldfield found himself eavesdropping on family intimacies. He was embarrassed, but he could not bring himself to stop the intrusion. There were family squabbles, a teenage daughter rebelling, tears, slamming doors, and a mother-cum-housewife trapped in the traditional role of peacemaker. All the nuts and bolts were there of family life and strife. All heard by Oldfield.

In fairness to the two men who undertook Oldfield's grubby work, it is important to appreciate that, in the absence of ground rules, all they could do was cast the widest possible net. They had no alternative but to include everything, just in case it meant something to Oldfield.

From the moment he was in possession of the tapes and the reports, Oldfield had not a clue what to do with them. He accepted that, for the purpose intended, they were worthless. They simply endorsed the obvious: that the rumours about Anderton were without substance. Oldfield's problem was that he allowed his personal dislike of Anderton to blind him.

15

On one of the tapes, Anderton was lampooning certain local politicians and a particular member of the Greater Manchester Police Authority. Another senior officer – in the car with Anderton at the time the jokes were made – also joined in the denigration. That is why Oldfield retained those documents for more than a month, before burning everything in his back garden.

How did a private detective find his way not only into a chief constable's home, but also into several rooms in the house and his official car, for the purpose of bugging?

Oldfield just smiled. If he did know, he was certainly not saying. My information suggests that at least two people were bribed to assist.

Did Oldfield ever consider keeping those tapes to release anonymously at a time when Anderton was vulnerable? 'Never. But some people would have done. Definitely!'

Who, for example?

'There are plenty of unscrupulous bastards about in this profession.'

Interesting, in view of developments the following June.

'I'm Jack. I see you are having no luck catching me. I have the greatest respect for you, George, but Lord you are no nearer catching me now than four years ago when I started. I reckon your boys are letting you down, George. They can't be much good, can they? The only time they came near catching me was a few months back in Chapeltown, when I was disturbed. Even then it was a uniformed copper, not a detective. I warned you in March that I'd strike again. Sorry it wasn't Bradford. I did promise you that, but I couldn't get there. I'm not sure when I'll strike again, but it will definitely be some time this year. Maybe September, October or even sooner if I get the chance. I'm not sure where. Maybe Manchester; I like it there. There's plenty of *them* knocking about. They never learn, do they, George? I bet you've warned them. But they never listen. At the rate I'm going, I should be in the book of records. I think it's eleven up to now, isn't it? Well, I'll keep on going for quite a while yet. I can't see myself being nicked just yet. Even if you do get near, I'll probably top myself first. Well, it's been nice chatting to you, George. Yours, Jack the Ripper. No good looking for fingerprints, you should know by now it's as clean as a whistle. See you soon. Bye. Hope you like the catchy tune at the end. Ha-ha.'

That tape-recording, packed in an ordinary envelope and posted in Sunderland, had landed on Oldfield's desk with the rest of his varied morning mail. The taunting male voice was distinctly Geordie, but during the three minutes and 16 seconds' running time, there was not one spark of spontaneity. 'Reading from a script,' Oldfield had concluded. He also made up his mind instantly that the dour voice on the 'I'm Jack' tape belonged to the Yorkshire Ripper and was not a hoax. A mistake that was to commit to a premature grave more innocent young women.

Early in 1987, six years after the arrest of Sutcliffe, a national Sunday newspaper ran a front page story alleging that the bogus Ripper tape had been sent to Oldfield by a disgruntled policeman. Later, this report was discredited by the chief constable of West Yorkshire, who stated that after 'a most comprehensive internal enquiry, [he was] satisfied there [was] no truth in the newspaper article'. However, my information from independent sources corroborates in essence the newspaper version. The chief constable's denials were probably technically correct in as much as they applied to his West Yorkshire force.

The rogue tape was actually the perversity of a friend and colleague of the two Manchester detectives who had arraigned Anderton at the conspiratorial assignation with Oldfield. Note in the tape the direct reference to Manchester: 'I'm not sure when I'll strike again, but it will

17

definitely be some time this year, maybe September, October or even sooner if I get the chance. I'm not sure where. Maybe Manchester; I like it there. There are plenty of *them* knocking about.' The tape was a protest at Oldfield's apparent lack of action against the Greater Manchester chief constable.

There were many other clues which Oldfield failed to heed, such as: 'See you soon'. This was inconsistent with the lines: '. . . you are no nearer catching me now than four years ago when I started. . . . At the rate I'm going, I should be in the book of records. . . . Well, I'll keep on going for quite a while yet. I can't see myself being nicked just yet.' But in the next breath, he was saying: 'See you soon'. How could the man on the tape be meeting Oldfield shortly and yet not be 'nicked'? Answer: because he was a fellow police officer and they would be meeting in the course of their duties.

The tape was a conundrum with a clue in virtually every line. 'I reckon your boys are letting you down, George', was a Lancashire torpedo fired broadside at the West Yorkshire constabulary. '. . . but Lord, you are no nearer . . . ' was a dig at Oldfield's God Almighty attitude. 'Maybe Manchester; I like it there', was just another demonstration of self-esteem and a further rebuff for the lads over the hill. 'I think it's eleven up to now, isn't it?' Would the Ripper have needed to ask? 'I bet you've warned them. But they never listen.' This was a subtle reference to Oldfield's own dogmatism and intransigence. The parable was: They're just like you. 'Well, it's been nice chatting to you, George.' The tape was a monologue, not a conversation; the 'chat' had been in Oldfield's office, when he'd admonished them. 'Hope you like the catchy tune at the end. Ha-Ha.' That was the ultimate give-away. The final twenty seconds of the tape consisted of a few lines from a ballad, 'Thank You for Being a Friend', which was a sarcastic allusion to Oldfield the enemy. Even today the police are unaware that the 'I'm Jack' tape was nothing more than a coded internal memo; an anonymous outlet for frustration and dissatisfaction.

'We were confident that George, the silly old sod, would never identify the voice on the tape,' I was informed. 'Neither did we believe, not for a second, that he could be so gullible and would readily accept that he was listening to the Yorkshire Ripper. I mean, for God's sake! For a start, there were so many anomalies. It was a joke! We were peeved; that's all. Angry men making a protest. There was no other way, it seemed at the time. We'd have been drummed out of the force if we'd put our feelings in writing. Only a man who believes that Hollywood is the Holy Land could have been duped by that tape. It just goes to show what an all-round sucker Oldfield was. However, in retrospect, we were rather harsh on him, but we weren't to know that he had acted upon our suspicions. I suppose we owe him – and Anderton – some kind of apology. But it's a bit late to say sorry to poor old George ... and Anderton wouldn't be amused. Neither would he forgive.'

Right and wrong. Too late, yes, to make peace with Oldfield, but I have a feeling Anderton would forgive, though still demanding the scalps of the offenders. Anderton believes in redemption but only after all the dues have been paid.

It was not until 1985 that the creator of the spoof tape and the two Manchester detectives who had clashed with Oldfield over Anderton learned of the outcome of the meeting in May 1978 with the assistant chief constable of West Yorkshire. They were at a pub in Mossley, just inside the Yorkshire boundary and only about 12 miles from the centre of Manchester, for a farewell party. A Lancashire detective was retiring and an upstairs room had been hired for the evening. It was mainly a stag night, but there were a few women present: a couple of wives, one or two girlfriends and a Manchester policewoman who was having an affair with a married officer, one of

19

the detectives from Leeds who had been involved in the covert manoeuvres against Anderton. In fact, quite a few of the detectives in that pub for the farewell party were from Yorkshire. Even the stripper, although hired from a Manchester agency, was a Yorkshire girl; she had two convictions for soliciting, having been arrested twice during Anderton's purges on vice.

It was a marathon, beer-swilling night. The drink was oiling memories and greasing egos. Soon it was story-time. Anecdotes massaged the night away. Life stories exchanged hands for the modest price of a round of drinks. And the Lancashire and Yorkshire detectives who had worked together on the Ripper case began comparing notes . . . and telling tales out of school.

Anderton would not be the least surprised to discover that a few officers had been conspiring against him behind his back, though the extent of the duplicity would sadden, and even shock, him. In recent years, there have been many threats to his life, especially after his speech on AIDS, which he said was being spread by people 'swirling around in a human cesspit of their own making'. Fear that one day 'some madman' may rape or even murder his wife or grown-up daughter, Gillian, as an alternative means of destroying him, is the ugly shadow that never leaves his side.

It is not uncommon for this big man, by reputation 'Europe's toughest cop' (he is 6 feet 2 inches tall and weighs more than 14 stone) to weep at home in the sturdy, supportive arms of his wife, while in public he is being pilloried.

'When I cry, it is not in anger, but sadness,' he explained to me. 'It's the price I pay for my high profile, but I shall never change. When you try to do a job fairly and honestly, and end up being publicly ridiculed, it is sometimes hard to bear.' He even believes that through his own experiences of persecution, he knows how Christ felt on the cross. 'I'm always being falsely accused of something by somebody,' he said. 'The subversives have projected me as a hardline, rightwing, repressive, jackboot cop. We all have our cross to bear.'

The two detectives who went to Oldfield with their malicious story are adamant that they were sincere, but I do not believe them; the story is too incredible. I think they were lampooning Oldfield, either because they despised him or Anderton, or possibly both. They were probably nervous during the meeting with Oldfield because they feared their artifice might backfire. Oldfield could very easily have alerted Ridgeway, or even Anderton, and their career prospects would suddenly have diminished. Certainly Ridgeway had no part in this reprehensible episode. What the detectives proved, beyond all doubt, however, was that Oldfield was in such a mental mess that he was capable of believing anything. This was further established by his ready acceptance of the 'I'm Jack' tape.

Cecil Franks, the Conservative Member of Parliament in 1987 for Barrow-in-Furness, referred to the Yorkshire Ripper case when entreating Anderton 'to retire gracefully' just after the chief constable had appeared to claim on a radio programme that he had a hotline to God. These trenchant remarks by Franks are not without weight because he is a former leader of the Manchester City Council, during which time he was a staunch ally of anything that bore the Anderton label: 'Every nutcase in history sooner or later claims guidance from God to justify what he is doing. Hitler laid into the minorities, claiming he had a divine right. And the Yorkshire Ripper claimed God told him to murder those girls. Throughout history we have seen man's inhumanity to man in the name of religion.'

2

A First and Lasting Arrest

Empire Day, 24 May 1932: Lord Inchcape, melodramatically muttering something about the rudeness of uninvited death barging unannounced into his house, died in a theatrical flourish in the arms of his faithful valet; eight miners perished in a pit disaster. The front page of the *Daily Express* related these stories, plus the woeful tale of the death of a farm labourer and a vicar's daughter who were very much in love, something their respective stations in life would not permit, while in Europe a German parvenu called Adolf Hitler was being voluble about his fascist vision of the future. Of less public interest at the time, though of considerable significance later, was the birth to a James and Lucy Anderton of a son. Ever since, Cyril James Anderton seems to have been repaying the media for having ignored him on the most important day of his life.

Anderton's father was a Wigan miner. Their home was a two-up, two-down miner's cottage in Northumberland Street, Goose Green, Wigan, dwarfed by a forbidding slag heap. The communal lavatory, shared with 20 other families, was sited across a cobbled courtyard. You really did have to be desperate to make the round trip after dark. Those cottages were demolished long ago.

The family could not live on a miner's wages and would have starved if his mother had not taken in sewing, which she did at night, after baby Jim had been put to bed. One of the comforting, familiar sounds was the clatter of the sewing-machine, audible at night but never on Sundays, which was God's day and devoted entirely to Him.

Although there was never a penny to spare, their home was always spotlessly clean. Lucy Anderton was house-proud, without being fastidious. James Anderton will never forget that first home: the linoleum-lined living-room, his play-den; the flagstone floor, the rush mat carpet; the dolly tub in which his mother did the washing every morning; meals cooked on an old-fashioned, black-leaded grate with a brass knob on the oven door. Anderton can still see it all so vividly, everything lovingly preserved in his mind. His father filling the doorframe: a formidable man; coal in his lungs and fire in his belly; the muck of honest graft and dishonest exploitation painting him the colour of a moonless night, while the whites of his eyes shone like stars. There was a daily ritual when Anderton's father came home from the pit. He would stand on the threshold, door wide open, take off his grimy miner's hat and aim it like a hoopla at the knob on the oven door. James, the toddler, would look on in wonderment as the hat raced through the air towards its burnished target and fastened on to the knob. Lucy Anderton's reaction on her husband's homecoming each day was a mixture of love and relief. It was to be a few more years before young James understood the thanksgiving celebrated by pit wives every time their husbands returned safely from underground.

Mining disasters in Wigan were common. So common, in fact, that commemorative serviettes of a standard design were mass produced. In the Pretoria pit explosion of 1910 – the second worst coal mining disaster in Britain – 344 men perished. The Pretoria colliery, straddling the Atherton/Over Hulton border, was devastated when the roof of a tunnel collapsed, followed by a blast and blaze, attributed to a defective safety-lamp. Two years earlier, 74 had died after an explosion at the Haypole Colliery,

Abram, near Wigan. And in the year that James Anderton was born, there was a death-toll of 27 in an accident at the Edge Green Colliery. Scarcely a day went by without a miner being killed or injured.

Lucy Anderton had held the hands of many desperate women, as they waited outside the colliery gates in silent supplication for news of the trapped men. Hope was not enough. You needed faith, which explains why the clergy preached to full houses three or four times on Sundays. James Anderton, senior, described coal mines as catacombs for the living. Often, though, they became graves for the real dead.

Religion, love, discipline and politics, probably in that order, prevailed over the Anderton home. Lucy was a strict Methodist, while James's father was staunchly Church of England, though running through the family like a coal seam was a strong atavistic Roman Catholic presence.

Anderton remembers his mother's cosy warmth and his father's volatility. Certainly it was his father who won the argument when it came to deciding where James should be baptized. The seed of Cyril James Anderton's Christian faith was first watered in Wigan's St. Matthew's Church. When Anderton was two years old, they moved to Brindley Street, Pemberton.

James's grandfather had been a devout disciple of the radical Socialist Keir Hardy. This fervid Socialism had been handed down like a precious heirloom. The family, like other mining families in the country, was loyal to Christ and the Labour Party, convinced of a divine connection; the poor had prayed for deliverance and God had answered by conceiving Socialism. Politics was a second religion in the Anderton household.

'I was surrounded by a family which had its roots firmly set in the community and the Church,' Anderton told me. 'The two always went together. It was a humble background, but I had no idea – not for a very, very long time

24

– that we were poor. I thought we were rich, and, in a way, we were. I had everything, or so it seemed at the time, through the eyes of a happy child: loving parents, enough food, a roof over my head, cloth on my back and leather beneath my feet. What other riches in the world were there!

'I accept now that we were deprived, perhaps, in the social sense, but that period was the stabilizing feature of my life – something that is sadly missing from the lives of too many children today. Love and discipline went together. I consider myself the luckiest person alive today.

'In retrospect, life must have been very hard for all the families like mine. It was the time of the Depression and we had very little in the way of material possessions.' Anderton's father had been caught up in the miners' strike of 1926, which lasted considerably longer than the General Strike of the same year. All mining families had been on the breadline during the 1926 stoppage and had survived only through outlawed coal-picking and the simple sustenance provided by the soup kitchen. Six years later, the hardship was still biting. 'But we learned to get by. Everyone was supported by the innate goodness of ordinary people. My parents were hard-working and they gave me everything. There was never any envy or bitterness in my parents' politics. Socialism for my father was not a desire to be as rich as the next man. Neither wealth nor social status came into his philosophy; it was all a question of justice. In any case, how could anyone be a Christian and be covetous? The two are incompatible. Certainly we were typical of working-class folk in south Lancashire at the time. There was a bond between chapel and the mining community. Our politics could not be a breach of faith. My father's Socialism, therefore, was loving and caring.'

Anderton has always been consistent about his childhood memories. Talking to one journalist about his father, early life and family, he said, 'He was a man whose whole body and life were racked by hard labour. My family were people of high intelligence, seeking to educate themselves and knowing that at the end of it, they would have no opportunity at all to convert that into something fulfilling. My father told me that he didn't want me to spend my life working so hard for so little. But he was uncomplaining. He was quite remarkable.'

And he was to tell Joan Bakewell, 'I would say I'm one of the luckiest men in the world. I say it quite often. I was born into a marvellous family: my mother a lovely person, quiet and homely, my father a little bit more fiery. I suppose I possess some of his temperament. Everything I got was a wonderful bonus to me, and I appreciated it. If I had to live my life again, I wouldn't alter it at all.'

He felt safe cocooned in the working-class domestic rituals. After a day digging coal, his father would strip off in front of the fire, while Lucy boiled water on the stove in saucepans and a copper kettle for the tin bath. The bath would be placed in front of the fireplace and his father would scrub himself down, simultaneously regaling them with stories about his day and asking questions about theirs. Friday was bath-night for James, another rite not uncommon to families of all classes throughout the country.

Despite the austerity, Anderton cannot remember ever going to bed hungry. 'My mother made ends meet on a pittance. I honestly don't know how she managed, but she did, and it all seemed so effortless.' No doubt a trick or trap of the memory. 'She was a miracle-worker.'

There was never any compromise on principles. One did not tell lies, whatever the motive. Impoliteness was inexcusable and insolence was physically swatted. For serious anti-social behaviour, his father would take off his pit belt, arch James across his broad knees, and strap him firmly. James would cry, and smart for days, but he did not resent the beltings, which he recalls as being neither

26

frequent nor excessively severe. He is in no doubt that the punishment was always deserved.

When he was five years old, there was an incident that he would never be allowed to forget. Two doors away lived a little girl called Joan Baron. He watched Joan, aged two then, toddle up the path to his house and enter the hall, where there was a bowl of fruit on a lace runner. Joan tugged at the lace, pulling along the bowl, then grabbed an orange and ran. James immediately went in pursuit and made his first arrest. He took the orange from his prisoner, wagged a finger in her shocked face, lectured her about the naughtiness of stealing, then put her across his knee and spanked her – a lesson he had learned from his own father. James returned indoors, feeling good in the role of policeman. The euphoria, however, was short-lived. Joan went home rubbing the tears from her eyes and showing the marks on her legs. 'Who hit you?' her angry mother demanded. 'That nasty boy!' Joan said, pointing to the Andertons' house. Mrs Baron went over and complained to Lucy, who asked James, 'Is that true?' 'Yes, Mummy,' he answered. 'She stole our fruit.' Whereupon James was promptly taken aside and spanked by his mother, which was another early lesson for him: no one is entitled to take the law into his own hands.

The little girl, Joan Baron, and the 'nasty' boy-next-door who beat her, James Anderton, were married 18 years later. By then, James had also learned something about forgiveness and rehabilitation.

Although Anderton insists that his family was ortho-dox, his contemporaries remember him as distinctly atyp-ical. 'He was a strange kid,' said Len Marsh, who is a year older than Anderton. 'I don't think I ever saw him smile, let alone laugh. He always looked so bloody miserable.'

Marsh followed his own father down the mines but had to retire at the age of 40 due to ill-health. He managed to re-train and found employment as a clerk with a transport company. 'Somehow he always got up my nose. There was something about him that rubbed most of us kids up the wrong way. I don't think he had a friend in the whole world. I lived in the same street. It was a tough town then, much tougher than anywhere I know today. We – the urchins from the miners' cottages – were always getting into scraps, but not him. Whatever he says, he was different. Several times I tried to pick a fight with him, but he just turned his back on me and walked away. He would say something like, "I don't want to fight you. I've never done you any harm, why are you doing this?" He could get away without fighting because he was very big. Although I wanted to give him one, I was also a bit wary.

'All the boys in the street went around in a pack, except for Anderton. Nothing was actually said, but there was an undercurrent feeling that he could look after himself, if necessary. We nicknamed him "Stuck-up Jim" because he was too good to be true. The rest of us used to do everything we could to get him into trouble. Once we threw a stone through a window, and blamed it on him. We got one of the girls to say ever-so-sweetly, "It was Jim Anderton, mister." We used the girl because we knew we wouldn't be believed. Anderton got a strapping for that, I think, but he didn't come out looking for revenge, which only made us more mad. When you taunt someone, there's no fun in it unless he reacts and retaliates. He never did. We never seemed able to get under his skin, which meant he won every time. It was maddening.

'We used to call his parents rude names to his face in an attempt to goad him, but still he wouldn't bite. Looking back, it was as if he had no real childhood. He seemed to jump a whole stage of development. He was a man in a lad's body. Being different is not healthy when you're a kid in a hard-nosed neighbourhood, but he had a remarkable flair for survival. In his own way, he had to be much tougher than the rest of us. It must have been a very lonely and painful childhood for him. He was always carrying books around and we'd tease him unmercifully, coming up behind and shouting "Bookworm!" then knocking the books out of his arms. He'd just stoop down and pick them up, and one of us might kick the books across the cobbles. The rest would join in a game of book football, with Jim groping around trying to get them back. We were always careful to keep our distance because of the instinct that, if ever he wanted, he could have dusted us all up. When he got home with dirty knees and torn books, he'd get another good hiding, I suppose, but I don't think he ever told tales.

'If we'd ever got to know him properly, we might have liked him, but when you're a kid, you're not interested in understanding people. You either rub along together or you're trying to rub each other out.'

Anderton, as much as anyone, recognizes that his childhood and adolescence were far from conventional. 'I somehow felt I was different as a youngster. Many things that seemed to please my contemporaries I found trivial and unimportant. Certainly, in matters relating to behaviour, I couldn't join in their thinking and very often stood alone as a consequence. In order to maintain my vision of life, I had to be at odds with a lot of my contemporaries. It was the same in my army life.'

Wigan in Anderton's boyhood days was a sooty, debilitating memorial to the Industrial Revolution. In the seventeenth century, it was a part of rural England, with a population of less than 4,000 and surrounded by hamlets. During the first 40 years of the nineteenth century, however, the population of Wigan soared to 40,000 to become one of the country's largest metropolitan authorities. It became famous, then infamous, for its coal mines, heavy engineering, textile mills, canals and railways. Wigan was the snakepit of every industrial vice, particularly the exploitation of child labour. In *Those Dark*

29

Satanic Mills (An illustrated record of the Industrial Revolution in South Lancashire) Alastair Gillies, archivist of the Wigan Record Office, wrote:

> The spiritual needs of the masses were also met, not so much by the Established Church, which often appeared remote to the poor disillusioned worker, but by the non-conformist chapels, and the Primitive Methodist ones in particular. With their small, unassuming buildings and simple, down-to-earth theology, they offered some means of relief to the worker and a belief that a better day would come. The Independent Methodists too established themselves in this area, which today (1981) still has the highest concentration of such chapels in the country.

The backcloth of Anderton's early life was one of square Victorian courtyards, bleak slag heaps, horse-drawn hearses, milk floats and coal-delivery carts, the street-corner smithy, hand- and foot-operated spinning-wheels, trams and trolley buses, cobbled streets and pavements, terraced miners' cottages with bulging outer walls and leaking roofs, and regimentally lined chimney stacks.

For entertainment, there was the Palace cinema in King Street and a few yards away the boisterous Hippodrome, which specialised in the traditional music hall bill of fare. Later, the Hippodrome was to become more risqué, staging such shows as *Reefer Girl* (billed as 'The Topical Sex Drama of the Day') and *We Never Clothed!* ('Brings you the Tops in Spice'), the theatre's last production in April 1956, before it was gutted by fire.

By the time Anderton was six years old, he was attending choir practice twice a week. On Sundays, he went to church four times, to communion, matins, Sunday school and evensong. Most of the children who attended church regularly were dragged there by their parents. Not Anderton. 'I went to church because that's where I wanted to be. I did not have to be ordered there. Even at that age, I felt close to God. Some people hate Sundays.

I've always looked forward to them. Church has been a second home to me, my anchor.'

As a family, they prayed to God for the food He put on their table. Anderton cannot recall ever forgetting at night to say his prayers when he went to bed. It was not something, he says, that he had to remember to do; it came to him as naturally as undressing before crawling between the sheets.

Academically, Anderton was a bright child and the fact that his parents were bookish was a constant help to him. There was never any money to buy books, but the Andertons were the best customers of the local public library. Even daily newspapers were beyond their budget, so they kept abreast of current affairs in the public library's reading room. At a very early age, James began a love affair with words and English literature, and he sailed through his examinations, winning a scholarship to Wigan Grammar School, an achievement he described as 'a very great honour'.

Every day after school, without fail, he would take himself to the Carnegie Library, where he read for hours, mainly non-fiction.

'At school, I was always in the A stream,' he related to me. 'I got by in maths and the sciences, but I had to work hard to keep up a reasonable standard. I enjoyed Latin, but I wasn't really good at languages. I was always in the top four or five of the class overall. Sometimes even top. I've still got all my school reports. They show that I never failed to do my best.'

Although his reading habits leaned towards the high-brow, schoolboy fiction was not totally excluded from his range. 'I was a great dreamer. I was going to be Biggles and fly the sky, or be a sea captain and ride the waves. I was always going to be a hero.' Even the mischievous escapades of *Just William* amused him. Over the years, the script changed, but never the theme of his dreams. The plot always concerned James Anderton making the top, fulfilling an ambition, conquering the world. Even saving the world.

On Saturday afternoons, he would pay tuppence at the cinema to see such films as *Flash Gordon* and cowboy movies featuring Roy Rogers. For weeks his mother saved to take the family to see *The Wizard of Oz*. Although nothing was said at the time, he knows now that it must have cost his mother at least half of her weekly house-keeping money. He does not think his image would benefit if he admitted being a romantic, but still he watches that film 'spellbound' every Christmas.

He cannot remember exactly how old he was when he had his first bicycle, but he knows it 'came off the back of a rag-and-bone cart', which is not the same as falling off the back of a lorry. 'It was bought for the price of a few rags.' The means of purchase did not inhibit young James. It was a bike and the wheels turned, and he was as thrilled as a teenager from a wealthy family would have been with a sports car. It was something of his own and he treated it with loving care.

The first time he saw the sea was a treat for which he had to wait several years and he still remembers it as one of the most exciting days of his life. From the age of about 10 or 11, holidays consisted of a day at Southport once a year, something he would look forward to for months. A week or two before the one-day trip to the nearby north-west coast, he would start to have sleepless nights. He likes to feel that the simple pleasures are still high octane to him, and link him to his past.

Through his daily excursions to the Carnegie Library, he was introduced to many of the icons of history, and Abraham Lincoln was one of his earliest heroes. Lincoln fitted comfortably into his embryo political vision. Anderton has always been attracted to sabre-rattling crusaders. Brave men who are prepared to gamble all or nothing for a principle are his natural soul mates; pragmatists are his plague. For Anderton, there are no pastel shades in politics; you cannot horse-trade with human life. Statesmen who have campaigned unequivocally for meritocracy and egalitarianism automatically find an honoured place in Anderton's hall of fame. He was slightly disillusioned when he read in a recent biography of Lincoln that his idol was reputed to be guilty of prevarication and brittleness of character, but he is forgiving, admitting that he, too, has weaknesses (none that he wishes to publicise, however). Even the legends of history must be allowed their peccadilloes, or they would not be human and fallible, and would, therefore, be unworthy of his admiration.

Even as a teenager, religion had him by the throat. He was appointed a Sunday school teacher and began disseminating the gospel with evangelical passion. Not unnaturally, the boys of his year at Wigan Grammar School wrote him off as 'eccentric' and 'a bore' – these were the slogans of the kinder kids. When he was twelve, he became a founder member of the 14th. Wigan Company of the Boys' Brigade. Years later, while Leicestershire's deputy chief constable, he continued this interest by accepting the office of Boys' Brigade battalion president.

One of Anderton's contemporaries at Wigan Grammar became a county councillor outside Lancashire. 'He [Anderton] was a target right from the start,' he remembered. 'What are most boys of fourteen and fifteen talking about? Sport and girls, right? Or girls and sport! Anderton didn't approve of that, although he liked sport a lot. We smoked in the bicycle-shed; Anderton disapproved. Sometimes we drank beer, though never in school; Anderton was appalled. We kissed girls in the street; Anderton probably prayed for our souls. To him, we were pariahs. To us, he was a stuffy goody-goody.

'So, we gave him a rough time. We were always passing around those so-called health magazines of our generation which were full of nude photographs, though very tame by today's standards.

'We considered it a great joke to tear out a pin-up and hide it in one of his school books. We wouldn't take our eyes off him in class as we waited for him to find the naked lady among his belongings. When he did, he went scarlet. We tried to get him in trouble by calling out, "What's that you've got, Jim?" "What are you trying to hide there, Jim?" I don't think we ever got him caught by the teacher, but we had a damned good try. He wasn't exactly a teacher's pet, as far as I can remember, but neither did he have the devil in him, like the rest of us.'

When he became chief constable, one of his first crusades was against pornography and the kind of photographs that had been used to taunt him as a child.

The senior boys at school frequently boasted about their conquests of girls. Explicit post mortems were obligatory. Anderton would squirm and walk away, at which point the other boys would immediately raise their voices.

'If you offered him an apple, he wondered where it had been stolen from,' said the Anderton contemporary. 'We should have known then that he would end up a policeman. When a girl smiled at him, he looked for the vamp anklet. Flesh seemed to frighten him, especially if it was female.'

Jane Cutler is the same age as Anderton. She married a teacher and is now a grandmother. Until the age of 20, she lived about 200 yards from Anderton. Before moving to London, she taught at schools in and around Manchester. 'I had a crush on Jim Anderton, but it was mostly from a distance. As a kid, I was quite attractive, even though I say so myself. Boys were always making a pass at me and asking for a date. I could pick and choose, but one date was very much the same as the next. The boys didn't want to talk, they didn't have anything to say. Their idea of a good evening out with a girl was an all-in wrestling match. But there was this different boy down the road who never wolf-whistled at girls. [Anderton disputes that.] That made him unusual for a start. He was invariably alone. I've always been attracted to loners, maybe because by nature I was one myself, although I was never without friends. I understand them. There are few people who are fully fulfilled by their own company, but he was one of the exceptions, and he intrigued me. I wondered whether he was always alone by choice, or whether the decision was made for him by others.

'Wigan has always been a macho town: Rugby League on Saturday afternoons, strong beer on Saturday night and hard labour the rest of the week. Virility comes free, so it was considered natural for every male to have it and to use it. When I told a girlfriend that I was interested in Jim Anderton, she warned me, "You're wasting your time."

'Jim didn't look like a cissy. In fact, he looked more man than most of the other lads. She claimed that Jim had said to a boy at school, "All you get from kissing is a cold." He might have said something like that, perhaps as a joke, but I doubt it. It sounded to me like one of those apocryphal stories that originate in the playground as a joke and suddenly takes off as fact.

'His religious conviction was constantly used against him. As if conviction meant he had committed an offence. Some small kids used to give the Anderton home a wide berth, having been told by older boys that Jim's parents sacrificed children in pagan ceremonies. Everything was so absurd, but in working-class communities, especially one as close-knit and claustrophobic as a pit town, this is what happens to nonconformists. There isn't the tolerance of Hampstead or Chelsea. Women were burned as witches just for being different. Ignorance can be deadly dangerous.

'Anyhow, I went after him, in the role of the predator, which was unusual for me. It was difficult because he never seemed to be hanging around with the other lads. I began following him to the library. I would accidentally-on-purpose bump into him as I was choosing a book. I tried to steer him into conversation, but it was not easy; he was so engrossed in what he was doing.

'Jim knew me by sight, of course, and he was always polite. Excruciatingly polite! In the end, I was the one who suggested that we might see one another somewhere other than the library. I was bowled over by his initial enthusiasm. What on earth are all the other girls talking about? I asked myself. "Great! Where shall we meet" I said. I should have anticipated the answer. He volunteered to escort me to church. I thought it was a joke and laughed. That was a mistake for which there was no second chance.'

Esther Leonard, a self-confessed demimondaine, was one of Anderton's pupils at Sunday school. She has been married five times, and five times divorced. She lost custody of her two children following a conviction for soliciting. A man she lived with was jailed for living off immoral earnings. An articulate middle-aged woman with no illusions about herself, believing that she has already had an explicit insight of the netherworld, she predicted, obviously with no fear of contradiction, 'Anderton would be ashamed of me. I went to Sunday school only because it was the thing to do. I messed around a lot of the time, but I have to say this about "Big Jim": he was one hell of a public performer, even then. His belief was total and it came across. There were no cracks; no areas for negotiation.

'The gospel was a true story to him and he told it with the sales pitch of someone who could truly recommend the product from personal experience. He was never intimidated by the scoffers like me. I wasn't really a sceptic then; I wasn't mature enough for that. I would just have preferred to be some place else.

'Anderton didn't turn me off religion, but neither did he inspire me, and I honestly believe I was up for grabs.

36

There was one flaw to his persuasive manner: he was too sure of himself. Cocksure! The story he had to tell was sacrosanct. Every statement he made was inviolate. I suppose I have to go down as the soul he lost. Or at least the one he failed to win.'

There are others who recall Anderton's early life with less clarity, people on whom his impact was minimal. 'He was a nondescript boy,' said one. 'Very ordinary. More shy than withdrawn. If he stood out from the other lads, it was because he was less aggressive. I think by nature he was much kinder than other boys of his age. He was basically a nice kid, which inevitably made him an Aunt Sally for jokes and cruel tricks at his expense. He took it all without hitting back. He was all right. Nothing special, but his heart was where it should be.'

Someone else told me: 'I think he had a strict upbringing, a harsh boyhood. He wasn't allowed to run wild like the rest of us. He was always well-mannered and polite, which generated hostility among boys of his own generation, but the girls liked him because he was considerate and didn't tease them. The one thing I remember more than anything is how kind and devoted he was to his mother.'

What many people recognised as arrogance was the opposite, according to Anderton, who insists that at school and as an early teenager, he suffered from a 'massive inferiority complex'.

Despite their highly developed intellects, his parents never thought in terms of a professional career for their son. A 'better future' than the life of his father was a job above ground, something – anything – in the sunlight. In any event, Anderton does not believe he had the alchemy for magical academic achievement. School was a chore for him, despite his love of English and his general high standards. He worked hard because it was expected of him by his parents, and for his own self-respect.

Although many of his contemporaries remember him

as a misfit, Anderton would not go that far. Never outstanding at games, he played his part. 'I was a moderate sportsman. Rugby League was my greatest sporting love; it had to be for a boy from Wigan!' He played for Worsley Boys' Club and was a keen fan of Wigan, always rushing home from weddings, throwing his choirboy collar at his mother, and scurrying off to Central Park to cheer the town team, his entrance fee paid for by the one shilling choir attendance money. Whenever he talks about Rugby League, it is to reminisce about the heroes of his boyhood – Bradshaw, Ryan and Gee. But his concept of his parents being archetypal mining folk is challenged. The connection between chapel and mining families is not disputed, but *there* the common thread seems to end. Few miners had the time, or inclination, for the kind of reading and pursuit of knowledge in which Anderton's father indulged. Neither was the majority as politically aware as the Andertons. Most miners and their families had a left-of-centre political commitment, but it tended to be historic rather than empiric.

The pub scene did not endear itself to James Anderton senior and this put further distance between him and his thirsty subterranean brethren. But those people who really knew James and Lucy found them generous, gregarious, compassionate and hospitable.

Two men shaped Anderton's life. First and foremost there was his father. The other was his great-uncle Nehemiah Occleshaw, a police constable in Manchester, who frequently visited the Andertons. For Anderton, his great-uncle was an hypnotic figure: rotund, with a florid face and an expansive waxed moustache. James would question him for hours about his life. Even tales of the expected riveted him. He feasted on morsels. Trivia was given epic treatment.

Anderton's infatuation with uniforms had become tantamount to a fetish. For Anderton, uniforms were symbols of stability. They represented authority, something

38

he literally worshipped. God he recognised as the ultimate dominion. The police and the Church were subordinate authorities, each having its own uniform, rules, rewards and penalties. He saw definite similarities between the two: they were on the same side, fighting a dual campaign.

Very early on, Anderton had decided that a policeman's calling was not unlike the vocation of a clergyman. In an interview with Lesley Garner, of the *Sunday Telegraph*, he said of the Wigan bobbies of his childhood, 'They were wonderful, majestic figures with an authoritative ambience about them. They enjoyed respect.'

While other boys hero-worshipped sports stars and pinups, Anderton was mesmerized by bobbies on the beat. He would watch them for hours, enthralled as they directed traffic, or with confident, flamboyant gestures gave directions to a lost pedestrian or motorist, or reprimanded a hooligan, ironing out the creases in town life.

He is prone to quote the words of Sanders Welch, who wrote in 1754 in *Observations on the Office of Constable*: 'Being a constable is a glorious opportunity of doing all possible good'.

As a young teenager, Anderton was first convinced that he should devote his life to Christ. He discussed with his vicar the possibility of taking holy orders, but eventually decided that a cloistered life was not for him. If he was to be involved in evangelism, it had to be at street level, amid the cut-and-thrust of daily life. 'I was fourteen or fifteen when I knew that I wanted to be a policeman,' he recalled. Even at that tender age, he had made a conscious decision about how he could best serve God.

'I was a dourly single-minded boy,' who became a dourly single-minded adult. Having decided on his career, he was determined to be 'the biggest policeman of all'. For any British policeman, the cornice must be Commissioner of the Metropolitan Police.

He talked over his plans with his parents and they were both behind him in his chosen career. Having his parents' endorsement was important to him. Adolescent rebellion is an integral part of most people's growing up, but it was not a component of Anderton's formative years. An occasional condescending air and a walk highlighted by a swagger were the only symptoms of youthful haughtiness. Even so, he feels ashamed whenever he dwells on himself as a teenager.

When he left school at the age of sixteen, he took a temporary job as a clerk with the coal board, marking time until being called up for National Service. Even at this age, he had the title of administrative officer at the coal board's No. 2 Wigan Area Office in Kirkless, New Springs. Without a doubt, those two limbo years were the most barren of Anderton's life. He had no stake in his interim job, but at a subliminal level he did learn something about office disciplines and structures, which gave him an edge when he was promoted into police management.

Anderton received his call-up papers with the intoxication of a football pools punter learning by telegram that he had won the jackpot. He was at last on his way in life and knew exactly where he was going.

The medical was a formality; he was promptly declared super fit A1. At his assessment interview, he was asked for the regiment of his choice. Without hesitation, he nominated the Military Police. Not easy to get into, he was warned. What was he doing in civilian life? What about the Ordnance Corps? The British Army, every army, needs clerks to handle the paperwork. Anderton recoiled. He had every intention, he explained, of becoming a career policeman. The army could give him the introduction he needed.

His academic record and school reference were examined. Also in his favour was his physique. Certainly he looked the part. The selection panel liked what it saw and Anderton began his police career in khaki uniform. The great game plan was under way.

As he said to Joan Bakewell, 'I wanted to prepare myself to enter the Force as a constable on the beat. That was a job that put together all that I saw in life, a profession that held dear all the ideals I treasured: integrity and a moral base for the work I had to do, a protective role in society which would match my expectation of myself as a Christian.'

He will never forget the day he left home for the first time. All his worldly goods were packed inside a cardboard suitcase. He walked tentatively from home like the reluctant partner in a trial separation. The street corner swallowed him and his boyhood was gone. The whole neighbourhood wished him well from the edges of neat curtains.

Two doors away, Joan Baron, then sixteen, noticed no change in her life.

3

A Uniform Man

For most 18-year-old males in Britain during the Fifties, National Service was a rude intrusion. It represented the continuation of institutionalised discipline that was identified with school or an austere home. It belonged to childhood; uniform was the emblem of schooldays.

Once again, Anderton was out of step, the oddball of the platoon. It is no exaggeration to say that he was besotted by army uniform – the cutting edge of the creases, bulled boots, blancoed webbing and burnished brassware.

'A love affair with uniform, tantamount to an adolescent crush, is not so uncommon among young men from Anderton's kind of background,' a psychologist explained. 'All their life their clothes have been handed down from older brothers or have come dirt-cheap from church jumble sales or charity shops. They've never known the feel of new clothing against the skin. Consequently, they've always felt inferior, like secondhand citizens, probably subconsciously, alongside their better-dressed classroom counterparts. Uniform is a great leveller; an instant equaliser. It fudges all identity. Uniform is the best disguise in the world; the ultimate mask. One nun looks like any other. They are stripped of personality.

'Three lads from the same town join the army on the same day. They come from rich, middle-class and poor families respectively. From the moment they are divested of their labels – their civilian clothes – there's no way of telling who's who. The world is stopped and they're pulled back to the same starting-line. They're issued with exactly the same number and type of clothes, even down to socks and underwear. Pay and opportunity are equal, in theory. It's the nearest one can ever come to Socialism. Even the suffering is shared equally. There are no privileges during basic training. Persecution is dispensed democratically.

'To someone like Anderton, I can understand the army and the police seeming like halfway houses to Utopia. What was undoubtedly spartan and frugal to others, must have been opulence to him. Everything is relative. If you are tall and have a certain deportment, uniform bestows upon you an inbuilt advantage, something akin to aureola; first it makes you equal, then it makes you more equal than others. I can fully see the reasons for Anderton becoming a uniform achiever.'

To many, the discipline of National Service was more of a shock than the icy water with which they had to shower and shave. But to Anderton, it was an old friend.

'It's possible to become too reliant on discipline,' said the psychologist. 'When babies are allowed to suck a dummy too long, it's difficult to break them of the habit. The same goes for any dependence. It becomes a drug, their crutch. They become slaves to a doctrine. If that doctrine is suddenly removed from their lives, so that it is unavailable to them, or is discredited, they flounder. These are very vulnerable people, often very unstable and prone to erratic behaviour. They tend to live the whole time very close to the edge. It doesn't take a lot to push them over. Often they appear extremely controlled. The truth is that they're probably over-controlled. All the time the pressure is building inside. Then one day – pop!'

Anderton cried himself to sleep on his first night away from home. He was far from alone in that respect. Despite their size and origins – mostly they came from blackboard jungle backgrounds – his fellow callow room-mates were just big babies really, fresh out of the home cradle. However bleak their life had been, it was the only one they knew, and it was missed.

Although Anderton loved and respected his father and was proud to have inherited his traits, including the temper, he was basically a mother's boy. Homesickness for Anderton was the trauma of being torn from the breast.

Anderton was an introspective recruit at the Military Police training depot, a former mental asylum at Woking, Surrey. While the others readily buried their past and prepared to reach out for what re-birth offered them, he never completely let go of yesterday. In his first few months away from home, it was as if he never truly felt safe on his own and did not completely trust himself. Everything, for so long, had been decided for him. His church gave him no room to manoeuvre on issues of religion and morality. Domestic disciplines had been strictly enforced by his father. His mother, through example, had taught him about relationships and the responsibility incorporated in them.

'Suddenly he was faced with a new set of rules, disciplines and relationship-demands, and subconsciously he would have feared that they might conflict with those which already constituted the James Anderton charter,' explained a military psychiatrist. 'He was probably very afraid, though he wouldn't have recognized the fear. People who believe they have all the answers are often more at risk, more emotionally flawed and in danger of aberrant behaviour than those who still have open – even empty – minds. It's common knowledge that mother's boys have a tendency to develop into adult loners. This can be good and bad. The loner is likely to have tunnel vision; he will have a goal and nothing nor nobody will deflect him. It's the reason why so many successful entrepreneurs and dynamic company chairmen are loners. On the deficit side, the loner has difficulty coping with personal relationships. He is not good at sharing and compromising. He needs to be winning all the time. That makes him a bad team member. He could win Wimbledon and the world chess championship, but is unlikely to be attracted to football or cricket. Even in marriage, he has to dominate and be boss. Children must do as they're told, without debate; there's no room for rebellion. Usually, he gets on better with animals, particularly dogs, which can be trained to obey commands, without questioning the sense of them.'

Anderton certainly made an impression with his fellow rookies, but not the sort he might have hoped for. Most of them quickly dismissed him as 'stuck up . . . aloof . . . a snob . . . a mummy's boy . . . a goody-goody'. One of them, now a transport policeman, had this to say; 'Almost immediately, Anderton stood out from the rest of us like the proverbial sore thumb. Within a day or two of being called up, most of us were belly-aching. We didn't take kindly to being pulled – literally – out of bed before dawn, while it was still pitch black. Nor being sworn at by the NCOs from morning 'till night. We grumbled about the food and cursed at being marched to and from the cookhouse. In the first few weeks, we didn't have any freedom. At night, weekends included, we were confined to barracks. I think it was several weeks before we were even allowed into the camp NAAFI in the evening. "Lights out" was incredibly early, but none of this seemed to bother Anderton. On the contrary, he appeared to be lapping it up, though he never said much.

'Not once did I hear him moan. The more he was chased around by the NCOs – and chase him with their sticks, they did, believe me! – the more he gave the impression he was loving it. He always did more than anybody else. Most of us did as little as possible, but he'd sit on his bed bulling his boots all night. One or two quickly caught on how to use him. They'd sidle up and say, "Hey, Jim, why aren't my boots shining the way

45

yours do? What am I doing wrong?" And he'd say, "Give 'em to me. I'll show you." And he'd do it for them and they'd be laughing and pulling faces at him behind his back.

'To be honest, I didn't think he'd make the grade, but he turned out the pick of the pack. He was very deceptive. When you talked to him, you could easily get the idea that he was both soft and a soft touch, but he was neither. In his own way, he was quite a hard nut, but it took a while for us to catch on.

'We'd be passing the fags and girlie magazines around at night, and he'd sort of shrink into a shell. We weren't exactly a sensitive bunch of choirboys, as you can well imagine, and no punches were pulled. Someone early on nicknamed him "Spit", because he was the spit-and-polish freak. He was the odd one out from the moment we found he didn't smoke. I'd been smoking since the age of twelve; I was normal, for that platoon. When he said he didn't drink either, someone asked him where he'd been all his life. He didn't rise to the bait. I don't think he answered.

'The majority of us stuck pin-ups on the inside of our locker doors, but not Anderton. Instead, he displayed photos of his parents; he took some stick for that, but if he was hurt, it didn't show.

'Anderton didn't emerge as a natural leader during basic training. One of the ringleaders, a bit of a hard case – from Merseyside, I think, a mouthy Scouse – told Anderton he'd have to drink twelve pints of beer on passing-out night. We needed to find a flaw. You don't feel at ease with someone who has no vices.

'Anderton replied that he wouldn't drink one pint, let alone twelve. There was a bit of confrontation, but Anderton held his ground. You could see the sullen stubbornness in him. Whatever the provocation, he wouldn't be intimidated. A couple of times he was dragged fully clothed under the cold shower, but he put on a brave face. He didn't lose his temper and thrash out tearfully like some did. Another time, he was stripped and blacked from head to toe with boot polish. I never felt sorry for him, though. He didn't evoke sympathy.

'He kept a Bible beside his bed and he never tried to hide the fact that he said his prayers morning and night. None of us at that age had ever come across anyone like him before. His Bible was always being hidden and he would dourly go in search of it, always polite, crawling under beds, sniffing around the ablutions, asking if anyone had seen it. "The preacher man has lost his battery!" was one of the taunts when his Bible had taken a walk.

'A few of us – I was one – wrote letters every night to our girlfriends. Do you know, I can't remember Anderton ever writing a letter, yet he must have done. I think it was army regulations to write at least one letter home every so often. But of all my recollections of Anderton, I cannot see him in my mind with a pen and writing-pad.

'He was always very starchy and square. Totally humourless. We were the first lot, so I understand, to call him "Upright Jim". It stuck for evermore, so I'm told – in the civilian police force, too. There was nothing else to call him.

'He developed, though. I don't want to give the impression that he remained a pain, because he didn't. It didn't take him all that long to come out of himself. He was like a hibernating animal, slowly but surely emerging from a long winter. On reflection, the humour probably had been there all the time, but we were too bigoted or thick to appreciate it.'

Joe Melling, now a security guard with a London store, still remembers distinctly the night they tried to get Anderton drunk. 'In the Mess, he'd have the odd drink. Just a beer. Maybe a shandy. He'd sit on the one all night.' Anderton's version is rather different. He claims that he 'never touched alcohol' at that time. Melling continued, 'It was an ambition to get him drunk. On the night in question, two or three of the others kept him in conversation while I slipped neat vodka into his beer. We chose vodka because it's colourless and doesn't smell. We waited. He sipped his beer. He didn't react. He hadn't noticed any change in flavour. A few minutes later, another opportunity arose and I poured a second shot of vodka into his glass. Everyone else knew what was going on and joined in the exercise of keeping him distracted. We knew if we were to get him legless, it would have to be done through that one drink, because not even God could talk him into having a second. Within half an hour, there must have been six vodkas in his glass and he finished it off without a word about it to anyone. We were all waiting for him to keel over. This was going to be the night we'd talk about for weeks, the night "Upright Jim", incorruptible keeper of the faith, was legless and had to be carried to his bed. We were already gloating over all the fun we were going to have at his expense. Next morning, when he couldn't remember a thing of the night before, we were going to be able to rib him with the most outrageous fabrications, such as how we were summoned to rescue some poor under-aged virgin from his clutches or to drag him from the bed of one of the officer's wives. But we never got the chance. He put down his glass and disappeared into the night as if he'd been on nothing but milk all night. Some of us followed him, thinking his legs would give way the moment he hit fresh air. Not on your life! He just kept going in a pencil-straight line.

'It's lucky he never did take up serious drinking. He'd have the capacity to knock back a skinful without turning a hair. I've often wondered whether he knew exactly what we were doing and was just proving a point – that he could beat us even at our own despicable game.'

A regular soldier who served in the Military Police with Anderton believes that many people's memories of the chief constable have been 'purpled' by 'extravagant' newspaper stories. 'Their recollections have been beefed up by everything they've read about Anderton,' he alleged. 'In the army, he was a skilled professional. If there had been anything particularly unusual about him, he would never have been promoted to a responsible position in the first place. Odd-men-out do not get on in the Forces. Anderton did get on, so there's your answer. If you read enough times that someone you once knew is unconventional in some way, your memory tends to rearrange itself accordingly. It happens to us all, without deceit intended. Anderton was a toughie, a barker and a disciplinarian. No one took liberties with him. I don't think he drank much or smoked, but there were others similar: he wasn't alone in that respect by any means and I don't believe his lack of vices particularly cut him off from the crowd.' He has a point. Most of the people who knew Anderton as a child talked about the "Jim" Anderton of their youth. Yet in those days he was known as Cyril!

Anderton is the first to acknowledge that his difficulties with relationships overlapped from school and office into the army. He has stark recollections of his comrades-in-arms ridiculing him mercilessly, mostly, he says, over his self-discipline in relation to chastity and alcohol. Only too well he remembers the 'Upright Jim' taunts, but not once did they make him waver or reconsider. 'It wasn't until much later that I questioned my commitment to my faith.' The more they mocked him, the more defiant he became. In fact, it is hard for him to call to mind a time in his life when he was not engaged in a crusade. He was quoted by one journalist, several years later, as saying, 'It was a matter of pride. No way was I going to humilate my parents.' When I saw that old newspaper cutting, it was the word 'pride' that leapt out of the page, because just a few days earlier, when I had asked him if he was proud of his record as chief constable of Greater Manchester, he had pounced, 'Pride is a sin.'

Anderton claims that the graph of his life is a straight line up to God, without a dip or a plateau. Consistency is almost a central thread of his creed, yet the reality is that although the Anderton theme music has survived virtually untouched the various social revolutions, the words most certainly have changed.

Many of the army stories about Anderton were confirmed in substance by his own comments to Joan Bakewell. 'Earlier, at school and in my teens, I suffered from a massive inferiority complex. Certainly in matters relating to behaviour, I couldn't join in their thinking and very often stood alone as a consequence. In order to maintain my vision of life, I had to be at odds with a lot of my contemporaries. It was the same in my army life.'

Although he has always recognized alcohol and licentiousness as demons of the devil, he has never skulked from them. On the contrary, he has relished open warfare, walking into the devil's den and jousting in the full glare of the public spotlight. For example, he never shunned the Mess in the army, although he knew that people there would always be trying to pressure him into something against his will. For him, this was the daily challenge to his religion and upbringing, and he welcomed being put to the test. He has always thrived on conflict and none more so than the battles on behalf of his faith.

His reputation quickly did the rounds and from then on he became a marked man. There was a lottery run by a number of rather immature and bawdy WRACs to see who could be first to seduce him. The tawdry prize was never won. No one came close. I don't suppose he objected to being tempted because it afforded him the opportunity to demonstrate his moral fortitude and durability, and he would have been uplifted by what he recognized in himself as a superior code of conduct. Every time he put Satan behind him, he was scoring a goal for God's team.

Sex for Anderton is something that goes with marriage

and nothing else. It has to be sanctioned by God, to serve His purpose, and must never be a gut reaction to a call of nature. Anderton's marriage is a contract not only with his wife but also with his Maker, and is a life-term with no chance of remission should it ever become hard labour. Long sentences have been a *cause célèbre* with Anderton ever since he found a public platform.

Although consistently a loner by temperament in the army, he was not always alone. There were one or two young soldiers who identified with him and became his disciples. By that time, Anderton's leadership qualities had blossomed and were being encouraged. He was made a substantive sergeant and then promoted to company sergeant major, but he declined a commission because that would have meant a longer engagement and his sights were set elsewhere. Although he insists that he enjoyed his National Service, which was extended into a short-service engagement, the Military Police was not for him; not as a career.

He has always considered the Police Force a bodyguard and custodian of Christianity. 'Jesus was at great pains to enforce the law. By enforcing the law, you are protecting life and property. What could be more Christian than that? The moral message is never a periphery. Morality and policing always go together.' But in the army, he was nothing more than a gaoler and troubleshooter, training others to break up bar fights, to throw the offenders into the guardhouse and to supervise fatigues. That was not his idea of real policing. Missing were the vital elements of reparation and rehabilitation. He wanted to be saving souls, not just storing them in the cooler.

When Anderton was 19 years old, he was already the senior NCO in charge of the company's toughest squad, comprising recalcitrant regulars and veteran barrack-room lawyers. You cannot bluff old soldiers. Stripes on his arms automatically gave him power, but he confesses

51

that he thrived on the responsibility that goes with authority. His confidence flowered and he began to suspect that he had been under-valuing himself through his maturing years.

Peter Frost, who became a hospital porter after serving six years in the army, more recently starting his own mini cab firm in the north-west, has never forgotten the influence Anderton had on him. 'I'd been brought up to believe in God,' he said. 'My parents were devout Christians. I rarely missed Sunday school when I was a kid. Even in my teens, I still went to church a couple of times a month. I tried to conduct my life in accordance with the Ten Commandments, but that all went out the window when I was called up for National Service.

'Like most people, I went with the tide. I told myself that only idiots swim against the flow. I began swearing and blaspheming because the others did. I wanted to be liked and considered one of the boys. You learn very quickly in the army that it can be a torturous life if you in any way vary from the norm. If you want a smooth passage, you conform. You run with the pack.

'I blasphemed about church parades and did everything possible to duck them, because that met with the approval of the pack. I began smoking and drinking heavily, which I'd never done before. I'd be cockeyed every weekend and although I had a fiancée back home, I was taking out girls who had the wrong kind of reputations.

'Then along came Anderton. He took me under his wing and said, "You don't have to be the way you are. You look miserable." And I was. I felt really wretched. But it takes courage to make a stand in isolation. Anderton did it, which made him a thousand times stronger than me. "No one will get at you, because I won't let them," he said. So I tested the water and he was true to his word. But I couldn't have done it without him. He led and I followed. I was not alone, and that made all the difference.

'He won over quite a few like me, and also some real tearaways who did not have the background of a caring upbringing. Anderton first had to establish that he was at least their physical equal, and he did that without flinching. There was nothing craven about Anderton, believe me. Because he talked religion a lot, the louts fell into the trap of thinking he would turn the other cheek if threatened with violence. That part of the Bible wasn't in Anderton's repertoire.

'He not only took care of himself, but he also looked after others too. It was Anderton who stopped me in my runaway tracks and put me back on course. I owe him a lot and I'm grateful.'

Anderton was the only National Service NCO in his company, the 170 Provost, and served most of his army days in Scotland, based some six miles south of Edinburgh. Most of his nights were spent arresting drunks and bar brawlers.

I managed to trace a man who had been arrested by a squad of Anderton's MPs for starting a fight in a pub one Saturday night. He agreed to talk only on the condition that I did not publish his name. He is married and has grandchildren. Since his army days, he has never been convicted of any offence and he has held down a responsible management job in industry since he was 35.

'I was in a terrible state when they arrested me. I didn't know what I was doing. I might easily have killed someone. I was drunk – very, very drunk – and I'd been molesting a girl who was already with someone else. I was told to "push off" in no uncertain manner. Instead of doing the sensible thing, like an idiot I picked up a bottle . . . and didn't remember anything else until I was being loaded into the truck.

'Anderton actually came to me in the middle of the night, asking how I felt and if there was anything I wanted. He was satisfying himself that I wasn't badly hurt. My head was thumping but my injuries were only superficial. I asked if I could have a mug of tea and he had one brewed specially for me. I also asked for aspirins, but he said he couldn't allow me any medication, especially as I'd been drinking. He asked if I wanted to see a doctor. I said I thought I'd be all right, if only my head would stop throbbing.

'He talked to me for a long time. He seemed genuinely concerned about me. I told him how ashamed I was of myself because I'd never been involved in anything like that before, and he sat down and virtually preached to me. At the time, it seemed like a dream; so unreal for an army MP to be talking that way to a prisoner. I said I was very sorry for what had happened. He said that I'd have to pay for what I'd done, that I'd have to take my punishment, but I should look to the future and learn from my mistakes. He said something about the army being a very forgiving institution and there was no reason why I still shouldn't have a bright future. He talked so wisely, yet he was younger than me. By the time he'd finished talking, my headache had gone. He even promised to put in a good word for me, though we'd never met before. He said he knew my record had been clean until that night. Before he left me, he said something like, "If I help you, then you must give me your word that you'll help yourself." That seemed a fair rate of exchange. He kept his side of the bargain, and so did I. There are not many ex-soldiers who have fond memories of the Military Police.

'Ever since Anderton became a chief constable, I've followed his career with interest. He's a remarkable man. From one encounter with him, I know exactly why he has gone to the top. He believes totally in what he's doing. Police work is not his occupation, it's a calling. My arrest was the beginning of his involvement with me, not the end. He locked me up and at the same time let me out, if you see what I mean. He made it possible for me to set myself free.'

Anderton could not have said it any better.

4

Poetry in Motion

Anderton joined the old Manchester city police on 30
March 1953, at the age of 21, becoming Constable DB2.
He was recruited by Robert Mark (not then knighted),
who was to become Metropolitan commissioner of police
and Britain's most outspoken policeman until being well
and truly upstaged years later by his own prodigy. During
a two-year period of energetic recruitment, Mark signed
up an elite cadre of cadets who were to become the next
generation of police mandarins. He was consciously looking for a new breed of policeman: academic high-flyers,
well-read and ambitious. Anderton met all the criteria.
So did John Stalker, another of Mark's recruits, who was
destined for a collision course with Anderton – an inter-
necine feud that was to entertain the media, serious and
otherwise, for more than a year.

Although Anderton had grown up only two doors away
from Joan Baron, they had never been friends. Joan had
long ago forgiven James for the harsh lesson he had given
her as a child, but she had not forgotten and had always
kept a healthy distance from the boy who had spanked
her.

In any case, three years is a generation gap in adolescence. They had much in common, no point of contact.
Both belonged to the mining community. Both were
deeply religious, though separated at that stage by denom-
ination: Joan was Methodist, while James was still Church

of England. Their parents were friends, so it was no mean feat to avoid one another consistently over such a span of time, but it had been achieved . . . until the Sunday – it had to be a Sunday – when they 'bumped' into one another on the way home from their different churches.

They walked home together, unable to stop talking. He did not want to let her go. Anderton says that, for him, it was 'love at first sight', suggesting he had never seen her before, not truly. They arranged to meet again – their first date. From that moment, they were officially walking out together. It was old-fashioned courtship from beginning to end. They would hold hands on walks, but that was all. It was a long time before they sealed their special relationship with a kiss. For them, a kiss meant 'I love you'. Joan has been the only woman Anderton has ever loved, apart from his mother.

Together, they joined the Christian Endeavour Movement and went on weekend rallies, gripped by evangelical fever. The Church had been matchmaker and now it served as chaperon. They enjoyed long walks and rambles which, in collaboration with their religion, packaged their engagement. In those days, the newest constables, the freshmen of the force, were on duty for a full week and then had the eighth day off, when Anderton would hurry back to Wigan to be with Joan.

Much to the approval of both families, they were married in 1955 in the Methodist church where Anderton's maternal grandfather, Silas Occleshaw, had been a preacher.

Anderton remained a constable on the beat for four years. His patch was Moss Side, once a select suburb of south Manchester, characterized by capacious Victorian residences, but by then it was on the slide, the rot made rampant by multiple occupation. It was also fast becoming a hotbed of vice. After dark – but often even in the day, before lunch – prostitutes postured under antiquated street lamps and littered every corner. Brothels were proliferating, but not the hedonistic type romanticized by Hollywood with crisp clean linen, floral finery, virgin whores and philanthropic madams. They were even a far cry from Cynthia Payne's good-humoured Streatham lair, where luncheon vouchers were exchanged for the sexual *plat du jour*. These were seedy rat-traps, run from damp basements and peeling attics, often curtainless, just a naked red light-bulb making the connection. Prostitutes would be leaning from windows, calling and beckoning to pedestrians. Pimps patrolled their territory like stalking night cats. There were illegal gaming dens and unlawful drinking clubs. Trade in pornography was growing fast. The only blessing was that drugs were not the problem they are today. This was the cauldron into which Anderton was plunged for his initiation.

'I was a happy bobby,' he remembers, not in any doubt. When he was on night duty, he used to spend many hours just reflecting or composing poetry. He never went anywhere without a personal notebook, into which he would scribble his thoughts as they occurred to him. His poetic works at that time frequently dwelt on the lives of miners and millworkers and their families. One of the poems he fashioned while on the beat in Moss Side was entitled 'Poor Souls', consisting of eight stanzas, the third of which is particularly revealing:

> The Law, the Church, the Lords, and business bosses
> Tend more and more to fashion all men's crosses
> Why is it that the feelings of real men
> Can be so subjugated time and time again?
> The day will come when unjust burdens fall
> Away from shoulders bent beneath it all.
> No man can live forever bound in chains
> Which take the shape of losses more than gains.

These are not the sentiments his fans on the political right would expect from their hero. But Anderton is not the man they think he is. He is a chameleon; he can change colour very quickly. As one leftwinger told me after Anderton had hinted to me that he might try to enter Parliament on his retirement from the police, 'It's doubtful whether even the Tories would have him. You see, you can never predict which way he's going to jump.'

When Anderton's poems were finished in rough and he was back in the police station, he typed them out and kept them.

Another of his poems, called 'Work', was written long after his bobby-on-the-beat days. Again, it has eight stanzas; the first two go thus:

> Days, weeks, months, and years
> A span of living touched by tears
> Produced by disappointment.
> Experience comes and with it grows
> Peaks of success and the right to know
> Moments of real satisfaction.

Terry Coleman, of the *Guardian* newspaper, pointed out to Anderton in 1978 that the 1960 interim report of the Royal Commission on the Police had stated that a policeman on the beat should have a sound heart and good feet, but should not be of too reflective a cast of mind. Had not Anderton, therefore, been a bad bobby, deserving admonition rather than recognition and promotion?

In his defence, Anderton referred to the occasion when Sir Robert Mark was presented with an honorary degree of Doctor of Laws. The professor who had given the eulogy at the ceremony was quoted as saying that Sir Robert had overcome a great obstacle when he joined the police: that of an educated and active mind. Anderton saw a distinct similarity between himself and Sir Robert. If he was in any way guilty, then so too was his mentor. A hint of: Is it really conceivable that two such great minds could possibly be wrong? Coleman understood

Anderton to mean that '. . . being a man of active mind should enhance one's performance of the most ordinary duties and should put "some gilt on the gingerbread"'. Certainly there is no evidence of any dereliction of duty. His reflections do not appear to have been at the expense of pavement-plodding.

Moss Side provided Anderton with a blinding kaleidoscope of infamy and temptation. There were financial inducements to look away from the vice and illicit gaming. Free sex was on offer in the brothels; free drinks in the underground drinking clubs. Some policemen, a minority, yielded. Not Anderton. The degenerates of Moss Side were perfect sparring partners to pitch against his probity. Their abject failure to penetrate his resistance was a confidence boost for Anderton, convincing him of the impregnability, and indeed sanctuary, that came with puritan rectitude. He was not intimidated by the low-life, because there was never any danger of it rubbing off on him. Neither was he tempted to despise the prostitutes who worked his patch, reminding himself continually of the special place of Mary Magdalen in the Christian tradition. All the time he was looking for redeeming features and when he detected them, he did his utmost to channel genuinely remorseful offenders towards people he hoped could help them, such as priests and community workers. But first they had to pay their debt to society (his phraseology, not mine).

Anderton was not afraid to talk with prostitutes in an effort to understand them, firmly believing that there was everything to be gained and absolutely nothing to be lost by taking the gospel on to his beat. The whores and their minders nicknamed him 'Holy Jim', without much affection. He wore police uniform and that designated him as the enemy, despite the small Bible he carried and the prayers he recited to himself in doorways and alleys.

Criminals are very conservative. A Bible-carrying copper was beyond their experience, therefore he was the devil they didn't know, making him a greater threat than the stereotype. Even so, Anderton had his street successes and pavement conversions, but nothing on a major scale.

Many moral puritans have developed an almost psychopathic hatred of prostitutes, but not Anderton. From the first moment people had a reason to listen to him, he was advocating emptying prisons of drunks and whores in order to make room for hardened, violent criminals.

Ever since he took his original police oath, he has been intrigued by the motives and chemistry that turned people to crime, and in 1960 he studied criminology at Manchester University.

Despite his four years in the front line of crime-fighting, Anderton was never really a natural street cop, unlike John Stalker. (Because of their parallel professional lives later, a brief comparison at this point is not inappropriate.) Stalker was not born to be a policeman and he became one by accident, almost against the grain. His strength was on the street, as a detective, playing cat and mouse, flourishing in the cut and thrust of combat. To Anderton, however, the CID never really appealed and he served as a detective for only two years. It was as a small boy that he first fell in love with police uniform, and that infatuation is as strong today as then. He never had any desire to disguise the fact that he was a policeman, hence his disenchantment with undercover work. Putting on his uniform each day was a solemn and edifying ritual, from which he drew strength. He has always been proud in the role of standard-bearer.

The suppressed extrovert inside Anderton was already agitating for expression. Working incognito was not the way for a crusader soliciting recognition, and certainly no role for a man who was once Oliver Cromwell.

Anderton is a steadfast believer in reincarnation and has reason to think that in a previous existence he was the puritan Cromwell. Apparently, the revelation came to him after his wife bought him a copy of Antonia Fraser's book, *Cromwell Our Chief of Men*. His mocking critics have reminded him of Cromwell's appeal in 1650 to the Church of Scotland Assembly, 'I beseech you, in the bowels of Christ, believe it possible you may be mistaken.'

Management has always been Anderton's *métier*, although after becoming desk-bound, he said once that he 'missed the hunt', adding, 'All policemen are hunters and I'm still a sworn-in constable.' But at the same time, he said also that he had 'always been a little leader' and had known from his first day in the force that he would become a chief constable. He is a fatalist and reads existential philosophers, often quoting Kant.

Stalker had no such belief in himself. Neither did he have a master plan. He lived by the day and for the day. Promotion came as a surprise, not by expectation. He had flair; Anderton had style.

Anderton's climb through the ranks was more than spectacular, it was unprecedented. Within ten years he had become a chief inspector. On 1 June 1967, he was appointed chief superintendent in charge of the Cheshire Traffic and Communications Branch. (He had been considered such an outstanding administrator that he had jumped straight from chief inspector to chief superintendent, missing out the superintendent rung on the ladder.) Now he was really racing. During that same year, he went on a senior command course at the police college and a mere 16 months after his posting to Cheshire, on 1 October 1968, he was promoted to assistant chief constable of the Leicestershire and Rutland Force. One former senior officer, who was on the command course with Anderton, remembers him for his 'unassuming' qualities. 'He was like a fly on the wall. He'd come into the Mess, sit down and quietly listen to everything that was being said. Although he didn't miss anything, he never attempted to impose himself or his views on others. He struck me as a man who could get things done, through diplomacy, and without conflict. I can't believe he's the same man who's made all those headlines for such controversial public utterances. It seems so out of character for the man I knew briefly. Either he has changed or the Press have consistently portrayed him inaccurately.' Four years later, on 1 August 1972, Anderton became assistant to HM Chief Inspector of Constabulary for England and Wales at the Home Office in London. The following year, he was the United Kingdom delegate in Paris to the Interpol conference, a gathering of the heads of police colleges from all over the world.

Meanwhile, his brief at the Home Office was training, traffic, telecommunications, computers, community relations, organisation and management, personnel, establishments and general police procedure. In 1974, he was despatched on a lecture tour of seven Asian countries. He had only just returned from that engagement when he was sent as the United Kingdom representative to the fifth United Nations Congress on the Prevention of Crime.

Cyril James Anderton clearly was being groomed for the highest office in the British police force. He was on course – and within his own demanding timetable – to reach chief constable by the age of 45. His next important breakthrough came on 1 February 1975, when he made his triumphant return to Manchester, taking over as deputy chief constable from Stanley Barratt, who had been made chief constable of South Yorkshire.

Then, on 2 April 1976, at the age of 44, he stepped up to the exalted rank of chief constable of Greater Manchester, in succession to James Richards, who was retiring on 30 June after 42 years' service with the police. Anderton's salary scale then was £13,275–£14,157. (Eleven years later this had more than trebled.)

At the time of Anderton's appointment, the Greater Manchester police force, the largest in the United Kingdom outside London, had an authorized strength of 6,628, though its actual establishment was well below the plimsoll-line at 5,953. The area covered was 500 square miles, with a population to protect of two and threequarter million.

It had taken Anderton just 23 years and three months to rise from raw recruit to Britain's youngest ever chief constable.

5

A City at War

Anderton is not the sort of executive who plays himself in quietly. He has taken each new challenge by the scruff of the neck from the first day. There was no moderating his mode when he took his place on the throne in the chief constable's spacious wood-panelled office at Greater Manchester's Bootle Street police headquarters. He came in like a storm and the wind continued to rage throughout his turbulent reign.

'Crime is rising here as everywhere,' he lamented. 'Our detection rate in the first half of 1976 was fifty-nine and a half per cent. This is extremely good. We can take a great deal of pride in that figure, though, of course, a hundred per cent would be better.'

Anderton's reputation in police circles had preceded him. Now the public also knew that the security of one of Britain's largest cities was in the hands of a hard taskmaster and an inflexible perfectionist.

Anderton was quick to diagnose and prescribe cures. 'The way to prevent crime is to have a powerful presence of policemen in uniform on the streets. I prefer prevention on the streets rather than the fire brigade type of response we now have to crime. I am prepared to accept the public disquiet about the apparent lack of foot patrols. This is not just a gimmick to placate people. We tend to be over-concerned with the result and not too much with how it happened in the first place. There is no social stigma to wrongdoing nor a question of changing moral attitudes. It may be long-term, but I would like to see the example being set by the adult population. We have to persuade people to set a better example. It is my ambition that I will seize every opportunity to visit every station to see and talk to my men.'

Explaining his meteoric rise, Anderton said, 'I have benefited from enlightened chief constables of the forces in which I've served. My career shows that every constable now has the chance of top command while he is still young. I made up my mind in my teens that I wanted to be a policeman. My parents encouraged me and I have never regretted it.' (By 'enlightened' Anderton means chief constables who have deliberately adopted an open forum policy of policing with the public.)

When questioned about his childhood, he said, 'I was mischievous. We got boxed on the ear by the local police. I never stole and I have never told a lie. Never. I had this great love of humanity and desire to stand up for the underdog.'

Of his army days, 'I thoroughly enjoyed my time.'

And of his police career, 'My work is a joy. From first to last.'

After being in office barely four months, Anderton was putting into action his pledge to try to make his domain a safer place, day and night. On to the streets of Manchester he launched decoy patrols, aimed at luring muggers into the open. Detectives were disguised as soft targets – reasonably well-heeled pedestrians suffering from a physical handicap, ranging from a limp to blindness.

Anderton chose the annual meeting of the Manchester Council for Voluntary Services to leak his 'declaration of war' against the muggers. It was a speech that was to set the temperature for his entire term of office. 'I aim to crack down on cowardly young thugs who, without provocation and for the sake of a few pounds, attack, terrorize and viciously assault defenceless and often elderly people.

'The offenders must be caught by the police and dealt with in such a way that they are not disposed to repeat their crimes. It may well be that there is a hard core of offenders responsible for most of the crimes. We must return to old-fashioned virtues of discipline, respect and obedience. If there was ever a moment, apart from wartime, when people everywhere should join forces in spirited citizenship to make a concerted and decisive effort to re-direct community life for the common good, it must surely be now.'

The reference to old-fashioned virtues, discipline, respect and obedience is classic Anderton rhetoric – and would become a feature of his public utterances, whether a homily from the pulpit or an oration from the platform.

In his favour, Anderton has never been the kind of general who leads from his fireside armchair. He earned the respect of his own force by putting himself on the street as one of the first decoys. 'It's a high priority,' he announced to the people of Manchester. 'I've put squads of highly trained detectives into problem areas.'

Meanwhile, his senior officers were telling people, 'It's Jim's own brainchild. You've got to give him credit, he's prepared to try anything. He's a chef who's brave enough to be first to taste his own cooking.'

This was just the beginning, a public wine-tasting, of Anderton's high-profile leadership. On the whole, the police and public responded positively to Anderton's aggressive and open style of management. The ratepayers, in particular, welcomed his robust and experimental approach to tackling crime on the streets. Many of them were weary of what they saw, rightly or wrongly, as an over-liberal approach of *let's understand the criminal and to hell with the victim*, which did not appear to be getting results.

Anderton speaks the forthright, no-frills language of the north-west. One of his senior colleagues in Leicester summed him up like this: 'Jim Anderton has the gift of feeling the pulse of the public and making it beat quicker. He's an uncannily successful populist.'

Most chief constables reach the top by proving themselves superlative administrators. More than anyone else, Anderton seemed to embody the academic breed of civil servant. Therefore, it came to his colleagues as a surprise – a pleasant one to most of them – to discover that there was another man beneath the image, one with a thirst for action, demonstrated at Wembley Stadium in 1976 when Anderton attended the Rugby League Cup Final. During the game, violence broke out in one section of the crowd. Anderton was off duty ('chief constables are never off duty') and was at the match purely as a rugby-loving spectator, but instinct took over and pitched him from his seat into battle alongside the Metropolitan police, who willingly accepted him on loan in their hour of need.

Although the public approved of the police decoys in the streets, many crime-prevention experts interpreted the move as nothing more than a gimmick, but it did focus attention on the problem and attracted extensive publicity. The citizens of Manchester were suitably impressed by the concept of the police, even their exalted chief constable, deliberately making themselves vulnerable and being offered as sacrifices after dark in the high-risk zones.

'Now they know how we feel,' one elderly resident of Moss Side commented at the time.

Of course, no one attempted to mug Anderton. However fragile he tried to make himself appear, there was no means of camouflaging his 14 stone-plus, or appreciably reducing his 6 feet 2 inches. Even with a muffler looped around the bottom half of his face, and leaning on a walking-stick, he would not have been appetizing to any mugger looking for easy pickings.

Anderton argued that the decoy squads were a deterrent, but their success, if any, is impossible to quantify . . . and the mugger is still with us.

In New York, the decoy approach to combating crime was being tried on the subway trains, with some notable coups, probably due to the restricted target area. Anderton had picked up the idea at the 1974 United Nations Congress on Crime. The decoy system is an offshoot of the principle of infiltration – very American in origin – and was ideal for an ambitious man who wanted to come up quickly with something new in Britain in order to make his mark and to help keep his country abreast of the latest crime-fighting philosophy.

Another controversy was already simmering, of a kind that was to pepper Anderton's administration. From the moment he succeeded James Richards, he despatched senior officers to all the Rugby League clubs within his jurisdiction, warning them against breaking the Sabbath laws by playing matches on Sundays. Rugby League officials immediately accused Anderton of being a lackey of the Lord's Day Observance Society. In a statement, the Rugby League secretary, David Oxley, said, 'We have no quarrel with the police. They are only doing their job. But what we're angry about is this harassment by the Lord's Day Observance Society. The police visits started only since the new chief constable took over and it's my understanding that he's having to act on complaints made by the Lord's Day Observance Society.' Oxley was displeased by Anderton singling out Rugby League, the police chief's professed favourite sport. 'Every other sport you can think of is played on a Sunday in this country,' Oxley complained. 'Why us? What have we done to upset him?'

Anderton retaliated, 'I am merely reminding clubs of the provisions of the Sunday Observance Act in relation to the admission of spectators to sporting fixtures on Sundays. Our advice to the clubs was thought to have been received in the spirit in which it was given.'

There were never any charges, but Anderton had given an unambiguous indication of the way he was going. This example of a quasi-moral/religious purge was to symbolize his tenure of office. He once said, 'Some say that in the light of what has transpired, I have been able to express my Christianity and reach more people than I otherwise could. You can exert a Christian influence in police work.'

Blatantly, he used his position as a platform to propagate his own morality and theology. 'When I advanced, I never let out a cry and said, "Now's my chance!"' he defended himself. Nevertheless, he joined the police in the first place in the belief that he could better serve God as a policeman than as a priest. It was a religious decision rather than a career choice, although he would say that the two are inseparable. Each promotion gave him more clout in God's name. When we were discussing the possibility of his one day standing for Parliament, he said, 'That would give me another platform.' Which party? 'Perhaps I should start my own!' I think he was joking. Despite his training, he thinks like a politician.

Rugby League fans were still seething when Anderton made a speech in November 1976 at the conference in the Piccadilly Hotel, Manchester, of the Police Federation, the policemen's union. However, even the lovers of rugby joined in the standing ovation when he said, 'For the offender, the crime may be no more than a flash of violent action, but for the victim it can be a haunting memory of fear. In my area, and many others, there is as wave of senseless violence, leaving in its wake too many wrecked lives.' Courageously you may think, considering his audience, he also made a scathing attack on the corrupt members in their midst. 'Bent coppers must remain a total disgrace to the entire community and a blatant denial of the integrity of the police service.' In a wide-ranging speech, he then rubbished plans to establish a police complaints board under the new Police Act. 'I have genuine anxiety and deep concern, along with Sir Robert Mark.' By then, Sir Robert was commissioner of the Metropolitan police. 'I never regard it as part of my responsibility to seek to defend or protect corrupt police officers.' During the same debate, Ken Mallinson, a former police sergeant who had become the landlord of the Ring O'Bells public house at Silkstone, near Barnsley, Yorkshire, called for vandals to be put in the stocks. He, too, was warmly applauded.

Almost every night Anderton had a speaking engagement. He was loath to miss any chance of exploiting his position to broadcast his views on policing, religion, morality and politics. He also collected public appointments the way other people stockpile rare coins or stamps and gained 32 in all: county director, St John's Ambulance Association, Greater Manchester; member, Council of the British Institute of Management; chairman, north-west region, British Institute of Management; president, Manchester branch, British Institute of Management; president, Junior League of Manchester NSPCC; president, Bolton Mini Le Mans Charity Race; president, Manchester and District RSPCA; president, British College of Accordionists; patron, north-west Eye Research Trust; patron, north-west Counties Schools' Amateur Boxing Association; patron, north-west Campaign for Kidney Donors; patron, Greater Manchester Committee, International Spinal Research Trust; patron, Sale branch, RNLI; hon. patron, Greater Manchester Federation of Boys' Clubs Challenge Appeal; patron, North Manchester Hospital Broadcasting Service; hon. national vice-president, The Boys' Brigade (1983); hon. vice-president No. 318 (Sale) Squadron ATC; vice-president, Manchester YMCA; vice-president, Adelphi Lads' Clubs, Stretford; vice-president, Sharp Street Ragged School, Manchester; vice-president, Manchester Schools' Football Association; vice-president, Greater Manchester East Scout Council; vice-president, Greater Manchester Federation of Boys' Clubs; vice-president, Manchester and District branch of Royal Life Saving Society; member, NSPCC executive committee, Manchester and district;

member, Manchester Advisory Board, Salvation Army; trustee, Piccadilly Radio Community Trust; trustee, Manchester Olympic Games Trust; hon. RNCM (Royal Northern College of Music), 1984; Cross Pro Ecclesia et Pontifice, 1982; and Chevalier de la Confrerie des Chevaliers du Tastevin, 1985. He is also a supporter of the Society for the Protection of Unborn Children, the anti-abortion lobby group, although he holds no title with that organisation.

He explained his insatiable public involvement this way: 'As a policeman, your job is your life and your family knows that. As a chief constable, you are public property; you have to be prepared to accept that. Whatever I do places a burden on others. I constantly have to question my actions as chief constable because there is always a price to pay, and often it is my wife who has to pick up the tab. I have to accept total loss of privacy and a good deal of hostility. I know in everything I do of a controversial nature, I am inflicting pain on my wife.'

He has also said, 'I give of my best. I don't look for public reward or approval, which matters not. If I was given a task, I would do it to the utmost of my ability. If I were asked to sweep a road, I would sweep it like it had never been done before. I can never cut off from my work. I can't. It's a lifestyle, an attitude of mind. I am committed.'

The national press quickly grasped that Anderton was a gifted producer of headline fodder. The dust had scarcely settled on his skirmish with the Rugby League hierarchy, when he came into conflict with the nation's more enlightened and progressive educationalists, exhorting teachers and parents to wield the cane. For his speech in favour of corporal punishment, he chose a gathering of the Greater Manchester Federation of Boys' Clubs, saying, 'The reasonable physical chastisement of wrongdoers, in my view, is justified in some situations. The conduct of some teenagers is so outrageous that some

71

form of corporal punishment would not be out of place.' He blamed the disruptive and hostile behaviour of rebellious young people on adults, 'for indulging in so many anti-social, immoral and irresponsible activities'. Quoting from the latest figures available to him, he said that juveniles between the ages of 10 and 16 committed more than 33 per cent of the known crime in Greater Manchester in the first nine months of that year. Burglaries had made up 53 per cent of those crimes; 46 per cent were robbery and theft (44 per cent from shops and market stalls).

On another occasion, he was to say of vicious criminals, 'I would have people flogged until they begged for mercy.' Penal work camps, where prisoners who had been convicted of crimes of violence would be 'humiliated into penitence' through a daily dose of unremitting hard labour, was another of his shock-treatment recommendations for scaring violent criminals off the streets. Although advocating corporal punishment, he was against the return of the birch or 'cat', believing them to be inhuman.

However, he was all in favour of firm floggings with 'a medically approved cane'.

Overnight he became the darling of the 'hang 'em, flog 'em' fraternity, but he did not believe everything they read into his artificially unequivocal pronouncements. When it came to the question of capital punishment, the reactionaries were dismayed to find their champion in the wets' camp. Anderton had decided that the taking and giving of life should be left to God's discretion. But he had not always thought that way. Early in his police career, he had been an adherent of the death penalty for all crimes of murder. Experience and his religion made him switch sides, but by 1978 he was going through yet another crisis of conscience. At a Rotary conference in Blackpool, he revealed that he had come to the agonizing conclusion that terrorists who murdered for political motives should hang. A decade later, he reversed this decision too.

Anderton would say that these dramatic shifts of opinion testify to maturity and enlightenment. Was it not the American liberal philosopher, Emerson, who wrote in his essay on politics: 'The law is only a memorandum. The statute stands there to say, yesterday we agreed so and so, but how feel ye this article today? Our statute is a currency which we stamp with our own portrait.'

Not known even to his closest allies was the bizarre source of their leader's bright ideas. They might have been somewhat pole-axed to learn that many of Anderton's brainwaves came as revelations in his dreams. In the middle of the night, as he slept alongside Joan, voices and visions would take over his subconscious. According to Anderton, this was God's way of guiding him. He would say his prayers just before going to sleep and God would come up with the answers during the night; the following day Anderton would act upon the divine messages and mental imagery. He has said that the more he tried to elaborate and expound this phenomenon, 'the more daft it seems'.

Already he was the most controversial police chief ever, and he had been in office a mere six months.

6

A Dream of a Solution

For the first time since their marriage, Joan Anderton felt settled. Until her husband returned to Manchester as deputy chief constable, they had lived as salaried gypsies, sometimes moving home as often as twice a year. At last they had a permanent place to live, a modern detached house in Sale, Cheshire, in the heart of the Manchester commuter belt and, during off-peak periods, a mere 15-minute drive from the office.

The education of their daughter, Gillian, was also becoming a crucial factor. She was attending Sale Grammar School and her mother was determined that there should be no further uprooting until Gillian had taken her GCE 'O' Levels.

Although Joan Anderton has always been a formidable woman, the impression given by much of the media is that she is totally dominated by her husband. Rumour has it that Anderton selects all the clothes that Joan buys and even dictates to the hairdresser what style to give his wife. Such a relationship is denied by them both.

It was Joan Anderton who converted her husband to her own Methodist persuasion. Not only did he take up his wife's faith and forsake his own, but he did so with such fervour that he even became a Methodist lay preacher. Anderton is impassioned about everything he undertakes, even his hobbies and recreations. When he puts on jeans, a tatty shirt and sweater to try his hand at painting and decorating, he does not dabble in the manner of most DIY dilettantes. 'I pay a tremendous amount of attention to detail in everything I do and it doesn't matter that no one ever inspects my decorating. For me to enjoy it, I must try to do it better than anyone else.'

So, is there such a thing as a typical day in the life of James Anderton? There is, but it has changed over the years.

From the time he became the chief constable of Greater Manchester, Joan would be the first up in the morning, rising at six o'clock. Anderton sleeps on until treated to breakfast in bed – seven days a week. At the time of writing, this would consist of plain porridge, a glass of fresh, unsweetened orange juice, lemon tea, vitamin pills, halibut oil capsules and yeast tablets. All the pills come by order of his wife, who stands over him, arms folded, watching him swallow every one; hardly the image of a downtrodden spouse. Joan contends that the tablets are essential if he is to maintain his mental and physical energy. Anderton is sceptical, but would rather take his medicine than the alternative, which would probably be no breakfast in bed. Every man has a price.

Back in 1976, breakfast had a very different flavour: grapefruit, eggs and bacon, toast and marmalade. His meals have changed in content according to the stipulations of his latest diet. He is always trying out the latest. Weight is one of his bigger problems and quickly gets out of control if not watched.

While eating his breakfast in bed, he reads the *Daily Telegraph*. As soon as he has finished eating it is time for a cold shower, in winter as well as summer. Joan is a yoga fanatic and makes sure that her husband does a few exercises before dressing. If anyone dominates in the Anderton household during the pre-work hours, it is Joan.

At some point during the morning scramble, he will say his prayers; possibly while under the shower or as he lowers himself in front of the bathroom mirror, slicking back his straight black hair and tidying his Moses beard.

In the army, Anderton made a ritual out of bulling his boots at night. He is no longer quite so fussy about his appearance, except when wearing uniform. Most mornings, he cheats and polishes his shoes on his trousers just before leaving.

His chauffeur-driven car arrives at about 8.15, sometimes a few minutes earlier, never late. Before leaving, he kisses Joan in the shadow of the doorway. Without that kiss, the whole day would be desolate for him.

From the moment the car pulls away from the kerb, Anderton's working day has begun. Sometimes he makes as many as a dozen calls on the car telephone between Sale and the Chester House headquarters in Old Trafford, which overlooks the Lancashire county cricket ground and Manchester United's football stadium. Alternatively, he may draft letters, make notes for a speech he is scheduled to deliver that lunchtime or evening, familiarize himself with the latest Government and Home Office circulars, or quickly finish his prayers and read a few passages of the Bible.

On arriving at Chester House, which was completed in 1979, he walks up the 221 steps to his security suite on the eleventh floor. Only Anderton and the builders have counted the steps: everyone else uses the lifts. Not once, even when pushed for time, has he ever taken the mechanical route. If he arrives with visitors, they take the easy way to the top and then have to wait for their breathless Tarzan. Occasionally he times himself, just to put his mind at rest that he is not slowing down. Now and again he will also monitor his pulse, to see how long it takes for it to return to a steady beat, a fairly accurate gauge of fitness. This daily demonstration that he can survive without a lift in life is yet another source of pride.

From the top of the stairwell, he goes straight to his office where, already laid out for him on his desk, are articles cut from the morning newspapers by members of his personal staff, who are equivalent to acolytes at an ancient Roman court; even if Anderton does not regard himself as Caesar, everyone else most certainly does. Among his very large entourage, amounting to as many as 16 officers, including some women, are two drivers, a couple of secretaries, researchers, a uniformed superintendent, who is his righthand man, and a constable whose main function in life is to perform surgery on newspapers and magazines, collecting press clippings which he feels may interest his boss. All the people who work on the eleventh floor are his flock. They are Anderton loyalists, his kind of people. He knows them all by their first name and in return they call him sir; that is Anderton egalitarianism. Before staff are drafted to the gods, they are assiduously vetted. They have to be the right sort of people, which means sympathetic towards Anderton's style of dictatorship.

'You won't find any heathens or libertines up there,' one veteran officer at Chester House said. 'Correction – you won't find anyone up there *admitting* to being a nonbeliever or anti-Establishment. They're skilled creeps, most of them. They know exactly what Anderton wants to hear and they hum the tune. The eleventh floor is another planet. It's similar to a germ-free oxygen tent. Bad news is kept out. Anderton is fed the bland food that his factotums know he swallows easily.'

Whenever Anderton is in the news, which is most days, even if only through the local media, the sorting of the mail is a full-time job for two officers. The letters fill several sacks every week and are stored in one of the outer offices. Anderton is extremely responsive to public opinion, but he is not all that concerned about the minutia of the correspondence.

Another officer at headquarters explained, 'His main consideration is how many letters support him and how many are critical.' Yet another example of the politician's mentality: *Am I winning the vote?*

One of his trusted team came clean. 'Some letters are just too terrible to show him. They get hidden. Not always, mind you. We tend to be very selective. Everything depends so much on his mood.'

Anderton is candid about his short-fuse temper, a flaw he inherited from his volatile father. When he is angry, he thumps his desk with his considerable fist and his long, fleshy face becomes bloodless, except for tiny red spots which spread in a rash of rage while his eyes roll. When piqued, he is prone to strong language, but he never blasphemes.

The *Observer* newspaper quoted a policeman who was reputed to be particularly close to Anderton – rare for a colleague – as saying, 'Anderton is a superb actor who has mastered the art of insincerity.' At a Police Authority meeting, Anderton once declared in a last-ditch gamble to swing the argument his way: 'Do I have to bring in the bodies of my dead policemen to convince you?'

Often he will interrupt his officers impatiently, with a dismissive wave of the hand, before they have a chance to finish a sentence, especially if the content is not to his liking. One indiscreet remark in his presence can spoil the climate for the rest of the day, which is the reason why many of the anti-Anderton missiles are intercepted.

One of his drivers had this to say: 'He's a good boss to work for . . . overall. He supports his staff; he backs us over pay claims and the need for more manpower. Despite his image, he's very much one of the boys. He can be a smashing lad. He's a copper's policeman through and through. But some of his public statements make life difficult for the rest of us. They create a diversion.'

Not bad strategy when you have something to hide, such as a climbing crime-wave, matched by a nosediving detection rate. Since the mid-Eighties, the morale among the Greater Manchester detectives has been on the decline, especially in the B and D divisions, which cover the daunting inner-city areas. By the end of 1986, the clear-up rates for B and D divisions were 25.3 per cent and 24.1 per cent respectively – dismal figures which incensed the honest residents trapped in those lawless and anarchistic parishes. Between January and September 1986, there were 220,259 crimes reported in Greater Manchester, a disconcerting rise of 13.3 per cent on comparable figures for the same period in the previous year. This increase put Greater Manchester near the top of the United Kingdom crime league. Neither was there any consolation for Anderton from the overall picture: the 27.6 detection level represented a downward spiral of five per cent on 1985. The number of burglaries had shot up by an intolerable 17.2 per cent, resulting in house-owners feeling complete lack of confidence in the police.

The Greater Manchester statistics were a disgrace, especially when compared with those of parallel regions. Through retirement, Anderton had lost a coterie of his most experienced and successful officers, including Detective Chief Superintendent John Thorburn, Assistant Chief Constable Charles Horan, and Detective Chief Superintendent Jack Ridgeway and Ken Foster, and the gaps were noticeable.

Anderton hopes to be remembered as 'the people's policeman'. Pressing that point, he emphasized, 'I belong to the people.' He is satisfied that he has always spoken their language. But what they found so difficult to understand was how a leader with so many absolute solutions and such impressive connections, upstairs and downstairs, could fail so consistently in the confrontation with crime. Especially with an annual budget of £168 million at his disposal.

Every morning at 9.30, unless he is out of town, Anderton chairs a round-table conference, attended by his deputy and seven chief officers.

At one time, he used to accept invitations to formal

luncheons, especially if he was asked to speak, but he started cutting back on those commitments when each one left its mark on his waistline. So, whenever possible, he eats lunch at his desk, settling for an apple, a grapefruit and an orange, a couple of high-fibre biscuits and a cup of lemon tea. Next to his office is a small room in which he says his prayers. He retires there at any time during the day when he decides that he needs to be alone with God. A copy of the New Testament is always by his side. If a crucial decision has to be taken, he will exhibit the facts, as he sees them, on his imaginary high altar for God's blessing. In addition to the Bible, he always carries a copy of his Catechism with him wherever he goes. The Catechism is kept in his briefcase and comes out when he has time to meditate, such as during train and plane journeys.

In the afternoon, he tries to put his paperwork aside for an hour or more while he walks the streets of Manchester with one of the officers from his personal staff. He is instantly recognizable, more so than many sports and pop stars, and he is used to being accosted in the street. 'I love it, every minute of it.' Old people stop him and talk about the fears for their safety at night and explain why they dare not venture out after dark. Anderton always produces a notebook and writes down details. 'As soon as I get back to my office, I shall attend to this matter,' he promises. 'I'm grateful to you for bringing these facts to my attention.' He is proud that his flock find him so approachable. His post-lunch meet-the-people sessions are tantamount to a prime minister's walkabout. He wants to be regarded as accessible and not the sheltered figure-head of an ivory tower. 'Just another stunt,' sneer his opponents.

As soon as he returns to his office, afternoon tea is served. Before committing his signature to important and far-reaching edicts, he might retire to his adjoining prayer-room for a final collaboration with his Master. Once God has given the nod, there is no turning back for

Anderton, whatever the supplication from other quarters. Most of his major decisions are made after five o'clock, when the flow of incoming calls begins to tail off.

Sometime between 7.30 and 8.00 pm, the duty driver is informed that Anderton is preparing to leave headquarters, but home is rarely the destination. Almost every evening he is committed to a public engagement. In one year, for example, he made 64 speeches, and attended 134 civic functions and 71 police gatherings. If he is an official guest at a dinner, he might have a pre-meal drink of vodka or malt whisky, followed by a glass of wine. Joan never expects him home before midnight, so she takes herself to bed between 10.00 and 11.00 pm, usually just after the 'Ten O'clock News' on television.

Anderton rarely goes straight to bed on his return home, whatever the hour. Before doing anything else, he sheds his clothes and changes into a tracksuit. Only then is he able to relax. If he is feeling a little hungry, he might put together a cheese sandwich, helping it down with a double scotch, while reflecting on the day behind him. Reclining in an armchair with his legs kicked out, he checks to see if there are any late-night movies on television. He is a real black-and-white movie buff and a fan of the late John Wayne, though any guns-blazing Western will suffice. *True Grit* is his favourite Wayne movie, which he has seen countless times. Wayne is a classical Anderton hero: patriotic, upright, swashbuckling, fearless, frank-talking, straight-shooting and illiberal.

Just before going to bed, he frequently listens to a tape of Luciano Pavarotti, which is not far short of a spiritual experience for him. He never allows sleep to creep up on him until he has said his prayers again, asking to be 'led through the new day by the good shepherd'.

Anderton expounded as we chatted in his office, 'Prayer enables me to get a problem in clear focus. I share that problem with God and ask for guidance to resolve it.

Prayer affords me comfort. It helps me to find a better answer, a way out. It is a moment for me to think and to reflect. I'm cast in the media as a crank. I hope this is not an unhealthy sign of the times, that to believe in God is to be a crank? I'm described as a self-publicist who wallows in it, but I don't need publicity. It has brought me nothing but trouble. But police work is a public matter. Speaking out is a part of my accountability.'

Most people quickly forget their dreams. Not Anderton. He files every one. He even records them, in writing, believing they have divine significance. Every morning he is excited by the communiqués of the night. Each dream is sedulously coded.

There are two dreams that dominate his nights. In one, he is always running down a steep hill with a pack of sharp pins in pursuit. His heart is thumping and he is gasping for breath. The pins are all the time gaining on him, until they are just about to become embedded in his back, but they never quite succeed. Anderton somehow always avoids the fate of the pin-cushion. In the other dream, he is levitating, looking at the world from outside himself, being refreshed with answers that eluded him during the distractions of the day.

But what is the import of the pins? That dream, perhaps, can be traced back to his mother, who kept a collection of pins in her pinafore. When he was a boy and his mother used to hug him, he was terrified that he would be impaled on the pins.

The Andertons have a second home, a holiday cottage in the Lake District, which is their weekend retreat. When they are at the cottage, Anderton turns into a different man, unrecognizable as the dynamic, superstar policeman who lashes himself through an 18-hour working day with zeal. In the wilderness of the Lake District, he reads – mostly history – listens to music, writes poetry about the trees, the rain and the landscape (he dismisses his compositions as 'pitiful stuff'), paints and decorates, walks for miles with Joan over the rugged Fells, and makes himself responsible for the odd jobs.

When Gillian was a girl, she loved to get away with her parents to their country cottage and enjoyed the outdoor life, but those halcyon days died long ago. Gillian's schooldays were not easy. She was a sensitive introvert, the very antithesis of her father, and wished to be judged on her own merits, but every time Anderton made one of his provocative pronouncements, it was Gillian who was stung by the backlash.

'My life has been threatened,' Anderton lamented. 'My wife and family have been threatened. What they both suffered could have been avoided if I had kept silent, but I never will.' And he had these words for another interviewer, 'My family see so little of me. We are told to get the balance right, but I know that if I had the time to do it over again, I would do it exactly the same way. It behoves everybody in every walk of life to improve the quality of life. I don't have to concern myself with matters confined to my police job. People cannot hide behind the façade of professionalism. We have to address life in its fullest sense. Too many people are negating a basic sense of duty. There is a desperate lack of purpose, an unwillingness to bare their souls, to demonstrate what they believe in.'

No one seems to have asked Gillian what she believed. Everyone assumed that she must believe in her father. She was seen as part of the Anderton package, and her father had no intention of modifying his brash and abrasive public mien for the sake of wife and daughter. Perhaps it never occurred to Anderton that his own flesh and blood could harbour religious and moral instincts dissimilar to his own. His duty took preference over all family considerations. If wife and daughter were hurt by the fall-out, it was unfortunate, but innocent people have been the victims of war since the first battle, he would argue. However, it was not Gillian's war. All she asked for was the freedom and peace of anonymity.

Joan had joined her husband's crusade, but Gillian was born into it; a big difference. When Anderton talked to colleagues about Gillian, he referred to her as '*his* future'. One of Anderton's police enemies leaked the lie that Gillian had dropped out of her Law course at Birmingham University as a protest against her 'dictatorial' father. The truth is that she not only completed the course, but left university with an honours degree. Anderton insists that he has 'a super' relationship with his daughter, but concedes, 'I think I have created difficulties for her because of my high public profile. She and my wife are my sternest critics.' From Birmingham, Gillian went to London and found a welfare job in one of the leftwing boroughs, helping to locate homes for the down-and-outs who were sleeping rough. Her office overlooked a small park and the job entailed touring during the night some of the capital's most dangerous streets and alleys, searching among cardboard boxes and under newspapers for human derelicts in need of rescue. She even kept from her closest friends the fact that she was the daughter of James Anderton.

When cornered by one tenacious member of the press corps, all she would say was, 'I am here to do a job and I don't give interviews.' She has since made it clear that the 'most precious' people in her life are her parents and that her father understands her better than anybody. 'I can tell him anything. He's so patient, so tolerant. But I'm proud of them both.'

One of her friends, who also worked as a social worker in London, explained, 'Gillian is a very gentle person. She doesn't believe in saying anything that might hurt anybody's feelings. The truth is, she's considerably to the left of her father. Gillian thrives on intellectual bargaining. She recoils from verbal thuggery.'

She had in mind such statements as, 'I abhor sexual

promiscuity. The condition of homosexuality, however we explain that, is not against the law. What used to be against the law, and should be, are some sexual acts practised by homosexuals and by some who are not homosexual. We know of people, thousands of them, who for their own sadistic and selfish pleasures and sexual satisfaction engage in buggery and sodomy and acts against children. They are just people with dirty, filthy minds, engaged in dirty, filthy acts, and I will speak out against them.'

During a lecture in Preston, Lancashire, he had implored society to afford 'short shrift' to social nonconformists, malingerers, idlers, parasites, spongers, frauds, cheats and unrepentant criminals. There should be 'rewards' for honour, hard work and dedication, he said.

Anderton is the first to describe himself as a nonconformist. But he is not the sort of nonconformist he was condemning on the public platform in Preston! Anderton's nonconformism is 'individualism and valour', Gillian's friend mocked.

7

'A Commie Yellow Belly!'

In the summer of 1977, the leader of the National Front, Martin Webster, announced his intention to head a procession of his organisation's members through the streets of Hyde in Greater Manchester.

Hyde is a predominantly working-class town on the A57 road eight miles due east of Manchester, almost straddling the Yorkshire/Derbyshire border. Continue eastwards for two miles and you come to Hattersley, where the Moors Murderers, Myra Hindley and Ian Brady, shared a council house. Although Hyde regularly returns a Labour Member of Parliament, it has a strong Conservative Association, with many of its members unashamedly on the far right of the Tory Party, as in nearby Ashton-Under-Lyne. In the past, resolutions with overt racial overtones from the Tory Associations of these two constituencies have been included in the Conservative Party Conference handbook.

Webster had not chosen Hyde at random for his party's march and rally. He had good reason to believe that in Hyde was a nucleus of support for the National Front, even if the area, as a whole, was not exactly a hotbed of fascism. It was equally obvious that the Socialist majority and the moderates of the other political parties would be enraged.

Anderton, who has always deplored anything that smacks of racialism, however obliquely, decided to take preventative measures. Unknown to Webster and many Conservative politicians, Anderton was negotiating secretly with councillors of the Tameside council to have the march and rally outlawed.

When the council backed Anderton and barred the National Front from Hyde, there was an outcry from alleged freedom-fighters. Overnight, Anderton was branded a 'Commie yellow belly', a 'Red Square Trotsky' and a 'Russian jackboot cop', as opposed to a Nazi jackboot cop. However, a spokesman for the Socialist Workers Party called the outcome 'a great victory', and the Anglo-Indian Association feted Anderton as 'a hero' who was 'bound to go down in history' as a humanitarian and anti-racist oracle. Meanwhile, three Conservative Associations were denouncing him as 'an errand-boy of the left'.

Jack Fletcher, the late president of Ashton-Under-Lyne Conservative Association, said of Anderton, 'He's a traitor to this country, a disgrace to his badge. He should be stripped of rank and uniform, and booted out. I'm sure he'd be welcomed with open arms in Moscow. It wouldn't surprise me if one day he led a Marxist revolution in Britain. I'm sure he sees himself another Castro. They even look alike!'

For weeks the death threats poured in, night and day. Extra guards were mounted around Anderton's home in Sale. Joan wasn't allowed out alone without a bodyguard. Gillian was escorted to and from school. Life was oppressive. Defending his action at the time, Anderton argued, 'The principle of absolute freedom, like many other things in our utterly selfish world today, is fine provided someone else is called to pay the price. How far is it necessary to limit liberty in order to preserve peace? That is a matter for Parliament, for the people, not for the police. I never realised how little is known by so many about an aspect of law and police procedure that has such grave constitutional implications.'

He felt the reaction from the right of the political spectrum was 'disgustingly abusive . . . mostly uninformed and emotive'. And of the death threats, 'Is there such a thing as a consensus of public opinion? I am sure there is. Perhaps now the sleeping conscience of a trusting populace has been aroused, though that was not my objective. I still have faith in the average man.'

How ironic that in one of his first political conflicts the man who was destined to become the symbol of the reactionary Victorian right, should have been portrayed as the darling of the revolutionary left!

However, the honeymoon with the left lasted barely a month. On 10 October, Anderton made it known that he had entered a secret pact with the National Front to enable them to organise a march in the Levenshulme district of Manchester the following Saturday. A part of the deal was that Anderton should help supervise the event for the fascists. By the time the Socialist Workers Party discovered the route of the thousand National Front marchers, it was too late for them to mobilise a counter-demonstration. 'That was the idea,' said Anderton. 'It was a big gamble, but I did it in the best interests of public safety and I would do it again.' Anderton claimed the credit for preventing street warfare, which had been widely predicted. When accused of conspiring with a racist political group, he defended his actions on the grounds that any conspiracy was undertaken 'on purely policing motives'. He added, 'If I paid a subscription to every political interest I am supposed to have a penchant for, I would be bankrupt.'

Later, Anderton was to provide massive police cover for a one-man parade through Hyde by Martin Webster. The cost of the operation was £140,000, half of which had to be met by the ratepayers of Greater Manchester's 10 district councils. 'I called the tune, now we must pay the piper,' he told the Police Authority.

By now, there were 10,000 people, including civilians,

on Anderton's payroll, making use of 1200 vehicles. And the chief constable's Daimler was traded for a Jaguar – an exchange of no significance then, but a thorny issue a decade later.

Anderton did not scorn any chance to spread his ideas. One day he was lecturing at Keele University. The next morning he was completing a complex questionnaire for an American publisher about police work in Britain. Then he was stealing the headlines again with another pugnacious address, this time to the students of a polytechnic. 'Don't join the far too prevalent contemptibles given to avarice, ridicule, envy and cynical indifference, not to mention a bit of thieving,' he beseeched them. 'We must stop pampering those who bite with increasing fury every single hand that feeds them. They, too, have their responsibilities, but they invariably command only their rights.' He dismissed as a 'tragedy of modern life' the fact that 'too many good people go unnoticed and unused'.

If he was making enemies in certain sections of the community, he was certainly winning friends among his professional brothers and sisters, with such emotive descriptions of a police officer's lot as, 'The police have become the industrial orphans of the twentieth century, almost driven to using their helmets as begging bowls.'

Anderton had taken office with the words, 'I am hopeful I can prove that the impossible can be done; that by casting aside precedents, I can show that there are better ways of doing things.' Proudly he had revealed his family motto: *Better a strong character than a bulging bank account*.

His promise of something new was delivered in full during his first few months as chief constable. His onslaught against pornography began in December 1977. At Anderton's behest, a hand-picked squad of officers raided 264 newsagents and booksellers in eleven months. They confiscated 160,000 newspapers and magazines with a total street value of £200,000. Included in the seized material was a photographic album of *The Sun*'s topless Page Three girls.

'Of course it was all about subjective judgment,' admitted Anderton. 'I was happy to shoulder the burden. We took the lid off a sordid Pandora's Box. Just as soft drugs can lead to hard drugs, so soft porn can lead to hard porn.'

The persistent pressure on the so-called pornbrokers was deplored by John Trevelyan, the erstwhile British movie censor, who had evidence of customers in Manchester shops, including some owned by such high street giants as W. H. Smith and the Tesco chain, being forcibly ejected by police officers during the impounding of alleged pornography. Not even council-owned kiosks were immune. The police padlocked doors and refused to provide receipts for the literature they took away. Even private homes and apartments were raided and searched. Traditional corner-shop newsagents claimed they were being hounded and harassed out of business by 'a religious maniac'. Anderton, predictably, remained unrepentant.

When we discussed this subject in his office, he stood at a window, hands clasped behind his back, looking for inspiration towards a murky, desecrated inner-city landscape, with the black canal coiling round disused warehouses, ugly flyovers and highrise monstrosities. 'On a clear day, you can see all the way to the hills,' he murmured dreamily.

But what about his purge on pornography? Had he any regrets? Any self-doubts? 'Manchester had a certain notoriety for licentiousness which has now been corrected. It was a response to public demand. In 1977, we had a strong public complaint. The people wanted something to be done and I did it. I guaranteed it would be sustained for as long as it was necessary and the public supported that. I set a standard and it has been maintained. It is so easy to abandon standards.' In view of the national furore, was there no time when Anderton considered a compromise? 'Oh, no. Never.'

He has always preferred a head-on collision, even a fatal one, to braking or making a U-turn.

During the height of the crackdown on literature deemed pornographic by Anderton and his Cromwellian court censors, he continued to justify his actions thus, 'When standards of decent behaviour fall, the abnormal becomes the normal, and people are almost brainwashed into thinking that evil is good. You can rationalise things to such an extent that evil conduct becomes acceptable in society and is morally condoned. Someone has to draw the line and it can be done only through the police. I am accused of bringing into play my own Christian principles, but those principles strengthen my hand as a policeman. The law is rooted in righteousness and Christian principle. I have no difficulty about enforcing it. Nor do I have a conscience about it.'

The year 1978 was only a few days old when Anderton was pitched centre stage into further controversy. He chose, rather shrewdly, the BBC's gentlemanly and urbane current affairs programme 'Tonight' to promote the radically reactionary proposition that everyone in the United Kingdom, without exception, should be compelled by law to carry an identification card and to be fingerprinted.

There was such a thing as 'too much freedom', he explained. 'I, too, believe in freedom . . . But freedom which enables people to act in a totally iniquitous fashion, in which they virtually sink to the bottom of the pit like sediment in a stagnant pond, is another matter.'

The nerve of revulsion which he touched should have come as no surprise to him, but he later professed disbelief at being 'so misunderstood'. 'Immediately anyone like me in this country calls for any reasonably severe measures and constraint, there are howls of protest and people feel outraged and descend on you in no uncertain fashion.'

While the debate raged among the National Council for Civil Liberties, the politicians, civil servants, sociologists, journalists, academics, the police and the judiciary, Anderton had already moved on and was whipping up fresh waves. He called a press conference to pass on the message to the world that he was 'wholly against' shorter prison sentences. He deprecated the fact that judges too often passed sentences fully aware that the offender would serve nothing like the full period. Continuing with the vilification of the British system of penology, he said, 'We have x pounds in the kitty and then tailor the situation to meet the budget, whereas it should be decided what is right in the interests of offender and offended, and then find the means to do it.' He conceded that his opinion could conceivably be considered 'an outrageous notion'. However, he went on to say that if a 10-year sentence was considered the appropriate penalty to satisfy the public conscience, to punish the guilty, and to serve as a deterrent, then 10 years it should be, and not one day less.

Lord Longford, who had been visiting Myra Hindley in jail, was singled out for castigation. 'I think we have an inverted logic where people like Lord Longford say, "Ah, they have been in prison for four years, they are now redeemed and have cleansed their souls." I believe that is the very time when a person should begin to serve their sentence, so that the real sense of shame and guilt imposes on him. Until that person feels that act of redemption, he does not feel the pain of punishment, and he could not care less. So I am wholly against the system of shortening penalties, no matter how contrite the person appears to be. But if he should only be inside for four or five years, then give him four or five. I believe that we have practically reached a stage in this country where peace and tranquillity are regarded by too many people as evidence of suppression and denial of human rights and that only trouble and disorder will satisfy a need for change.' He was convinced that so many people 'in the not too distant future' would be in prison for crimes of political subversion or violence that the Government would have to 'devise some temporary means of keeping them out of circulation'.

He has an amazing ability to win friends – often the most unlikely people – and to lose them within the same day. When he went to war against the Page Three girls, he became the hero of the feminists. The extreme law and order brigade worshipped him for his vision of a Britain in which everyone carried ID cards and had fingerprints on file in a 'Big Brother' central computer centre. They denounced him as Judas when he began to cool on that idea. He is the equivalent of a Member of Parliament who crosses the floor of the House of Commons, changing his colours, every day of his life. Some people say that that makes him an outstanding man, who is in nobody's pocket. Others take the view that it demonstrates capriciousness and intellectual instability.

By February 1978 he had become dubbed 'Hammer of the Northern Pornographers'. He told a club for business and professional captains, 'If Greater Manchester police is the rock against which the instant wave of pornography in this country breaks and eventually ripples away, I shall not be disappointed.'

The following Sunday, he was in the pulpit, selecting for the text of his sermon a passage from St Paul, 'The powers that be are ordained of God', which was an insight into his own view of himself.

On the tenth day of the same month, to prevent a National Front rally erupting into a full-scale riot, he took 2000 police 'troops' to Bolton, put helicopters in the air and set up road-blocks. 'My policy of containment worked. It was costly, but worth every penny.'

The controversy he had created over his call for ID cards would not go away and almost daily he was besieged by diverse groups, demanding that he back down or elaborate. It was put to him that his remarks sounded as if he was pushing for a police state, to which he replied, 'I am a Christian democrat. I am not looking for a police state. I was crystal-gazing on the supposition that some time in the future our whole social order might be challenged by subversives. As a matter of fact, our pockets are full of ID cards, which we rush to pull out if we want credit. Why is it an infringement to do that for the good of the state?' And when accused of arrogance, he retaliated, 'I am the most humble person I know'.

Still in February, he was cracking down on all forms of late-night drinking, especially in clubs that were serving alcohol outside their hours of licence. Due to police objections to renewal, 24 nightclubs had their licences revoked by magistrates.

If he was losing friends in clubland, he was making them among motorists, announcing a police policy of positive discrimination in their favour. After issuing his 7000 officers with a 'go easy on the motorists' directive, car stickers were on sale throughout the region declaring: *This driver has god on his side – JA is OK!*

Anderton had become so worried by 'the popular lies in general circulation' about himself that he considered it necessary to make a statement repudiating them. It was downright calumny, he said, that he: 1. instructed officers to oppress the working-class; 2. harassed homosexuals and intruded on their haunts; 3. selectively enforced the licensing laws; 4. possessed a huge police armoury of firearms, including sub-machine guns; 5. had carefully created a personal paramilitary army that might be used one day to back a coup to overthrow the democratic Government and instate a rightwing dictator; 6. encouraged racism by his officers; 7. deliberately abused the law when it suited him.

In June, a lobby of homosexual protesters disrupted a

massive Christian rally in the Free Trade Hall, Manchester, at which Anderton was speaking. From the balcony, they pelted him with abuse and missiles, also hanging banners bearing the slogan: *Homosexuals say Anderton OUT – OK!* A gay petition was presented to the Home Secretary demanding that Anderton be dismissed on the grounds of bigotry. Once again 'pained', Anderton said he could not understand the antipathy because he believed himself to be the avuncular Dixon of Dock Green among chief constables.

His October torpedo-of-the month was aimed at the Advisory Council on the Penal System, rubbishing their recommendation for reduced jail sentences as 'morally bankrupt'. Instead of lighter prison terms, he championed the scrapping of all maximum sentences and pressed for the fixing of minimum periods of confinement.

In November, he announced plans to recruit policemen who were shorter and older than the nationally accepted requirements, which sounded to the Home Office very much like the drum-beat of revolution. 'Even if the entire Association of Chief Police Officers was against it, I would still go ahead,' he vowed defiantly. And he did. Until then, any male below 5 feet 8 inches and older than 30 was excluded automatically from consideration for the police. Anderton changed all that at a stroke, much to the consternation of other chiefs.

Anderton relied on the Sex Discrimination Act (SDA) for riding roughshod over traditional regulations governing entry to the Force. Since the SDA was passed, women of 5 feet 4 inches had been doing the same job as men on the beat. 'So why should we be prejudiced against men of the same size?' Anderton knew very well that he had logic as his ally. But his real motive was to prove that acts like the SDA were double-edged. Others saw his action as a swipe at women. Would he employ a woman if there was a man of the same height and age on the job market? Anderton countered by saying that he did not believe recruitment should be influenced by physical measurements. The murder squad, for example, rarely needed brawn, but could never do without brain. In an emergency, beefy back-up could always be mobilised.

After an unusually low profile for almost three months during the bitter winter of discontent, in February 1979 he took up the entreaty for legislation to change the laws on trade union picketing, the war cry of Mrs Thatcher, who was waiting in the wings to tip Prime Minister James Callaghan off stage at the imminent General Election.

Midway through March, Anderton made this speech in St Helens, Merseyside, to a branch of the Magistrates' Association. 'Views on crime and punishment are endless', he began. 'We are living in the middle of a period when people fully expect the police to catch criminals and the courts, given sufficient evidence, to convict them. But what the long-suffering public want most of all is the reassuring satisfaction of knowing that someone who does wrong will be effectively punished for it. Unfortunately, it is an expectation rarely met these days.

'It is a demoralising prospect. Glamorising crime and violence through books, plays and films has lessened the stigmas of wickedness inherent in criminal conduct and softened its impact upon the community. With the advent especially of television, crime is now classed as entertainment, to be hawked around for public consumption like some frightful circus.

'Everybody seems to have a finger in the pie, and there must be more people making a living by researching, writing, and talking about crime than there are policemen dealing with it. There are too many dabblers, meddlers and daydreamers, and not enough decision-makers and law-enforcers. It is time crime was looked at only as an offence against humanity and treated accordingly. We can close the cover of a book and switch off our television pictures, but we cannot hide the truth that crimes are committed by flesh and blood people, and real people get hurt.

'When dreadful incidents come up for consideration in our courts, we would do well to re-enact in our minds the terrible circumstances of them and try more purposefully to put ourselves in the place of offenders and victims, suffering the shame and guilt of the former and the agony and loss of the latter. Some criminal trials have become mere battles of wits and technical struggles, with lawyers testing their considerable capacity for oratory and semanticism at the expense of the truth. Indeed, I suspect that some lawyers belong to the Society for the Prevention of the Conviction of the Guilty.

'We have come unstuck on the basic question of attitudes to sentencing and punishment. For example, we seem to find it easier to punish for absolute traffic offences, where true guilty knowledge hardly applies and no person is physically hurt or consciously deprived of his freedom and civil rights, than for crimes of a much more serious kind, causing lasting harm, crimes committed with malice and deliberate intent to satisfy a wicked motive. Courts seem more concerned about straightforward, relatively technical matters, like parking, vehicle licensing, obstruction and speeding, in which possibly selfishness and inconsiderateness represent the worst anti-social elements, than they are about crimes of damage, violent assault, large-scale theft and burglaries, which leave the victim shattered and shaking from the effects. It would appear that the control of vehicles and drivers often has priority over the control of thugs and thieves.

'Now, all this is linked to the public's increasingly curious conception of crime. There is an urgent need to get back to first principles in our consideration of crime, starting with the simple truth that it is wrong to steal, rape, assault, ravage and cause damage. That everybody except the insane and mentally deficient clearly knows and understands this. That we all have a choice whether

97

to conform or not, to obey the law or not. And that if we are caught and convicted, we should be punished and expect to be punished, without complaint. It is just as easy to behave as to misbehave, and when innocent people get hurt, they are entitled to seek ample retribution. The extent to which we condone and excuse anti-social behaviour today is quite ridiculous.

'It is hard to pinpoint the commencement of what can only be described as the worst period in recent history of communal weakness, which seems to coincide with the fostering of a crazy notion that people are not really responsible for their own actions or account to their fellow men, but rather have been failed conveniently by something they loosely call "society", of which they insist they form a part. As far as I'm concerned, people who behave inhumanly to their fellows should expect to be treated with the severity such conduct merits, until they mend their ways. The choice is theirs and they know the answer. The best and most effective remedy is in their own hands.

'Regrettably, there has built up over recent years in this country, and in other supposedly enlightened places, a gradual feeling that, although it is still basically wrong to commit crime, it is an even greater nuisance to be caught, because you then put so many more people to the trouble of trying to decide what to do with you. That kind of reasoning brings stupid criticism of shopkeepers for displaying their goods in an insecure and tempting fashion; criticism of everbody at large for not insuring or adequately protecting their property; criticism of the law for being too effective; and criticism of the police for doing a good job. We may be losing the desire to protect ourselves, but we must not give in to the guile of those in authority whose commonsense has been plundered by a lifetime immersed in theory and spent in ivory towers.

'We pay far too much attention to the sex and ages of offenders. Whether an offender is male or female, boy or girl, sixteen or sixty, does not matter a great deal in the final analysis. We should ask ourselves: What have they done? How did they behave? And what harm are they doing to the rest of us? And then make sure that our leniency does not turn to lunacy. There is no need to return to the Dark Ages and the dungeon, to stocks, leg-irons and the gibbet in order to strengthen our forms of punishment. But we do need a level of punishment sufficient to cause people to think twice before they choose to commit crime.

'I am concerned over a current threat to the autonomy and effectiveness of the police, although I remain absolutely convinced that the vast majority of the public support the police. It is not the ordinary man in the street who presents a problem, but very active minorities who find favour among those holding positions of power and influence, in Parliament, the universities, and elsewhere, and see in the police a substantial obstacle to the wider public approval they need to achieve their objectives. When the police and the law-abiding majority are in harmony, there is little risk of serious civil unrest or a weakening of our parliamentary democracy. Anything, therefore, which embarrasses the police and challenges their integrity is seized upon by the few virulent opponents of the police, who press it for all they are worth. This campaign is backed to some extent by a so-called free press and aided and abetted by fools who seem to care little for the security of the state and the future of this country.

'In conclusion, let me say this: the police are the lifeguards of the community. Let us, therefore, ensure that the tide of freedom does not turn so suddenly that those whose job it is to protect the innocent and unwary majority are drowned in the unchecked breakers of criminal licence.'

The following month, he was having to defend members of his force against complaints of gun-toting and turning 'crime-busting into a Wild West Show'. He strenuously rejected that the 400 men trained to use guns were a 'bunch of cowboys'. His revilers were not assuaged; they never are. 'So be it,' said Anderton, as obdurate as ever.

Speaking at a Manchester luncheon club, he returned to one of his favourite themes: tough penal work camps, where 'hooligans could sweat as they've never sweated before'. Hardened criminals, he believed, should be subjected to hard labour and discipline, 'until their violence has been vanquished by penitent humiliation and unqualified repentance. Tender mercies are wasted and ill-spent on some offenders.'

Mounting criticism was being directed at Anderton's commando-style Tactical Aid Group (TAG), formed in 1977 and comprising 72 highly trained combat policemen. Anderton defended TAG, stressing that none of its members was armed 'as a matter of course', and that in 1978, the previous year, 774 arrests had been made by this streetwise special unit.

For Anderton, the year went out the way it had come in: with a lion's roar. 'Trendy teachers' and their 'half-baked notions' were the butt of his caustic Christmas message. Cannabis, he said, had replaced caramel-chewing in schools and 'boozing' was more popular than sport.

Gillian, who was still a student, suffered as a result of her father's condemnation of teachers, schools and children. It was not her best Christmas.

8

Blitz

Only Anderton could think of turning a meeting of the organisation Animal Rescue into a platform for a swingeing broadside on subjects as diverse as race relations, child prostitution and treason. He managed it effortlessly at Windermere, Cumbria, on the night of 26 September, 1980, in a blitz on random scapegoats.

'Ethnic minorities have suffered miserably from overexposure by Government,' he alleged. 'They have been stuck like goldfish in a bowl and made to feel different when they are not.' He talked about 'creepy and dangerous minorities' and backed the abolition of Britain's 'race relations industry', which he berated as 'outmoded and expensive'. Clashes of culture, he predicted, would lead to misunderstanding, mistrust, fear 'and even violence', which would have to be written-off as 'the price of progress'. He described as 'a volatile explosive mixture' the presence of disparate numbers of black people, whites and Asians, whether British subjects or not. His prescience of violence was not something he willed, he emphasized, but prejudice, ignorance and hatred provided a natural breeding-ground for conflict.

One cannot help but observe a certain parallel between Anderton's rhetoric and Enoch Powell's infamous 'red rivers of blood' speech.

'But the answer is not to be found in attempts to separate them like cattle in pens or opposing factions at a football match,' he declared. 'Such solutions might secure a transient peace but would remain forever unproductive, harmful, undignified and wrong. It would be a policy of apartheid. And neither will legislation by itself mend the wrongs in this particular theatre.' The 'solicitous attention' devoted to the ethnic minorities was 'counter-productive', he went on, undeviating. Social ideas had become 'lost in a web of political intrigue and opportunism'. He conceded that there was 'still an ingenuous desire on the part of many decent workers in this field to help disadvantaged racial groups towards a better quality of life'. He believed, however, that such efforts were frequently 'completely nullified by others who blatantly employ the system as a catalyst for promoting racial disharmony and antagonising the police!

'I am particularly concerned,' he continued, 'about several organisations, including some community relations groups, whose activities are useless to those most in need. In short, they have been infiltrated by anti-establishment factions, one of whose aims is continuously to impede the police. Black racialists and revolutionaries grab every opening to alienate black youths from their families, the police and all established systems. White racialists flaunt their sickening gospel of hate under a banner of rude nationalism, creating atmospheres of conflict and tension.' Attempts had been made in numerous districts, he claimed, to exclude police representatives from approved community relations councils. Anti-police propaganda of a 'singularly scurrilous kind' was 'churned out from centres aided by public funds'. He deplored the waste of public money and public effort, saying that despite everything that had been done to further the cause of race relations, 'the main problems of prejudice and discrimination remain unresolved'. Attitudes remained 'polarised, hard and inflexible'. Real understanding he dismissed as 'scant', and the blame for the perpetuation of suspicion and the lack of progress, he felt was 'wrongly apportioned'. Urging a new approach, he said, 'There has been far too much talk and not enough action and it is evident that social ills will not be cured by the grinding wheels of bureaucracy. In my personal opinion, the race relations industry, set up with all good intentions and claiming significant success, has now become an obstacle to progress, as it features obsessively the sole question of race.'

In 10 years in England and Wales, indictable crime had increased from 1,498,000 cases in 1969 to 2,395,000 in 1979, Anderton informed the meeting. In 1929, when the population of Manchester was greater than in 1980, there had been a combined total of 789 burglaries and house break-ins, compared with 10,219 in 1979. Juveniles were responsible for nearly a third of all crime, he reported. 'Ten years ago, robberies were usually confined to organised attacks by experienced criminals on vehicles and personnel carrying wages or collecting cash for commercial concerns,' he pointed out. 'Now we have large gangs of young people, boys and girls, roaming city streets by day and night, attacking defenceless people, both young and old, and stealing money, wallets and handbags. Favourite targets in Greater Manchester are unaccompanied old ladies and pregnant women; such is the "courage" of the thieves.'

The number of 'little girls' turning to prostitution was a new degrading social phenomenon, he said. 'In one incredible instance, the little girl was only nine. Apart from the stunning realisation that girls of such tender years so easily become hardened, experienced prostitutes, we also have to come to terms with the fact that there are men who will pay for their services. One girl, then aged twelve, admitted, in addition to her prostitution, that she had introduced seven other girls to a man who is now serving a term of imprisonment.' Two years later, he said, the 'little madam' was still a headache for the police.

Continuing his wide arc of fire, Anderton unloaded on

the 'well-known public figures' who were seeking to 'undermine and displace the constitution'. Treachery in high places was rife, he insisted. He did not name names, but it has become apparent that he was alluding to certain Members of Parliament, a number of leftwing trade union leaders and radical Socialist politicians, plus a majority of his own Police Authority, and those he disparagingly refers to as 'influential wreckers who hide under the cloak of do-gooder'.

During 1981, there was a bitter industrial dispute at the Openshaw engineering factory of Laurence Scott. For 11 days, pickets blockaded the roads around the factory. 'No one will ever breach our picket line,' vowed one union spokesman. The inevitable heated exchanges and scuffles broke out, prompting the management to seek police protection. Anderton had been taking a personal interest in the development of strife at Laurence Scott and he made himself responsible for the police response to the management's appeal. Anderton promised that any lorry driver wishing to cross the picket lines would do so.

The policing of the 11-day siege cost £100,000. During the climax of the strike, Anderton deployed 300 officers in the area of the factory, day and night. Because of Anderton's action, all the lorries got through and the strike was crushed. This time, the leftwing Greater Manchester police committee were really gunning for their chief constable. They accused him – not for the first time and certainly not for the last time – of being a 'jackboot puppet of the capitalists' and a 'fascist management skinhead'. His men were likened to street-corner louts spoiling for a fight, spurred on by the bully boy gang-leader. Workers' lives had been endangered by policemen who had encouraged lorry drivers to crash through the human barriers, some committee members alleged. This feud simmered for 10 months, finally reaching a head in March 1982, when the committee passed by 16 votes to 12 a vote of no-confidence in Anderton and his policy.

Anderton retaliated by demanding the abolition of all police committees in the country and replacing them with non-political bodies. It was as he left this meeting that Anderton delivered the immortal line, 'Now I know how Christ felt when he was crucified.'

I questioned Anderton about police involvement in industrial conflict. I wanted to establish exactly where he stood, without ambiguity.

'The vast majority of policemen are from working-class homes, like myself. We have a love and respect for the families on the picket line. We understand their feelings, their culture, their struggle. Many times a policeman has come face to face with a loved one on the picket line. It's hard, but preserving law and order is all that matters to the policeman. He's not on anybody's side. He's not the representative of management or worker. He's for order and against disorder, wherever it might be and whatever the cause. It's as simple as that.

'I have a tough job to do. I am a tough policeman. When I am putting down riots, there can be no halfway measures. I have to do what has to be done. I am known in the United States as the toughest cop in Europe, a hardline, rightwing, repressive, jackboot cop. But there's a compassionate, human side to police work that goes unnoticed.

'I have deep compassion. So do most of my detectives. After arresting offenders, they have been so deeply moved by the plight of the criminals' families, they have collected money for food and clothing. They find jobs for criminals when they come out of prison so they can make a fresh start. They even run marathons to raise money for them. I'm running the biggest social service agency in Greater Manchester. We're a charitable trust in our own right. The fact that I don't dress up my speeches in sociological language doesn't mean I'm not aware of all the pressing social problems. I'm just as concerned about the plight of the homeless and unemployed as you. There is more in my annual reports about unemployment than in most of the speeches by the MPs who attack me for being uncaring. They have double standards. The moment I go against the grain, they yell, "Out of court!" I don't change for political reasons. Some politicians believe the police should be subordinate to them, having a say in police tactics and strategy. They are acting against the public interest. They say chief constables have too much power. They say chief constables have too much autonomy. They say chief constables have too much independence. They say chief constables should be answerable for their conduct.

'I believe in rehabilitation, but an offender must be punished. He must pay the price and then I'll move heaven and earth to restore that person to society. There's not enough attention focused on what brought a person to crime. There are lawbreakers who do so out of desperation. We have to examine the motives. We need a return to simpler days, thinking more of providing for people's spiritual needs.'

Anderton has made several pilgrimages to the Holy Land and Rome, and in 1982 he had an audience in Manchester with the Pope. More recently, he attended private meetings at Tirley Garth, the northern headquarters of Moral Rearmament. It was his meeting with the pontiff, however, that turned Anderton towards the mandate of the Vatican and away from no-frills Methodism, the 'People's Express' to heaven.

From Church of England to Methodist to Roman Catholic – is Anderton a conservative who believes in change or a man who doesn't know his own mind? He had been quoted as saying that 'everything attracts me to Roman Catholicism; its good order, its lack of compromise, its principles and its total belief in family life.'

Yet it was not so long ago he was telling Joan Bakewell that he was no longer a regular churchgoer. He made a special point of disassociating himself from 'Sunday Christians', saying, 'I'm not a Sunday Christian; never have been.' He let on that he did not worship regularly in any church, apparently exhorting others to do as he preached, rather than as he practised. He wanted it to be made known, however, that he was not decrying people who were habitual Sunday churchgoers. Other people needed a weekly church visit for succour, but for Anderton it was surplus to requirements. His spiritual life, he said, came from his home and his work, an ideology that is in direct conflict with the strict disciples of the Roman Catholic Church, with which Anderton purports such accord. For a Roman Catholic not to attend church on Sunday, if at all possible, is a sin. If Anderton defies that rule, then within the Catholic Church, he will always be a bad Catholic and a fair-weather Christian – not at all the Anderton he would have us recognise.

If a policeman is ever to be congratulated for his work, Anderton invites both the officer and his wife to the chief constable's office, turning the event into an emotional occasion. Tea would be laid on and the wife would be presented with a bouquet of flowers.

'I was as proud as punch,' I was told by one wife who had been given the treatment with her husband. 'I now know why ninety-nine per cent of all coppers in the country believe Anderton's the best boss any bobby could ever have. He's real smashing! I don't care a damn what the knockers say.'

Not a Christmas Day goes by without Anderton visiting all sick and injured officers from Greater Manchester who are in hospital. But for those who fall from grace, it is a very different story. His wrath is explosive, and he will not hesitate to dismiss or demote, if so inclined.

'He can be pig ignorant,' complained one officer who was once reprimanded by Anderton for improper use of a police vehicle. 'He didn't give me a chance to explain anything. He treated me as if I was a common crook. He waved and shouted. Anyone would have thought I'd committed murder. He's allowed to make mistakes, but not anyone else. Anderton's a classic hypocrite: one law for god, another for his flock. He's a laughing stock all over the world and I won't be sorry to see the back of him.'

Anderton's idea of a relaxing holiday is trekking and hill-climbing, especially in the Western Highlands of Scotland. Neither he nor Joan are sun-worshippers or beach people. If they go abroad, it is on cultural tours to countries like Germany, Austria and Italy. They never tire of visiting stately homes, churches and cathedrals, and they used to belong to the Hallé Society.

Anderton has never become a Freemason or Rotarian, believing it would be wrong to belong to organisations which are viewed by some sections of society as motivated by self-interest. He claims to have read every political doctrine from Marx and Engels to Mao Tse-tung, Sartre and Kierkegaard. He is rarely without a small silver-edged, black pocket notebook, which he uses to record any non-blue anecdotes he hears during the day, either at work or while mixing socially at night. He likes to have a fund of funny stories with which to regale his audiences: he is a master eclectic, gathering as he travels.

Making friends has never been easy for Anderton. Several senior officers have become reasonably close to him, but the relationships have always fallen short of friendship. Scarcely anyone from the Force has been invited across the threshold into his private life. Real friends can be counted on one hand. There is Freddy Pye, who once owned Wigan Athletic Football Club, and Archie Thornhill, the former chairman of the Police Authority, and Luis Anton, at one time the Portuguese Consul in Manchester. Pye, a prosperous industrialist from humble origins, occasionally has the Andertons round for dinner. Once Anderton went salmon fishing in Scotland with Thornhill, a bookmaker by occupation.

Despite not being a sun-lover, Anderton did spend a holiday in one of Anton's apartments on the Algarve. But when socialising within his small clan of kindred spirits, he never discusses his work. He talks about family, music, the countryside, nature in general, sports, politics and religion. If someone mentions declining standards, he will not miss his cue. If he is out to dinner and his host pinpoints a specific crime, such as an old lady being brutally attacked, and asks what the police are doing to safeguard the public, Anderton will not dodge the issue, but his answer will be a generalisation and not attributable to his own force.

One of his old allies commented, 'You don't overnight become a friend of Anderton. It takes years to be really accepted by him as a blood brother, and even then he would lock you up if you cheated the Inland Revenue of a bean. I admire him for that, though. You know where you stand with him. There's nothing more corrosive than privilege: he'll have none of it. If you believe that a friendship with the chief constable places you above the law, you'll never be a friend of Jim Anderton. He's one of those people who's perfectly content with his own company. He's at home in the countryside; he's very much an outdoor person. He takes it in and likes to jot down his thoughts at the time. You wouldn't think it, but he's a dreamer, without being too abstract. He's what I call a man who speaks from the belly of mankind. Everything with him is a gut reaction and he's always in step with the mob, the pulse of the people.

'He'll hear something political on TV and will react to it. I can't see him making friends with someone who has very different political or religious views from his own. I'm a die-hard Tory. Most people who don't know Jim Anderton all that well will have him branded a Monday Clubber, but he's more convoluted than that. His Labour roots are as dear to him as the family silver.

'There was a persistent rumour at one time that he

would be the Liberal SDP candidate for Rochdale when Cyril Smith stood down, but he's always at the centre of bizarre speculation. Anderton-gossip has always been a thriving cottage industry. I never mentioned the Cyril Smith rumour to him. On anything like that, I always wait for him to tell me. If he says nothing, I assume it's rubbish what I've heard. The Manchester Central Conservative Association tried to induce him to resign from the force to be their Parliamentary candidate in the 1987 General Election, but Anderton didn't give it serious consideration. Manchester Central is a graveyard for the Conservative, let alone other factors. If you really want to know his politics, I should say he's a reluctant Tory, that he sees nowhere else to go, he's there because, to him, the alternatives are deadends.'

Certainly the severest test of his authority came during the Moss Side race riots, which he had been forecasting two years previously in 1980. They began at three o'clock in the morning of Wednesday, 8 July, in the wake of incidents of similar street anarchy in Brixton, south London; Southall, west London; and Toxteth, Liverpool: 100 black youths going on the rampage, wrecking shops, burning, looting, wounding and raping.

Anderton left his bed to take charge personally of the police operation from the front line. Greater Manchester, under Anderton, became the first police force in Britain to be equipped permanently with riot gear, which is now standard equipment for every constabulary.

For four days, Manchester was a city torn by civil war. During that time, Anderton never left his 900 officers, who were battling on the blazing streets to try to restore order, continually coming under attack from petrol bombs and improvised deadly weapons and missiles. The chants of 'Kill! Kill! Kill!' echoed through the suburbs from Gorton and Moss Side to the adjoining city of Salford.

'It was organised anarchy,' said Anderton. 'All attempts failed at appealing to reason through a low profile. The organisers wanted a showpiece insurrection and they were not disappointed.'

The rioters kept each other informed of developments via CB radios and used the same means suddenly to switch the eye of the storm to an unprotected area. In the aftermath of the pillage, Anderton prepared the most provocative speech ever contemplated by a serving police chief, but it was never delivered in public.

9

The Riots of '81

Anderton's most controversial speech of his six years as Greater Manchester's chief constable was to have been the second Lord Hewlett Memorial Lecture. It was never made because the lecture was cancelled. He was going to begin by quoting General Brinkerhoff, who in 1896 was president of the National Prison Association of the United States, 'The lessening of the crime of a country is an object worthy of the best efforts of our best man.'

Taking that as his theme, he had intended to speak as follows: 'General Brinkerhoff's comment long ago was as obvious and timely then as now; timely in that we seem, yet again, in this country to be enduring an agonising period of recrimination on questions of law and order, when we need to be reminded not only of the universal benefits which a peaceful society brings, but also of the perpetual difficulty of securing lasting improvements in a world in which more and more people seem less willing to comply with steps taken for the common good, less ready to limit their personal freedoms in the wider public interest.

'Unchecked liberality has indeed marched apace with unchecked crime, and the predominant human emotion now is fear. It is not really within the law's capacity to shape men's feeling. That can only come from the spirit which guides men's souls. And so many things influence crime and public disorder. For instance, the relaxing of self-control by eroding discipline, the cynical promotion of envy for the sake of profit, and the ruthless denigration of those morals upon which valid social progress is built. These and other similar factors make people who recklessly serve their own personal ends feel somehow vindicated.

'The main purpose of this address is to enable policing to be viewed in fair perspective. The police lately have been given a tougher time by critics than by crooks, their old traditional enemy; so it is imperative that some sort of balance should be struck.

'Judged by the fortunes of history, the police stock seems to rise with the perceived capacity of politicians to cope. Paradoxically, as social and economic events turn bad, and public disorder and crime increase, the police, who deserve unqualified support, become the political scapegoats for recurring community failures. Now, during a critical phase in the political transmutation of this country, out of which, whether we like it or not, will eventually emerge a whole new social structure for the future, the police are being deliberately isolated and pushed aside to be constantly harried and often abused for political gain.

'The great strength and eminence of the British police over the decades has been their undoubted popularity with the general public, derived from the moral force attaching to their work. Now, even this unique partnership is severely tested as the whole essence of British life reacts to change. Somehow or other, aided largely by a persistent leftwing press, an idea detrimental to the police service has grown that chief constables are seriously divided over the best means of policing our increasingly complex society. This is not so. It is, of course, true that one or two of the more independent and forthright 'Top Cops' choose occasionally to express personal opinions of a markedly contrasting kind, reflecting their professional experience. The social and political environments in which chief constables operate differ very dramatically, shaping their personal attitudes and development as much as they influence the responses of the local community. In short, a chief constable, just like anyone else, can be conditioned by the limits of his own experience, when reality blurs and comparative judgments are difficult to make.

'Surely we all know that responsible grassroots policing is a solvent mixture of applied social care and sensitive law enforcement? A healthy combination of two complementary doctrines, not an abiding conflict between them. We know in our hearts that, if through kindness and compassion people can be persuaded not to commit crime and violence, then the joint task of the police and the community will be eased. But we do not live in Utopia. There are vicious villains about who will not be appeased or alter, and strong police measures will always be necessary to protect the law-abiding from the law-breaker, and to put the interests of good people first.

'The fear engendered by the terrifying riots of last summer should still be pulsing through our veins, otherwise the dead hand of complacency is upon us. For those, police and public alike, who suffered personal injury or serious damage to property which, in many cases, shattered the spirit as much as the bricks and mortar it had taken a lifetime to build, the scars will remain forever, as a kind of memorial to madness. For them, there will be no return to normal. Things can never be the same again. And, you may ask, why not? Because certain factions in the community, either with criminal intent or stupid bravado – the motives of individual rioters differed enormously – threw caution to the wind and plunged into an orgy of violence that shortened the threshold between the civilised peace we have come to take for granted and the terror of total lawlessness. Of course there were many who regretted their actions almost as soon as they found themselves involved. But there were many who did not, and will not, and they could easily cross that threshold again.

'The police also turned a corner which took them down a very different road. They faced unprecedented levels of blind fury and hatred, and suffered injuries, savagely inflicted, on a scale never before experienced in this country. From this frightening confrontation sprang a resolve among the police – certainly in Greater Manchester – that no matter what the odds that might be stacked against them, they will not retreat from their duty. They realise, of course, that circumstances could arise where the police would be physically overwhelmed, but should that time ever come, the peace-loving citizens of this country will have one unavoidable choice to make – to come at once to the aid of the police.

'Why, in a country renowned for its stability, racial tolerance and good humour, did those terrible events occur at all? What factors and grievance, so deeply felt and as acute as to precipitate such an awful, hateful violence, could possibly go unnoticed? Although most people have the capacity to be violent, whatever their education and background, it is unusual for the collective control of an apparently entire community to snap in this way. But did it? And how much of it had to do with race? What are the facts? I estimate that in a nation of 49 million people, only a maximum of 11,000 or so ever become involved in rioting and probably half of those get swept along on a crazy tide of boiling emotion. In Greater Manchester, all kinds of people got embroiled, including university students and journalists; and housewives joined in the looting. After the first and unexpected outbreak of violence implicating mainly black youths, the raison d'être altered. The initial explosion of frustration, no matter what really conditioned that mood, led to further rioting without cause, and criminals jumped on the bandwagon. The tragedy is that the inherent political objectives, such as they were, of the rioters and potential rioters, were

115

achieved when the first petrol bomb was thrown in London.

'My chief officers and I in the Greater Manchester Police knew as long ago as May and June 1981 that there would be rioting in Moss Side, probably towards the end of July; not for any sane or defensible reason, but to fulfil a much publicised prophesy. Yet there was nothing we could do to prevent it. After Southall and Brixton, we knew it was only a matter of time before the violence erupted in Manchester, and that little could be done to guard against it. The inner cities had been primed for trouble and it was clearly on its way. There were frequent and – in my opinion – thoroughly irresponsible references in the national press and in television programmes to the likelihood of clashes between police and young blacks in Moss Side, although there was no compelling evidence to support it.

'A dangerous kind of solidarity began to breed, and the police knew that an excuse for criminal violence would be found. The trigger for Manchester was Toxteth, but it need never have happened at all.

'For several years now in this country, young blacks especially have been brainwashed by an increasingly intense campaign to promote hostility between police and black people. Even well-intentioned workers in race relations, whose honest motives were not in question, unwittingly lent support to this menacing and misguided propaganda. Problems were fostered in peaceful places and discontentment in innocent minds. Such difficulties as there were in our main inner cities were gradually cultivated, and this insidious work still goes on. Even now, influential people, including some in high office, continue to spring to the defence of certain groups whose principal activity is crime.

'The riots of '81 brought police in full focus again and soon after the emergency abated, it seemed almost certain that yet another special inquiry into the police would begin. As it was, Lord Scarman's report on the Brixton disturbances dealt mainly with the role of the police, and the Hytner investigation in Moss Side had nobody but the police in mind. It is sad that the Scarman Report and many subsequent discussions have given the unfortunate impression that the police are not sufficiently in touch with the public and that this somehow contributed significantly to a genesis of community dissatisfaction that sharpened the prospect of impending public disorder. What a lot of silly nonsense that is. And how unfair. What other organised public body exists with such a wide outreach to the people? None.

'It is time to put the record straight; time the police boasted openly of their achievements and stopped being on the defensive. What on earth should cause the police to be ashamed? Certainly nothing following the events of last summer. The largest blame should be put where it belongs, at the door of the rioters and criminals and upon all who chose to inspire them. People must realise that when police have to resort to tougher tactics, it is generally the fault of the community and not of the struggling police. We should stop making excuses for conduct that is palpably wicked and nothing else.

'And now the magic word "consultation" has been offered as a panacea to all our plagues. What a wistful delusion that is. Experience has shown, especially in the field of race relations, that formal liaison committees become bureaucratic, political and often unproductive. In other words, they tend to exist for their own sake and are guilty of too much profitless talk and too little positive action. I think, nevertheless, Lord Scarman is right to emphasise the need for responsible communication, but any machinery must be established with care. To make sense of Lord Scarman's ideas, I would much prefer to see each district council (10 in Greater Manchester) set up a "Liaison Committee on Police Affairs" which would at least represent the interest of the local community through its elected members, but without any political or executive powers. Other people from different walks of life could be co-opted as necessary. It is the only really workable proposition.

'One of the most fashionable terms today is "accountability", beloved but shockingly misrepresented by the new vogue of political aspirants now making their voices heard. In the context of police organisation and control, it means one thing and one thing only – the power to give orders to the police and to expect them to be obeyed. It is said that chief constables and their senior officers should be prepared to discuss general problems affecting both the police and the community and to take appropriate advice. There is nothing wrong or radical in that. It has been done for many years. But it is really not so simple. The ultimate objective of those pressing for changes in the role and functions of the police and their accountability to local councillors is the statutory power to require chief constables to consult with councillors before any police strategy is employed. That is a very, very different matter for it effectively destroys the impartial status of the police.

'But the revolutionary proposals go still further. Certain politicians have recently stated quite unequivocally that elected members of police committees should have the power to order the chief officer of police to disband police units like the Special Branch and the Special Patrol Group – or indeed any unit which offends their political stance. The next call obviously to be paraded under the banner of accountability is the power actually to overrule the operational decisions and professional judgments of the local police, no matter how carefully and soundly based, if they run counter to the dominant political will of the elected police committee. Is that really what the people want?

'Concern about the police now being expressed by certain people, distinguished more by the regularity than

118

the relevance of their interventions, has precious little to do with better community participation in police affairs or any notion of the police service without which the dream of a Marxist totalitarian state in this country cannot ultimately be realised. A police service, immune from the ideological pressures of any single political party, provides the surest and only guarantee of the people's individual freedom. Unless the present independence and impartiality of the police can be preserved, then the struggle for our traditional democracy will be over. If some of the new proposals affecting police accountability were introduced, the character of the British police would be changed for ever and life in this country would never be the same again.

'A quiet revolution is taking place around us and the prize is political power, to be wielded against the most cherished elements of the establishment, including the monarchy. It is as much the duty of the police to guard against this as it is to guard against crime. I sense and see in our midst an enemy more dangerous, insidious and ruthless than any faced since the Second World War. Let none be in doubt about this, for the first calculated steps have been taken. I firmly believe there is a long-term political strategy to destroy the proven structures of the police and turn them into an exclusive agency of a one-party state. I am also convinced that the British police service is now a prime target for subversion and demoralisation.

'The police must not be tricked into dropping their guard or their standards, and chief constables especially must ensure that their forces are not infiltrated by undesirable people who could wreak havoc in the years ahead. The most trying situation for the police is the changing behaviour of some Police Authorities since the local government elections last May. Of course, I do not challenge or deny the right of a political party to pursue the line of its own manifesto, but it must surely offend the

119

public interest to use the Police Authority structure for that purpose. A Police Authority must not be a forum for party politics, but this now is a very frequent occurrence. Basic issues in the field of law and order are increasingly submitted to a vote. The time-honoured practice whereby police committees put aside internal political rivalry and invariably sought a consensus of opinion in the wider public interest has disappeared completely in some areas.

'It is the statutory duty of a police committee to maintain an adequate and efficient police force, but it is not the job of police committee members to approach the management of police business within their jurisdiction from the standpoint primarily of party politics and any emerging political theory. Police business should be discharged without political bias. For years I have been an ardent champion and devotee of the need for police to be linked with local government, but now the picture has changed and I cannot support that view. Gone are those relatively halcyon days when the interest of the people clearly came first. Gone are the days when chief constables could look confidently for unqualified encouragement. Gone, too, it seems are the days when politicians were more prepared to temper their ideological differences for the wider public good. Now there is shameless suspicion, undisguised acrimony and distrust, and deliberate secrecy between the various political factions as they vie for advantage and power. It is a very sorry sight indeed.

'Everyone knows the police should not be caught up in this. But now chief constables have to play a conscious political game in their own basic war against crime. It is a very distressing trend for the suffering public to witness. So serious are the problems now arising that I believe a way must be found urgently to remove the police completely from the realm of local politics, no matter how radical and painful that may seem.

'If things I see around me are allowed to go on much

longer, then incalculable damage will be caused, for it must be obvious even to the layman that some local politicians surely intend that their grip on the police should be tightened.

'Police committees should be re-constituted to avoid the exercise of a political majority. There is a very strong case for giving magistrates at least half of the committee membership. Better still, I recommend that police committees should be totally abolished and replaced by non-political police boards, the members of which would surely be much more objective. Police boards should be empowered to precept upon the district councils, following the practice in Metropolitan London.

'Let me conclude my lecture on the reality of community policing. This reality requires that the police must not succumb to post-riot propaganda by which dying issues are kept alive and dead problems are resurrected.

'Police sensitivity to minority group feeling must not be so heightened as to give free reign for the perpetration of crime. And police must not be pushed so far back on this issue, whatever local pressures are involved, that they fail to enforce the law. When people are being beaten on the head, what they want from the police is protection. When shop premises are being raided and ransacked, what they want above all is protection. When schools are set on fire and burned to the ground, what they, too, want is protection. When the elderly are being robbed in the street, what they want from us all is protection. That is the reality of community policing.

'Police officers are well tuned to the perplexities of human nature, but it is hard to preach conciliation and compassion when someone has got you by the throat. It is hard to meet people halfway when they refuse to take a step forward. It is hard to appeal to reason when there is no understanding of that word. That is the reality of community policing. So let us stop fooling ourselves.

'It will inevitably come to pass in all states clinging on

to democracy that the survival of their ideals will increasingly depend upon the ability of the police alone to halt the rise in terrorism, serious crime and public disorder, against which an uncompromising deterrent will be needed. And the United Kingdom will be no exception.

'It is, furthermore, my honest belief that our police will be the one body left to erect an umbrella of public confidence and safety under which all social agencies can shelter: the one truly trusted profession attracting the unwavering support of the public.

'The heaviest burdens will unquestionably be discharged by police in the seven Metropolitan areas where 41 per cent of the population is concentrated, and where the police chiefs who happen to be in command will hold the key to the future of this country.

'The next five years will be the testing time and the pressures are already building up. Police performances in this coming trial period will determine not only the shape, standing and strategy of police forces for years to come, but also the kind of society in which we shall be required to live.'

In that draft speech, Anderton seemed to be favouring a political initiative by the police, as an institution, which would make it almost an alternative choice of government, with its own manifesto and mandate. There was also the strong hint that, in a given situation, police rule should be imposed without choice, for the sake of democracy. This is a novel concept, reeking of: *I believe in democracy as long as the result of the ballot-box agrees with me*.

Anderton is on record as being opposed to the principle of police states. But is he opposed in practice?

10

'Put Your Life in His Hands'

Anderton's career has been beleaguered by crises, many of them self-inflicted. At a seminar on AIDS in December 1986, he spoke of homosexuals, prostitutes and drug-addicts 'swirling in a cesspit of their own making'.

Amid the inevitable uproar, Anderton refused to retract one word. He explained his rhetoric this way, 'I believe I was moved by the spirit of God to say exactly what I did. I felt compelled to speak. When I got out of bed that morning, I had no idea what I should say. As the moments went by, the more I felt it was in my heart that I had to say what I believe to be true. I have never felt such peace of mind in my life before. I was completely calm and contented. I have no regrets at all. I did what was right.' He reiterated that he believed his speech had come directly from God.

The Church, in all its shades, the medical profession and various social help agencies, were dismayed by Anderton's inflammatory intervention. The most modest criticism focused on the 'unhelpful' nature of the speech, while the most acrid reaction came from Anderton's own Police Authority, which sought permission from the Home Office to discipline him. The majority of the police committee members wanted Anderton gagged on matters of public morality for the remainder of his tenure. Anderton defiantly responded that no one would ever deprive him of the right to free speech.

Dr John Habgood, the Archbishop of York, spoke out against Anderton because he was concerned that the speech would succeed only in driving sufferers underground and away from seeking vital medical treatment. He told 300 doctors at York University, 'If one goes too far in stressing fear and guilt, one is simply adding to the burden which sufferers already have to bear and one is making the notification of AIDS much less possible. As long as sufferers are labelled morally as well as medically, they will try to hide or will react with excessive fear or guilt. There is a fear throughout the Church that a growth in adverse attitudes towards sufferers is driving AIDS victims into a moral ghetto.'

In his defence, Anderton claimed that he had sackfuls of supportive letters in his office and only a handful of derogatory ones. The people who backed him were the 'moral majority', while the antis were the 'moral lepers'. He said, 'I have letters signed by whole congregations. Hostility rests with a tiny minority.' But his life had been threatened again and security at his home had been tightened, particularly for Joan. He confessed that both he and his wife had cried together at nights because of the ferocity of the odium towards him from some quarters. 'We have been reduced to tears, through sadness not anger, that people could do it to us. When you try to do a job fairly and honestly, and end up being publicly ridiculed, it is sometimes hard to bear. Then you pick yourself up and face the world. It must happen to a lot of people. There are nearly ten thousand to help me. Some have no one to help them. So, I'm lucky.

'On my last day of service, I shall look at the oath I took as a newly installed recruit, and I shall ask myself, "Have I fulfilled my pledge?" If the answer is yes, then I shall have done my duty.'

A poll conducted by London's LBC Radio produced a 74 per cent response in favour of Anderton's comments on AIDS. Of the 1,018 listeners who participated in the

Brian Hayes phone-in, only one in four disagreed with Anderton condemning homosexuals for the AIDS epidemic. Two national newspapers, who organised a similar survey, reported comparable results. An 89-year-old woman from Solihull, in the West Midlands, told one of the newspapers by telephone, 'The homosexuals who have brought this plague upon us should be locked up. Burning is too good for them. Bury them in a pit and pour on quick-lime.'

Anderton has a flair for adding the flame to smouldering fires. Most intellectuals accuse him of appealing to base instincts, the lynch mentality, the guillotine solution. He says that he merely supplies a voice for the reticent majority.

Something positive, however, did appear to emerge from Anderton's irascible involvement in the AIDS debate. Through his initiative, a potent anti-AIDS spray was developed and was demonstrated to kill the virus 20 times faster than any other known chemical. The spray is a disinfectant for anyone who comes into contact with an AIDS sufferer. Some 30 police forces immediately bought the chemical, called Phoraid, and it is now sold throughout the country to dentists, funeral directors, schools and colleges. Orders were also received from the police in the United States, Hong Kong and Denmark. It was first used by Anderton's officers to wash out the cells in police stations if they had reason to suspect a prisoner was an AIDS sufferer. Phoraid can also be used as a skin-wash.

All of Anderton's officers were kitted out with an infectious diseases 'briefcase', containing rubber shoes, a mask, gloves and synthetic 'spacesuit'. Stanley Sexton, the health officer of the Greater Manchester police force, said that where there was heavy spillage of body fluids in road accidents, policemen would arrive on the scene 'clad in the full equipment'. The special briefcase was marked with a green cross.

Phoraid was developed by Smyth-Morris, a Yorkshire-based subsidiary of the Kalon chemical company, whose managing director, Mark Silver, said that his firm would never have imagined there was a demand for the special disinfectant if the idea had not been *sold* to him by Anderton.

Even this contribution from Anderton did not meet with universal approval. For example, Dr Donald Jeffries, head of virology at St Mary's Hospital, London, said that Anderton had gone 'way over the top'. And Nick Partridge, education officer of the Terence Higgins Trust, the gay helpline, believed that the whole exercise was 'a waste of money', which could have 'been better used in educating Manchester police, from the chief constable down, to better understand HIV infection'.

A month after Anderton's speech at the AIDS seminar, he was back in the headlines, this time for floating the proposition in a BBC radio religious programme that God might be using him as a prophet. During the broadcast, he remarked, 'God works in mysterious ways. Given my love of God and my belief in God and Jesus Christ, I have to accept that I may well be used by God in this way.' Given a chance on the programme to expand on his previous AIDS speech, he continued, 'Something was speaking to me inside and the words that I was using in my speech just flooded into my mind. I couldn't qualify them. I couldn't change them and I couldn't alter them. I had to say what I was compelled to say. If Jesus were here today, He may have spoke in terms similar to the ones I used. I must say I am completely dismayed by the attitude of some of our churches, and particularly some of their spokesmen, who never seem to say anything unequivocally. It is their duty and their responsibility to give a moral lead to the nation. I would argue that an acceptable moral code in this country is far more important than an enforceable criminal law. If we had that code, then you would need fewer laws and, hopefully, fewer policemen.'

In a radio interview, the Right Rev. Stanley Booth-Clibborn, Bishop of Manchester, commented, 'I would say that sometimes when people say strong things about moral issues, they tend to over-simplify. I believe that we have to realise that we live in a very complex world with many influences on people's behaviour.'

The police monitoring committee of Manchester city council announced plans 'in the interest of natural justice' to instigate allegations of professional misconduct against Anderton. The committee called for his immediate resignation. Anderton, true to form, was scornful. John Commons, the Liberal Party spokesman on the committee, said of Anderton, 'If he is to hide behind the shield of divine inspiration, he is not a fit and proper person to hold office,' while Tony McCardell, the committee's chairman, had this to say, 'If Mr Anderton was the chief executive of a firm, you would be asking him to seek medical help. His superiors are beginning to distance themselves from him.'

Peace talks were convened hurriedly in London. The chairman of the Greater Manchester Police Authority and his deputy were invited to the Home Office to make their charges against Anderton.

Allies of Anderton at the Home Office advised him 'not to rock the boat' at this critical juncture. Threats never succeed against Anderton. If anyone barks at him, he bites back. Therefore, the nature of the Home Office approach was conciliatory.

A few days after the Police Authority had levelled complaints, Anderton was afforded the opportunity to plead his case. These meetings were with Sir Lawrence Byford, Her Majesty's Chief Inspector of Constabulary, and Michael Partridge, the Home Office's deputy secretary in charge of police. After a further 'cooling off' period, a joint meeting was set up at the Home Office, lasting most of a full working day. The outcome was a wary, porous truce. Anderton had not been silenced, but he would strive for a closer and more amicable working arrangement with his Police Authority, taking its members into his confidence, especially before going public on contentious issues. Both sides gave an undertaking not to disclose anything that had been discussed during any of the Home Office negotiations.

If there was a winner, it was certainly Anderton. There was no pressure on him from within the Home Office to resign, and he had defended and successfully protected his right, as a free citizen in a democracy, to uncensored verbal freedom. The Home Office line was that all parties should behave more responsibly in public for the sake of the good name of the police. This could be achieved only by a spirit of unity and mutual respect between the chief constable's office and the Authority.

However, the fresh winds of a new storm were already blowing from the north-west. The chief constable's official car, a 17-year-old dark-blue XJ6 Jaguar, had 120,000 miles on the clock. Anderton asked the Police Authority for a new Jaguar. 'No,' they said, 'we'll give you a Mini!' After yet another public slanging match, the Authority compromised, but not much. They earmarked a maximum £10,600 for the new car and finally decided on an Austin Montego. Anderton said that the decision amounted to 'an insult' and, the moment the Montego was delivered, he ordered rigorous speed and safety checks on it, to see if it was capable of emergency high-speed anti-terrorist manoeuvres. He also issued a statement saying, 'The substantial reduction in standard and power of a car thought to be appropriate for the performance of official duties by the chief constable of the largest provincial police force in the country would appear to reflect the low opinion some members of the Police Authority seem to have for the force and its chief constable.'

On 31 October 1986, Myra Hindley, who was serving a life sentence at Cookham Wood Prison in Kent for her part in the Moors Murders, received a letter from Winifred Johnson, the mother of Keith Bennett, who had disappeared on 4 June 1964, at Longsight, a few miles to the south-east of Manchester on the A6, while on his way to visit his grandmother. Keith was 12 years old. His body had never been found. Mrs Johnson (formerly Bennett) pleaded in her letter for Hindley to reveal to the police where Keith's body had been buried. Ever since the trial in 1966 of Hindley and Ian Brady, at Chester Assizes, there had been no doubt that Keith Bennett and 16-year-old Pauline Reade were further victims of the Nazi-worshipping sadists. Pauline had vanished near her home in Gorton, Manchester, on 12 July 1963, while on her way to a dance at a nearby youth club.

At their trial, Brady was convicted of the murders of Lesley Ann Downey, aged 10, 12-year-old John Kilbride, and Edward Evans, aged 17. Hindley was found guilty of murdering Downey and Evans, but not guilty of killing Kilbride. However, the jury convicted Hindley of harbouring Brady, knowing he had killed Kilbride.

On 18 November 1986, Hindley made up her mind to help the police to find the bodies of Reade and Bennett. Contact was made with Greater Manchester Police and Detective Chief Superintendent Peter Topping had numerous meetings on the subject with Anderton. They were both of the same opinion: if there was any possibility of discovering the remaining bodies and thereby finally putting to rest a horror story that had haunted the nation for more than two decades, then Hindley's offer should be accepted. Accordingly, in December 1986, Myra Hindley was flown by helicopter from Kent to the snow-swept landscape 1700 feet above Oldham. To protect Hindley from assassination attempts, 300 police officers cordoned off the area of search. Hindley wore identical clothes, including a hood over her head, to her guards – except for one item. She was the only person on the helicopter wearing red gloves. Within an hour of landing, this information was in the possession of two men who had pledged – one publicly and the other privately – to kill her if ever she was released from jail. One of the men – Patrick Kilbride, the father of John Kilbride – broke through a police road-block leading to the moors and, when finally restrained, he was dispossessed of a knife. 'I was going to kill her,' he said.

The other man, potentially much more dangerous, was an ex-Lancashire police officer who received a telephone call from 'a faithful friend in the Force', but not from anyone within Anderton's private office or Topping's special squad. The Moors Murders had affected this former policeman very badly – this was one of the reasons for his premature retirement. Part of his grudge against Hindley and Brady was that they had ruined his career by letting loose demons in his head, nightmare devils that could be exorcised only through the extermination of the source.

Unknown to the police, he went to the moors that morning armed with a telescopic-sighted rifle. But the light and visibility were poor, and from a distance it was impossible for him to define precise colours. 'I didn't get in one shot,' he said. 'I went home crying. Three times I was sure I had her in my sights, for at least thirty seconds on each occasion, but I wasn't a hundred per cent certain. I couldn't take a chance. If I'd killed an innocent man, a policeman, that would have been murdering family. I'd have been reducing myself to her level.'

But who told him how he could pick out Hindley on the moors? He smiled whimsically. 'That would be telling. That I'll never do.'

Hindley was on the moors that day for seven hours. Nothing was found and digging had to be suspended for the winter when the grim weather closed in.

There were considerable misgivings, within the police as well as from politicians, for what some critics saw as pointlessly opening old wounds, but Topping denied that he had become 'caught up by the spell of the moors'. And Anderton dismissed as 'rubbish' suggestions that the new dig was nothing more than another of his publicity stunts. Both Anderton and Topping were soon to be vindicated.

Hindley was returned secretly to Saddleworth Moor in the spring of 1987, after she had made voluntary statements to Topping on 19, 20, 23 and 24 February. On 1 July, the police dug up the remains of a body from a shallow grave among an exposed outcrop of rocks on the crest of a hill above Oldham and near the A635 road. Those remains were taken to the public mortuary in Oldham and the 24-year search for Pauline Reade was over.

In June 1988, Topping, then aged 48, announced his premature retirement due to ill health. In the same statement, he made a plea to the Home Secretary, Douglas Hurd, to allow Hindley to be interviewed under hypnosis, believing it the last chance to find the remains of Keith Bennett. But even though Hindley said she was willing to be hypnotised, the Home Office refused to give its approval, annoying Topping, who failed to see the logic of the 'negative decision'.

Anderton would have been horrified to learn that he had become one of Myra Hindley's heroes. In fact, Hindley so admired Anderton that she wrote to him on three occasions. All the letters were intercepted before they landed on Anderton's desk. 'He'd have had an apoplectic fit if he'd seen those,' said one officer.

The first letter was written just after Anderton's suggestion on the radio that God could be using him as a prophet. Hindley wrote that she knew he was right because she had shared a similar experience. 'God talks to us all, if we're prepared to listen. I wish I'd listened years ago. I'm allowing Him to guide me now, the way you are. I agree with you; if you place your life in His hands, you cannot go wrong.' She said that she respected his moral strength and rejection of compromise and pragmatism. 'Yes, you're a good man,' she wrote.

The second letter was sent just after a newspaper stated that Anderton was becoming a Roman Catholic convert. She said that she was sure he would not regret his decision. 'We're following parallel paths, although arriving at them from very different directions.' The third piece of fan mail to the chief constable from the child-killer was written following a speech by Anderton in September 1987, at the International Crime-Fighting Conference in London, at which he advocated castration for rapists. On Independent Radio News, he said, 'If an offender has some form of medical problem, if one can call it that, clearly he should be physically prevented, by whatever means, from repeating his offence. And if that means removing his uncontrollable sexual urges by some form of castration, then I would support that as a proper course of action.'

As Anderton expected, he was assailed from many directions. Typical of the criticism was that of Martin Flannery, the Labour MP for Sheffield Hillsborough: 'Frankly, this is just the kind of nonsense that the British people here come to expect from Mr Anderton. There ought to be some kind of inquiry into a chief of police who talks nonsense like that. One wonders where he is heading for, but his remarks will be condemned all over the country.' Flannery was wrong with his prediction.

Myra Hindley thought Anderton's 'constructive' proposal should have been considered years ago and she praised him for his courage, writing, 'Some men will never be able to control themselves. If castration prevents one rape, one murder of a little girl or woman, it is justified.'

And the leftwing dominated Greater Manchester Police Authority, so often the sack on Anderton's back, which was expected yet again to press for the chief constable's resignation, astonished everyone, especially Anderton, by rallying behind him. Stephen Murphy, the Authority's chairman, blamed the media for 'grossly distorting and sensationalising' Anderton's comments. Mrs Cicely Merry, the Labour Party group leader on the Authority, who had attended the conference at which Anderton made his castration speech, said the press coverage was 'dramatic and degrading . . . an absolute disgrace . . . and their treatment of Mr Anderton was totally unfair'.

Anderton had said that he knew from personal experience how Christ must have felt when crucified. Now he knew what it was like to be resurrected.

Part Two

11

The Stalker Affair

Anderton admits to having a demanding, possessive mistress who dominates his life for 18 hours of every working day. Her name is Duty. Even though she is not always attractive and comforting, she has to be obeyed, without equivocation. She has heart, but no sentiment. And it was she, 'that stern mistress of the soul', who compelled him to call, in May 1986, for the suspension of his popular and distinguished deputy chief constable, John Stalker, and to have him permanently removed from what was to become known as the 'shoot to kill' inquiry into Northern Ireland's Royal Ulster Constabulary. 'But it was the blackest day of my life,' Anderton insists, explaining that he was under the influence of an uncompromising force that allowed him to make no concessions. Thus began one of the most complex mysteries in the history of the British police.

Politicians at both national and local levels, business tycoons, mobsters involved in organized crime, conmen, petty criminals, gay rights activists, M15, other Secret Service agencies (including the CIA), Church leaders, prostitutes, pimps, the Home Office, the Special Branch, the British army, Freemasons, the Conservative Party, the Mafia and even the deposed president of the Philippines, Ferdinand Marcos, were to become embroiled in this cauldron of conspiracy: an extraordinary Lancashire hotpot.

By the time 'Long John' Stalker was re-instated in

August 1986, as Greater Manchester's deputy chief constable, there were still very few people privy to the essence of the Stalker Affair. Stalker himself, even today, and despite what he has written in his own autobiography, has never been convinced about the motivation for, or indeed the nature of, the main thrust of a saga that bristled with all the tantalising and speculative components of an extravagant television 'soap'.

But how did it all begin? Why did Anderton decide that his immensely talented junior partner, whom he had respected for more than 20 years, should be investigated? Was it Anderton's decision or did the orders come from an even higher eminence? Could this extravaganza possibly have been rooted in something as simple as a personality clash? Had Anderton become jealous of his high-flying deputy and seized this opportunity to eliminate a counter-attraction to his own razzamatazz? Was there a British Government and/or RUC plot to smear and discredit Stalker? Were the Freemasons a factor? Had Stalker become a liability to the Thatcher Government, threatening the fragile Anglo/Irish Agreement? Was he even jeopardising the special relationship between Britain and the United States? Did we witness a witch-hunt inspired as a smokescreen to camouflage something more sinister? Or was the Stalker Affair merely another publicity hype that was all wind and little sail?

A crucial date in the chain of events was 24 November 1982. In County Armagh, Northern Ireland, it had been raining since dawn. Clouds were gathering and the temperature was hovering shakily two or three degrees above freezing.

Two youths were on a Montessa 250 trail motorbike, travelling out of Lurgan towards an unoccupied farmhouse in Ballynerry Road North. The driver was Martin McCauley, aged 19. His passenger was 17-year-old Michael Tighe.

This was IRA territory – dangerous, border country-side. A potato crop could be the innocent mask over a minefield. An old woman clutching her chest and pleading for a doctor might well be a decoy. A car with a puncture was likely to be a boobytrap. The oxygen cylinders in an ambulance, apparently responding to an emergency, might well be bombs. Ammunition belts have been responsible for countless 'pregnant' swellings.

Alongside the ramshackle, stone farmhouse stood a hayshed with a cluster of small windows, resembling a Highland crofter's cottage. Tighe knew it well. He had been inside on at least six previous occasions, using it as a lover's nest. Only the previous week he had taken an 18-year-old Catholic girl to the shed after dark. There, they had made love on a bale of hay in a corner, in exactly the same place where Tighe had had sexual intercourse with his previous girlfriend, the daughter of an RUC police-man. The romance with the policeman's daughter had come to a bitter end shortly after she broke the news to Tighe, in the hayshed one evening, that she was expecting his baby. He immediately offered to marry her. She promptly turned him down. 'My mother would kill me,' she said. 'I can't have the baby. Neither dare I marry you. I must go to London to get something done about it. Will you help me, Michael?'

But Tighe refused to contribute towards an abortion. 'I'll go with you to London and I'll marry you there,' was Tighe's alternative proposal.

Upset, the girl ran in tears from the farm. Tighe pursued, pleading with her, which only made her more distraught and resolute. They parted for the last time at the roadside, where the girl mounted her bicycle and pedalled towards Lurgan, while Tighe tramped disconsolately after her.

In his short-trouser days, Tighe had been to the farm at nights with friends to spy on lovers, and the two of them that cheerless 24 November were wondering what hanky-panky they might encounter.

They were 'looking for a laugh'. They did not find one.

The owner of the hayshed was an old woman, Catherine (Kitty) Cairns, whose late husband had held high office in the IRA during the 1920s. The crumbling property was not lost to civilisation like so many remote Irish farms: there were a cottage and other houses nearby, and children and domestic animals were always roaming across the boggy land. McCauley was later to say that he had promised to act as watchdog at the farm for Mrs Cairns while she was out of the country.

As the youths approached the hayshed, an RUC Special Branch constable, in a nearby police Portakabin, was sitting with earphones on at a desk in a special telecommunications room. He was listening for noises and conversations from premises that had just recently been bugged. All quiet so far. Nothing to report. He looked at his watch; not too long before his tedious shift would be over. With him in the Portakabin were several army intelligence officers. The constable had a direct line to the Special Branch's Tactical Co-ordinating Group headquarters in Gough Barracks, Armagh. Most of the military intelligence officers were also equipped with earphones.

McCauley led the way from his motorcycle to the hayshed. Immediately, he noticed that the leftside window was open. Peering into the hayshed through the opening, he spotted 'a metal object sticking out of the top of some hay'. With the help of his friend, he climbed on to the windowsill, at which point he spied two rifles inside. He told Tighe what he could see and both of them squeezed through the open window into the hayshed. As he landed on the straw-covered floor, McCauley caught sight of a third rifle. What happened next will always be in dispute.

All three rifles were more than 50 years old. The bolts

140

were missing from two of them, which meant they could not be fired, and there was no ammunition. Both youths began fondling the antiquated weapons. They aimed the rifles at each other and made mock war in the hay.

In the Portakabin, all these noises were monitored by the eavesdropping constable and the intelligence officers. The constable was having some difficulty deciphering the sounds. An army major stood by his side, being entertained to a running commentary. There was a constant flow of policemen and soldiers in and out of the Portakabin, playing havoc with the acoustics.

'I'm getting something,' the constable announced excitedly. In front of him was a microphone, linking him by radio to a senior officer of one of the RUC's Mobile Support Units (MSU). 'I can hear whispering.'

'Another couple screwing, more than likely!' quipped an intelligence officer by his side. Since the electronic surveillance of the hayshed was started, they had snooped unwittingly on several courting couples and the return on their efforts had been various symphonies of grunts and groans. Hence the officer's scepticism.

The MSU had been created in 1981 to provide the RUC with its own military wing, believed necessary in the campaign against terrorism if the fortunes of this uncivil war were to be changed. Mr Michael McAtamney, the RUC's deputy chief constable, had announced that all members of the MSU would 'be handpicked and trained to react with firepower, speed and aggression'. Furthermore, all those recruited to the RUC's paramilitary units would be 'kept at a constant high peak and trained to neutralise and eliminate any threat'. Warning shots would never be fired. There were 30 marksmen to each unit, which were divided into 'quick-reaction squads'. Each squad was led by a sergeant and incorporated its own self-contained surveillance team.

The bug in the hayshed of that unoccupied farm was planted by E4A, which had been formed two years earlier. E stands for Special Branch, 4 represents the department's Secret Service number, and A means undercover. In 1982, E4A comprised an establishment of between 25 and 30 agents. It is now known that many of those agents received combat training in England from the Parachute Regiment. However, their prime function was spying on subversive subjects, rather than filling a front-line role.

More indistinguishable reverberations crackled from the hayshed, sounding like a scrape of metal and the cocking of guns. Still the constable in the cabin could not make out exactly what he was hearing.

Unknown to Tighe and McCauley, the farmhouse was being staked out by one of the Mobile Support Units. The officer in charge of this particular unit, which lay in wait at the farm, was anxious to know what was happening inside the hayshed. To try to help him, the constable in the Portakabin removed his earphones and held them against the microphone, bridging a direct link between the MSU chief and the hayshed. Seconds later, the 'Go' command was issued to the assault squad at the farm.

The hayshed was peppered with bullets as it was stormed by the military-trained policemen – a sergeant and two constables – firing submachine guns, rifles and semi-automatic pistols. During the commando-style raid, not one shot was fired at the policemen. The door was kicked in. Bullets were sprayed inside the hayshed. The three members of the assault squad who did all the shooting were armed with Smith and Wesson pistols. In addition, the sergeant carried a Stirling submachine gun and the constables had Ruger rifles.

McCauley's description of the attack went thus, 'Within the space of a couple of minutes of being in the shed, two loud shots made my ears ring. There was a pause between them. They hit Michael, who had scrambled on to the bales of hay. He fell, disappearing among the bales. Then there was a rake of shots across the doorway.

'Someone outside shouted, "Right, come out!" I looked towards the door and saw a dark figure moving very fast across it. Almost immediately, there was a burst of gunfire through the door. I dived for cover and was hit twice in the back and once in the leg. There was another shout for us to come out and I yelled, "Right! Right!"

'More shots were fired through the door, which was then smashed down. I was dragged out. They were screaming at me. They wanted to know my name and were shouting questions about guns and explosives. They wanted to know where the explosives were. I hadn't a clue what they were talking about. Someone wanted to finish me off and there was an argument about that. I was in a daze. It seemed years before the ambulance arrived.'

Michael Tighe was already dead.

The original offical RUC line on the shooting was that a mobile patrol had been on routine anti-terrorist duty in Bellynerry Road North when a sergeant, in one of three unmarked Cortina cars, had seen a gunman moving stealthily towards the hayshed from the direction of a nearby cottage.

The sergeant had radioed the other cars for back-up, which was provided by the two constables. From outside the hayshed, they heard a rifle being cocked inside, whereupon the sergeant shouted, 'Police! Throw out your weapons!'

When there was no reply, the command was repeated. Still there was no answer. One of the constables then lowered a plank from a window, only to find himself looking down the barrel of a rifle. That is when the officers opened fire, in an act of self-defence. As soon as the shooting was over, an ambulance was called, without delay. There was no conversation with McCauley because he was too seriously wounded.

This description of the tragic sequence of events at the hayshed was flawed. For a start, 60 cigarette butts were found in an outhouse near the hayshed, making irresistable the theory that there had been some form of stakeout at the farm and that the assault squad had not merely 'stumbled across' the hayshed and a suspicious gunman.

Just 13 days earlier, three IRA sympathisers were gunned down at a police road-block near Lurgan, not far from the hayshed where Tighe was fatally wounded. On that occasion, however, none of the suspects survived. The dead men were: Gervais McKerr, Eugene Toman and Sean Burns. There were no independent witnesses to the killings, so we have only the word of the RUC for what actually happened. The Establishment version is that the three men tried to crash through the barrier in an attempt to escape across the border. A total of 109 bullets were pumped into the car by the crack MSU squad which was manning that frontier checkpoint. When the bodies were pulled from the car and the vehicle was searched, it was established that the occupants had not been armed. Three MSU officers who had been on duty that day at the road-block were charged with murder. When they were acquitted by a Belfast court, the judge commented that they should have been commended rather than subjected to a trial.

On 12 December, some 18 days after the hayshed blitz, Seamus Grew and Roddy Carroll, who both belonged to the outlawed Irish National Liberation Army, were cornered in their car outside Armagh by another MSU squad. One officer alone showered 19 shots into the car. By the time the shooting stopped, both Grew and Carroll were dead. Once again, neither of them was armed. The constable who had discharged the 19 bullets in rapid fire claimed, in a statement shortly after the killings, that he had honestly believed his life was in danger and had acted in self-defence. He too was cleared of murder.

But back to the hayshed drama . . .

The truth is that E4A knew that a consignment of explosives had been hidden in the barn, because the delivery had been observed by undercover agents. Shortly afterwards, during September, MI5 had installed bugs in the rafters and among the explosives, apparently with the authority of the Home Secretary, Willie Whitelaw. The Nothern Ireland Secretary of State, James Prior, also seems to have been briefed.

However, the bugs were defective and the explosives were smuggled from the hayshed unknown to MI5. The same explosives were used to make a landmine which killed three police officers at a politically sensitive location less than a mile from the venue of a lecture by the chief constable of the RUC, Sir John Hermon. Two suspects were reported escaping towards Lurgan on a red Honda motorbike. A similar machine was found abandoned a few hours later in Lurgan. After the murder of those three policemen, a new bug had been planted in the hayshed and a round-the-clock stake-out initiated.

The original official tale told by officers involved in the hayshed raid was later admitted to be nothing more than an elaborate cover story, designed to protect the identity of a mole within the IRA.

It was also conceded that all the weapons – the Stirling submachine gun, Ruger rifles and Smith and Wesson pistols – were fired during the killing of Tighe and the wounding of McCauley.

Inside the hayshed had been three ancient Mauser rifles, a sack and a screwdriver kit. There were definitely no explosives nor ammunition.

The tape from the hayshed was immediately taken to Gough Barracks, where it was signed for by one of the Tactical Co-ordinating Group's top-ranking officers.

McCauley was subsequently charged with possessing firearms in suspicious circumstances. At the trial, at which he was convicted, it was admitted that neither McCauley nor Tighe had any terrorist connections. Nor was there a shred of evidence to suggest that Tighe was even a

Republican. On 16 February 1985, McCauley was given a two-year jail sentence, suspended for three years.

The tragic, premature death of Michael Tighe probably aroused more anger and resentment in the local community than all the other similar bloody clashes put together, especially among the Protestants. Everyone outside the RUC readily accepted that Tighe had been an innocent victim and had never been a Republican urban guerrilla. There was talk in the bars that he had been set up because of his romance with the daughter of an RUC constable. No longer than a week after Tighe's death, the father of his former girlfriend declared scornfully in a pub, among mixed company, including other off-duty policemen, 'He [Tighe] got what he deserved. He was guilty all right. IRA or no IRA, the rotten little buck rabbit was guilty!' It seems obvious that by then he had heard about Tighe's association with his daughter, but did that information reach him before or after 24 November? And from whom? Why should he have been so ruffled about his daughter going out with Tighe, if the young man was not a Republican? If he had knowledge of the pregnancy, that would explain a lot, of course. His daughter, who stayed in London after the abortion and has never been back to Ireland, concedes that she telephoned home when she learned of Tighe's death.

I tracked her down to a bedsit in Cricklewood, north-west London, where she confided, 'I was hysterical. I screamed and screamed at my dad. I accused him of murdering Michael. But I didn't mean him personally. It was a collective accusation. I was pointing a finger at the RUC, the whole bloody lot of them. They're paranoid and jump at the sight of their own shadows.'

When had she made that call?

'I can't recall exactly. It seems so long ago now. It might have been as much as a month after Michael died: I didn't hear immediately. I heard about it from a friend; someone close to me from the same part of the world. I was numb for weeks. I've no recollection of the timetable of events. I'm sorry.'

Had she told her mother or father that she was pregnant?

'You must be joking!'

How many people knew before she left Ireland that she was pregnant?

'Just me and Michael . . . and the doctor, of course.'

Did she have the same doctor as her parents?

'Of course.'

Might he have indiscreetly leaked the news to her parents?

'It's always possible, but I doubt it . . . I can't say.'

When she telephoned her parents, was it self-evident that they were aware of her friendship with Tighe?

'Absolutely.'

Who could have enlightened them?

'It wasn't a big secret . . . only the pregnancy.'

During that hysterical call, did she mention the baby?

'Definitely not.'

Did her mother or father broach the subject?

'No, but they knew; I'm positive of that. My mother just pleaded with me to return home. In the end, I hung up.'

Tighe wouldn't have told the girl's family about the baby, so who might have?

'Michael must have talked to someone, a friend, a mate.'

Was he a Republican?

'That's the crazy part; no.'

Was there any possibility that he might have become involved with a terrorist organisation?

'It's absurd! He was a lovely boy. Now I just want to forget.'

Had she ever seen him with a gun or any kind of weapon?

'Never.'

Was he politically motivated?

147

'Not to my knowledge. Occasionally he talked about politics . . . unemployment, the cost of a drink, fags . . . just like anyone else.'

Was he anti-English?

'No more so than anyone else in Ireland. If anything, he disliked the Irish police more than the British army, but it wasn't an obsession with him. It wasn't something that burned him up.'

Why did she think he was killed?

'Because of me. It was family. Someone lied; putting Michael's name forward as an IRA soldier. That person must have been someone who knew Michael's habits. I'll never be persuaded otherwise.'

Shortly after the hayshed incident, there was a persistent rumour in circulation that a fierce argument had broken out at the farm among members of the MSU, reinforcing McCauley's account. One of them reputedly said, 'I thought we weren't supposed to take prisoners? Why doesn't someone finish the job? There'll be hell to pay if that fucker lives.'

Someone is alleged to have replied, something like, 'It's too late now. We've reported back. An ambulance is on the way. We can't top him now. The shots have already been counted.'

The first speaker apparently then fumed, 'What a cock-up!'

A third person was said to have muttered, 'We thought he [McCauley] was dead.'

This story is supposed to have originated from a member of the RUC who was at the farmhouse on that fateful November night. One can only make an objective judgment by analysing all the evidence that was collated during the next five years.

During the trial of McCauley, it was proven that a number of RUC offiers had lied when giving details of events surrounding the death of Tighe. 'Acting on orders from superiors', was the lame excuse from the discredited

148

law enforcement officers when ruthlessly cross-examined. According to their testimony, at all costs they had to protect the Special Branch and military intelligence from a public scandal and ignominy, plus shielding the informer who had given the tip-off about the hayshed being used as an IRA arsenal.

By now, there was a growing disquiet about the Mobile Support Units. There had been a dawning of suspicion that they were being turned into execution squads, posses of scalp-hunters and a law unto themselves. Politicians were picking up reports of cross-border sorties. A squad would nip over the frontier into territory out of their jurisdiction, meting out instant, cowboy justice. Some bodies were buried in woodland, while others were secretly incinerated back in barracks. Robbing the dead was one of the perks of the job. All their targets came from military intelligence. Most of the quarries had a history of IRA entanglement. The border was their tight-rope: they would choose carefully their moments to jump into Ulster on bombing sprees, scurrying back to be quickly lost in the labyrinthine network of their own intricate underworld. All the conventional ferrets had failed to flush them out. Of course a large number of these stories were apocryphal, but far too many had the ring of truth, and a file of disturbing allegations had reached the learned ears of the Northern Ireland director of public prosecutions, Sir Barry Shaw. Sir Barry, a man of the utmost integrity, was becoming alarmed by his feed-back, propelled at him from so many different sources.

The supplementary questions on Sir Barry's mind were more agonising: if the accounts of the killing orgies were fundamentally true, at what level were they instigated? Were the raids acts of revenge or were they a part of policy? And if it had become procedure, whose dictum was it? The RUC's? The British army's? The Westminster Government's? Or could it be that there was a joint approach? Had there been an agreed 'shoot to kill' directive? If so, where did it come from? Sir Barry had a headful of questions, but no answers; an omission he intended to waste no time rectifying.

Sir Barry immediately took up the matter with Sir John Hermon who, in turn, briefed his deputy, Michael McAtamney. The nature of that briefing has never been adequately clarified, but the outcome of McAtamney's inquiry did not satisfy the director of public prosecutions, who voiced his criticism, which he sustained. Under pressure from various fronts, Sir John consulted with Sir Philip Myers, the inspector of constabulary for Northern Ireland and the north-west, and that is when the hard bargaining began.

Into the arenas stepped Douglas Hurd, who by then had become the Northern Ireland Secretary of State, an MI5 liaison officer based in Belfast, other high-ranking agents with military intelligence in Ulster, and Bernard Sheldon, the head of MI5's legal department. The negotiations also included Sir Barry Shaw, Sir John Hermon and Sir Philip Myers.

Understandably, Sir John resented the push for an independent inquiry. He argued robustly that the RUC was more than capable of conducting its own spring clean. Sir Barry was not impressed, and said as much. He pointed out that the RUC had already been given a chance to look critically at itself in the mirror, but the opportunity had been squandered. Sir John considered these attacks a slur on his deputy and he pursued a stubborn policy of retrenchment.

Meanwhile, Sir Barry was becoming increasingly convinced that perjury had been committed on a grand scale by some RUC officers during numerous trials relating to shooting deaths of IRA suspects. In the back of his mind were the earlier allegations of the systematic ill-treatment of detainees in Castlereagh Barracks, during the time that Sir Kenneth Newman was chief constable of the RUC, before he became the Metropolitan commissioner at Scotland Yard.

Inevitably, all the Secret Service agencies were intransigent in their opposition to any form of official inquiry. The predictable objections were trotted out *ad nauseam*: undercover agents in the field would be put at risk, only the IRA and other terrorists could possibly benefit, Intelligence *modus operandi* would become universal currency and public confidence would be destabilised.

Caught in the middle was Sir Philip Myers. Anyone with an understanding of Anderton's philosophy would have been able to predict which way he would jump if he was consulted. Anderton commanded the largest provincial police force in the United Kingdom, which also happened to be in Myers' province, along with Northern Ireland. In terms of operational experience, Anderton was second to none.

Once Anderton ordered his driver to chase a police car that was speeding. A 'copper's nose' told him that the uniformed officer in the vehicle ahead, despite the whining siren and flashing blue light, was not responding to an emergency call.

You can imagine the ghastly look on the shocked young officer's face when he was forced into the side of the road by the chief constable's car and asked to explain where he was going in such a hurry. Sheepishly, he replied, 'Home for tea, sir. I'm late and it'll be cold.'

Anderton was enraged and in a matter of a few scorching seconds, the offending patrolman was reduced almost to tears. To Anderton this was a serious matter, not something to smile about, even in retrospect. 'This is just the kind of thing that gives us all a bad name, lad. It takes five minutes to do and a lifetime to live down.' In Anderton's critical eyes, it was a classic example of a flagrant misuse of privilege. He makes no allowances for himself nor his peers. According to his code, compromise is another word for corruption. 'The law is the law;

anything else in unlawful. There is right and wrong. Consequently, anything in between cannot be on the side of right.'

On the question of a public inquiry in Ulster, Sir Barry Shaw, the DPP, and Sir Philip Myers were lined up against Sir John Hermon and all the heavy military brass. Everything depended on which way Douglas Hurd would lean. Hurd made up his mind and Sir Philip Myers was in agreement: there *would* have to be an independent inquiry, despite the risks.

With the door closed on that dilemma, another door opened: who should lead the inquiry? It would be Myers' decision, now the talks were confined to Sir Philip, Sir John Hermon and Anderton, who ruled himself out for the appointment right from the outset. It was obvious to everybody that whoever was entrusted with the assignment would have a vastly reduced amount of time for his regular duties. Anderton's deputy, John Stalker, had been at his desk only a matter of weeks, therefore the overall running of the Greater Manchester police force could hardly be left solely to him. After all, he was still finding his way around the eleventh floor of the relatively new headquarters at Chester House in Old Trafford. Neither was it to be the kind of inquiry that could be conducted from a base on the mainland, with occasional visits to Belfast. The team would have to be grounded in Northern Ireland, although the officer-in-charge would be allowed a more floating role. Demanded was a solution that would create the least disruption, without undermining the operation by opting for anything less than excellence. It was against this backcloth that they all concluded there was one man only for the job.

It would have to be John Stalker.

12

The Plot against Stalker

Undoubtedly, Stalker had all the credentials for this demanding commission. More so even than Anderton, he typified the local-boy-makes-good fable. He was born in Miles Platting, a derelict neighbourhood of Manchester, which made him *really* local. His father was an aircraft engineer and John grew up with three brothers. During his schooldays at Chadderton Grammar, his heart was set on a career in journalism, but he changed his mind at the last moment, instead joining the police cadets. He was recruited into the old Manchester city police force in 1956 and his early stamping ground was another decaying suburb of Manchester, Moss Side, following in the footsteps of Anderton. His rise was as meteoric.

In the 1970s, he headed the city's Special Branch and was responsible for tracking down the IRA bombers who had been guilty of murderous outrages in 1973 and 1974, an important gold star for him to have appended to his personal file in May 1984, when the Belfast appointment was being made. It demonstrated that he had already a commendable track-record in the field of anti-terrorism and harboured no sympathy for the IRA, despite his own religious roots. His mother, Teresa, was born in County Westmeath in the *Republic* of Ireland and all her children had been brought up as Roman Catholics; a point not missed when Stalker was being considered for the sensitive and highly emotive leadership of the 'shoot to kill' inquiry.

Anderton had no reservations about Stalker's impartiality nor his ability to cope with the inevitable resentment from a staunchly Protestant RUC, steeped in Freemasonry which, until recently, had been anathema to Catholics. Anderton himself was in the throes of conversion to Catholicism, but that would not stop him arraigning a murderer just because he or she happened to be Catholic.

It is unlikely that an investigator whose knee bowed to Buddhism, Islam, atheism, agnosticism or the Archbishop of Canterbury would have been any more acceptable to the RUC than a page-boy of the Pope. Anybody other than the bodyguard of Ian Paisley, the leader of the Democratic Unionist Party, would have been held in suspicion by most of the RUC. The concept of religious neutrality was outside their experience.

Stalker was the right policeman for the job, so he got it. His religious inclinations and commitments were irrelevant.

Stalker's 28 years at the sharp end of policing had done nothing to blunt his appetite for success. By nature, he was what the Americans call 'a street cop'. He had excelled as a detective, rubbing shoulders with villains and building up an impressive portfolio of contacts in the criminal underworld – an essential element of the job. Blessed with a predator's instincts, he had thrived on the chase and the final kill.

Anderton's strength was in management. He is an administrator, a natural leader, but essentially a deskman and bureaucrat. He could run a hospital, a factory, a railroad or an airline with equal flair, because he has an intrinsic aptitude for delegation and organization. With little recourse to fanciful imagination, he could see himself occupying a seat on the front benches of Parliament or the chairman's throne in a boardroom. Unfortunately, he suffers from the restrictions of a uniform mind and has never been totally happy with the *modus operandi* of the

CID. It is with reluctance that he accedes to the necessity for detectives to socialise with villains; it goes right against the deep-rooted Anderton puritan grain. The sight of officers, while on duty, in jeans, cowboy boots and sweatshirts, perhaps also with a medallion looped around the neck, is an Anderton nightmare.

All but two of Stalker's 28 years as a policeman had been spent in Manchester. The brief hiatus had come when he was put in charge of the Warwickshire CID. He had a reputation at street level for being 'the nice guy'. Not soft or credulous, but always approachable. It was hard to find anyone, outside Ulster that is, with a bad word for Stalker.

'Your rank was immaterial to John,' said one detective who had worked in Manchester under Stalker. 'He would always listen and try to help. He certainly had the gentle touch – very compassionate and a humanitarian. It didn't matter whether your problem was personal or professional, he'd give you his time, his wisdom and confidence. He was known as Gentle John; that says it all, doesn't it?'

Whereas Anderton has always been a loner, Stalker is gregarious. He has the ability to rub along with everyone, keeping all his relationships well oiled. As for his superiors, they had him earmarked for the dizzy heights. 'Diligent' and 'tenacious' were the epithets most commonly used in the private reports of Stalker's progress in the Force, and his advocacy of community policing installed him in the minds of the hierarchy as a progressive and radical policeman, yet also soundly entrenched in tradition. Nothing illustrates more the esteem in which he was held at the Home Office than his selection in 1983 to attend, with 30 other people, the Royal College of Defence Studies for a course designed to groom those who would lead the nation in the event of nuclear war. This college dates back to 1922, the result of a decision by a Cabinet committee, chaired by Winston Churchill, who at the time was Secretary of State for the Colonies. When originally founded, it was named the Imperial Defence College. Churchill saw its role as a cadre for men who would be responsible for preserving the British Empire. Nowadays, Western defence is its main consideration.

It was in May 1984 that Anderton was asked by Myers to approach Stalker, and the appointment was confirmed officially on 24 May.

Stalker, naturally enough, was flattered to be singled out for the high-profile assignment across the Irish Sea, and Anderton congratulated him warmly. They had known one another a long time and had charted similar courses, setting sail from similar bleak ports. Backgrounds paved in poverty had served as a tenuous bond, but they had never been friends; never could be. The chemistry was all wrong for friendship, and Anderton has avoided any close associations within the Force that could prove compromising. Anderton has an overpowering, dominant personality; he is an extrovert and loves the spotlight. His opinions are important to him . . . and should be equally important to other people, he feels. He is much more comfortable talking than listening. One high-ranking enemy of Anderton told me bluntly, 'He's an articulate bullshitter.'

By contrast, Stalker never sought the limelight or used his position as a platform. Making arrests was message enough. Unlike Anderton, he was always 'one of the boys', but he is also a family man. All his leisure hours are devoted to his wife Stella, daughters Colette and Francine, and their bungalow and smallholding in War-burton, now a part of Greater Manchester but historically in old Cheshire.

On the day he kissed Stella goodbye and departed for Northern Ireland, he could never have imagined the furore that was to follow. For Stalker, it was the biggest challenge of his life, the chance to achieve a result that would make swift promotion to chief constable, somewhere, inevitable. Many eminent pundits saw him as a future Metropolitan police commissioner, possibly after Anderton.

Before he left jauntily for Belfast, Anderton told him, 'Remember, you can't make an omelette without breaking eggs.' Numerous commentators construed that remark to mean Anderton was warning Stalker to tread carefully and to restrict his digging to the top soil. In fact, Anderton meant the opposite. A strict translation is, *If you do the job properly, you're going to upset a lot of people. Start upsetting!*

All the officers in Stalker's team – a total of seven, excluding himself – had been handpicked by Stalker from the Greater Manchester force. He knew and trusted them all. He had to be certain that they were beyond reproach, immune to bribery, incorruptible.

For his deputy, he had chosen Chief Superintendent John Thorburn, a rugged and tenacious Scot. The other six were all detectives, one a woman. Thorburn was to be in day-to-day charge of the investigation, while Stalker concentrated on overall policy and strategy, also fulfilling as best he could his deputy chief constable role in Manchester. He decided to make two teams from those going with him to Ulster, but he declined the offer of RUC sleeping accommodation and Mess hospitality, for obvious reasons. Instead, he opted for an hotel outside Belfast. Their office was to be a former hotel that had been turned into a non-operational police station.

Sir John Hermon, fleshy-faced, flat dark hair brushed back severely, might have underestimated Stalker on their initial encounter, shortly after the arrival of the Manchester deputy. 'Well, Mr Stalker, you're in a jungle now,' declared Sir John.

Such a welcome made Stalker feel at home immediately. After all, he was one of the kings of the jungle. His self-effacing manner did not mean that he was inadequate or insufficient. When he blinked behind silver-rimmed glasses, which were always slipping halfway down his nose, he gave the appearance of an artless schoolboy, lean and lethargic.

Sir John might have been forgiven for thinking to himself: *What a dunderhead! No wonder Anderton dumped him on me!* Sir John was one of many people who, at their own peril, underrated Stalker.

Stalker and his team approached their task no differently from any other police investigation. They sifted through the evidence, studied statements and court transcripts, then started knocking on doors. PC Plod will still be in employment long after the last computer has been made redundant. Methodically and painstakingly, they followed the fading trails of the cases that had triggered this inquiry, but it was six months before they heard about the bug at the hayshed where Tighe was killed and McCauley was wounded.

The RUC were still trying to hide the fact that they knew the disused farm had been an ammunition depot and refuge for IRA terrorists. No one was owning up to planting the three old rifles in the hayshed either. However hard Stalker tried, there was no escaping the possibility that two innocent young men had been set up for murder by policemen in a premediated act of revenge, not caring too much who died.

Stalker went personally to see McCauley, whose first reaction was to try to slam the door in the deputy chief constable's face. 'To me, he was just another nosy policeman,' McCauley recalled. 'I detest them all! I'd talked enough to them to last me a lifetime. All I could think was: Now what do they want? Why can't they leave me alone? He wedged his foot in the door, the way they do. The more he talked, the less he sounded like a policeman, but I thought it must be a trick, that he was a bit cleverer than all them others I've ever met. He told me he held no brief for the RUC, but I didn't really believe him. I thought they must be having another go at stitching me up. I know there are a lot of people who regret that I didn't die with Mick. It must have been considered a monumental blunder when I was taken alive from the farm.'

So monumental the blunder that there was a joint unofficial meeting of the Special Branch, MI5 (the Security Service) and MI6 (specializing in espionage) to consider the ramifications of this 'botched up job'. The meeting took place in Liverpool's Crest Hotel exactly one week after Stalker's unwelcome arrival in Northern Ireland. A double room on the second floor had been booked in a bogus name by the Special Branch. Although the three men were at that period stationed in Northern Ireland, it was considered safer for such a policy meeting to be held 'away from the heat of the kitchen'. In any case, whenever possible, they liked to get to the mainland for a few days as an antidote to island madness.

'Special Branch' checked into the hotel around 6.00 pm, indicating that he would be the only person occupying the room. When he registered, he gave a false address. Before heading for the bar, where he waited for the others to show up, he took aside a member of the staff and tipped her five pounds for an innocent little favour.

Despite their close professional ties, the MI5 and MI6 agents arrived separately. It was almost seven o'clock before the third man, from MI6, made an appearance. While in the bar, they posed as salesmen in Liverpool on business. They drank beer and regaled each other – and the bar staff – with anecdotes and jokes. They played their parts convincingly.

A table in the dining room had been booked for eight o'clock. They took their beers with them into dinner and at the table ordered two bottles of red wine. They finished with coffee and liqueurs. Still no real business had been touched upon. When they returned to the bar, 'Special Branch' suggested, rather clamorously, that they should all retire to his room 'to watch a bit of TV'. This was agreed.

But when they reached the lobby, 'MI6' demurred. He was worried that 'Special Branch' might have bugged the room earlier in the evening. After whispered exchanges, 'Special Branch' volunteered to change his room. This satisfied the others. The reason given to the receptionist for a request to change rooms was that the television wasn't working properly.

The moment they were ensconced inside the new room, they searched one another perfunctorily for bugging devices. None was found.

Before throwing himself on the bed, 'Special Branch' called room service to order a bottle of whisky, three glasses and ice.

'MI5' occupied the seat at the writing-desk. 'MI6' stood at the window, leaning on the ledge. Only one item was on the agenda: *What should be done about McCauley and Stalker?*

All three expressed the opinion that McCauley was a liability. They were also astonished that such a mess had been allowed to occur. Their understanding was that MSU squads were under strict orders 'never to take prisoners'. For a couple of hours or more, they talked around the subject. 'MI6' said he would have been prepared to have gone to the hospital to 'finish the job' during the night of the same day that McCauley was wounded, but concluded, 'It's too late now. If anything happens to McCauley now, we'll all go up in smoke. There's nothing I can do for you. You'll just have to ride it out.' Nobody was comforted.

'MI5' floated the idea of McCauley 'disappearing' without trace. The others listened quietly while he elaborated. The plan went like this: MI6 should 'remove him'. The RUC could 'take care' of the body and then announce that McCauley was on the run to avoid being charged with 'something or other pretty terrible on the mainland'.

A week later, someone could file a report that McCauley had been seen in the Republic 'up to no good'. The inference would be that he had been a Republican all the time and had been 'lying his heart out'.

'Better we blow him up and make it look as if he had an accident with his own explosives,' said 'MI6'. 'But even that has been left too late. Stalker wouldn't swallow it. McCauley's untouchable. He's found the answer to eternal life.'

By eleven o'clock, they had reached the conclusion that they were left with nothing better than a smear campaign against McCauley, in the hope that it would invalidate any testimony he might give to Stalker and the court, when he came up for trial. 'MI6', it was promised, could assist with planting 'poison ivy', a cryptogram for false evidence.

One of them wanted to know, 'What's Stalker really like?'

'Trouble,' was the terse reply from 'Special Branch', who added, 'But we know every move he makes . . . before he makes it. He won't get far. He hasn't a chance. We're keeping a close tab on him.'

'But whose side is he on?' one of the others asked.

'Not ours. He wants to be a hero, so I'm told.'

'God gave us Stalker!' 'Special Branch' reminded them. They all laughed when the meaning dawned on them. 'Pious Jim' had even become an Irish joke.

That entire conversation was taped. 'Special Branch' had anticipated the reluctance of the other two to hold the meeting in a room which they would be unable to verify as 'clean'. He guessed that they would demand a last-minute switch. So, he had arranged in advance, when giving the five-pound tip, to swap rooms, concocting a convoluted story about wanting to play a practical joke on a couple of old friends. The receptionist told him which room he would be moved into. Before going to the bar, he had persuaded a chamber-maid to let him into the second room, where he concealed a simple voice-activated recorder. If one of the others had not demanded a room-change, he would have, bringing about the same result.

Their night was rounded off at the casino, where between them they won £120 at roulette and blackjack. None of these men was acting on authorised orders, and their activities that night were not a part of their legitimate job. This was something personal.

After hearing about the hayshed tape-recording, Stalker again went to see Hermon. It seemed to Stalker that the recording, if the sound quality was good, would go a long way towards resolving all the unanswered questions relating to the shooting of Tighe and McCauley. Stalker asked who had the tape. Hermon replied that it was the property of the Special Branch. 'I should like to hear that tape,' said Stalker, hardly surprisingly. Hermon referred Stalker to the Special Branch, whose senior officer promptly informed the Manchester deputy police chief that the tape would not be made available to him.

However, after protracted and frequently rancorous negotiations, Stalker was given permission to interview the RUC constable and an army major who had both listened in to the recording while it was being made. Stalker and his detectives went about taking statements from the two witnesses in the conventional manner of policemen at work. Therefore, they were astounded when both witnesses refused to answer questions on what they had heard from the moment the shooting began. Parrot-fashion, they replied to every question relevant to the actual blitz on the barn, 'Sorry, that's classified.'

The head of the Special Branch in Northern Ireland confirmed to Stalker that the RUC constable and the army major were acting on orders and he still refused to hand over the tape. Stalker returned in a rage to Hermon, expecting support from the top.

'I intend to get to the truth, however long it takes me,' Stalker vowed.

'That's why you're here,' Hermon retorted acidly.

'Do I get your full co-operation?'

'Of course.'

'Thank-you. What about the tape?'

'Ask the Special Branch.'

Stalker then turned his attention to the car ambushes in which all the occupants had been killed in a hail of bullets. By now he accepted that he could not rely on the independence of any of the Northern Ireland police experts, so he recruited his own ballistics scientists from England, causing a further deterioration of relationships in Belfast.

The scientists were adamant: the trajectory of the shots proved beyond doubt that the sworn statements of the policemen who gunned the suspects were flawed. Those armed policemen could not have been standing where they claimed they were at the time of the shootings.

Stalker was beginning to establish a rapport with McCauley. It had not been easy, but patience prevailed. McCauley finally came to the conclusion that Stalker wanted to unravel the truth, rather than to preside over its burial.

Stalker had stressed from the outset that he was not on anybody's side: not the RUC's, not the IRA's, not McCauley's. He was, however, hungry for information, no matter what or where the source. He alone would assess its worth, free from religious or political bias.

McCauley opened his heart, although never fully trusting Stalker. In his turn, Stalker did not accept the story at face value: inspired by healthy scepticism, he stuck it up as a target and did his best to shoot it down. When he had finished, there were remarkably few holes in it, in marked contrast to the implausible RUC line.

Once again, Stalker appealed to Hermon to release the hayshed tape. Once again, Hermon refused.

When it was leaked that Stalker was sympathetic towards McCauley, one very senior RUC officer retorted,

'What do you expect from a Catholic!' This anger was shared by the Secret Service agencies in Northern Ireland. They believed that Stalker should be making allowances for the 'special circumstances', the fact that in Ulster war conditions prevailed. 'No one worried too much about our boys shooting to kill the Argies in the Falklands,' was typical of the protests heard by the leaders of the security forces. 'The frontline conflict is just as real here. Why the double standards?'

Stalker retaliated by opining that it was not his business to compromise his criteria. He had been appointed to investigate and to report his findings. It would be up to the politicians to decide whether or not the RUC had exceeded their mandate, taking into consideration the paramilitary theatre of war in which the plots, sub-plots and counter-plots were enacted.

Both Stalker and Hermon were in constant touch with Sir Barry Shaw, the DPP, and Sir Philip Myers, although this was a breach of protocol. It is accepted practice that an inspector of constabulary has no contact with an investigating officer from the moment an inquiry begins until it is offically over.

However, Stalker could see that he was to lose his battle with Hermon unless he could persuade the big guns in Whitehall to give him support-fire. Hence, a meeting was arranged in London between Stalker and the legal adviser of MI5, Bernard Sheldon, who argued forcefully that the dispute over the contentious tape should be 'put on ice' until after McCauley's trial. Stalker had objections but was prepared to horse-trade if, in the end, he was going to make significant headway. Sheldon laid a set of ground rules to which Stalker reluctantly agreed to adhere.

After the McCauley trial, Stalker would make another approach for the tape. If that application failed, he should then re-apply in writing to Hermon, with a copy of that letter going to MI5. By the end of that meeting, Stalker felt bound and gagged by red-tape shenanigans. But the more they gave him the runaround, the more determined he became to complete the course. By now, he was getting his second wind and a long-distance rhythm. To the chagrin of Hermon and the Security Service, they were to discover that they had pitched themselves against an indefatigable marathon man. (Later, Sheldon was to figure prominently in the case of *Spycatcher*, the memoirs of former MI5 agent Peter Wright, which the British Government tried to have banned in Australia and elsewhere.)

Stalker, always a gentleman, played by the rules. Immediately the McCauley trial ended, he once more pressed for the tape. Application refused.

The same day, he put his request on paper, with a copy to MI5, as arranged. Application refused – this time on the express authority of Sir John Hermon himself.

In the interests of the investigation, Stalker believed it was advisable for two senior officers to be suspended from duty for the duration of the inquiry to avoid anyone at a later date being able to accuse him of having been pressured. Hermon, backed by the head of the Special Branch, Trevor Forbes, dismissed Stalker's appeal on the grounds that such action would debilitate morale. The personality clash between the two men was beginning to worry Whitehall and, in Manchester, Anderton was kept abreast by Stalker of the feuding in Belfast, without there ever being a violation of secrecy.

On a cold night in March 1985, Maureen Connolly (that's her professional name) picked up a client near the Piccadilly bus station in Manchester. It was just after 11.00 pm and she had spent the previous two hours in a pub. The man she had solicited had been in the same pub, his face obscured for most of the evening by a beer glass. As far as she knew, they had never seen one another before. In reality, her 'pick up' was well-acquainted with Maureen

Connolly, who made a living as a kissogram girl, part-time nude model, semi-professional stripper and pin-money prostitute. Her client that night was the same Special Branch officer who had tape-recorded his meeting with the MI5 and MI6 agents in the Crest Hotel, Liverpool. He was aware, for example, that until six weeks previously Connolly had been living in Belfast, where she had a two-year-old daughter, Mary. The child was being cared for by Connolly's widowed mother, who suffered from chronic arthritis. The fact that Connolly had gone to Manchester to broaden her horizons was sheer coincidence.

'Special Branch' was asked if he was 'looking for business'? He replied casually that he 'could be, depending on the terms'.

'Depends what you want?' she countered, changing gear into the hard sell. 'Straight sex is twenty.'

'Pounds?'

'Not pence, that's for sure!'

They both laughed.

'Where do we go?' 'Special Branch' wondered.

'Are you staying at an hotel?'

'Sorry.'

'That's all right. I have a flat.'

'Not too far away, I hope?'

'Only Fallowfield. Where's your car?'

'Round the corner.'

'We'll be at my place in ten minutes.'

The sparsely furnished, two-room flat was on the ground floor of a shabby house that had been built between the wars. Ms Connolly led her client directly into the dimly lit bedroom.

'Special Branch' removed his trenchcoat and tossed it on the bed. Connolly began to unbutton her blouse, stipulating, 'Money first before you take anything else off.'

Four fivers exchanged hands. She had just slipped out

of her blouse and was struggling with her bra clip, when 'Special Branch' said, 'That won't be necessary. I only want to talk.'

'Oh, you're one of those!' she sneered, not understanding. 'Suit yourself, you're the customer.'

Connolly, a Catholic, had been singled out by 'Special Branch' several weeks earlier when it was established that the likely father of her child was a staunch Loyalist with criminal convictions for fringe terrorist activities. Ever since, she had been the subject of surveillance. When she moved to Manchester, she became an even more 'attractive proposition'.

'Special Branch' sat on the bed beside her and took out a black-and-white photograph from his jacket's inside breast pocket. 'Do you know who that is?' he said, passing the photograph to her.

She shook her head, asking, 'Should I?'

'Special Branch' responded, 'You don't forget your *regulars* that easily, do you?'

'I've never seen him before in my life,' Connolly said adamantly.

'Special Branch' contradicted her, advising that she must be mistaken, working his way purposefully towards the punchline, 'You've been to bed with him on three separate occasions.'

'Not true. Who are you? What's this all about?'

'Never mind that. Are you interested in making a lot of money?'

'How much is a lot?'

'A few hundred.'

'What's involved?'

'Very little.'

'I don't do anything kinky.'

'But *he* does.'

When she looked at him curiously, he explained that the man in the photograph enjoyed dressing in women's underwear. 'I shall be wanting a statement from you to

167

the effect that you helped dress him in your underwear on three occasions, before turning a trick for him. He paid you fifty pounds each time. Three weeks ago you told him you were pregnant and that he could well be the father. He immediately offered to pay for an abortion. You said you couldn't do that because you're a Catholic.'

'How do you know that?' she interrupted hotly.

'We know everything there is to know about you.'

'*We?*' Now she was frightened.

'Hear me out. He pleaded with you, talking about his wife and family. All this was happening in Belfast. I can give you dates.'

Connolly's fear was sharpened. He read her eyes. 'He showed you photographs of his wife and children. Then he offered a thousand pounds on top of the abortion fee . . . and that's why you came to England.'

Connolly tried to make 'Special Branch' take back the £20, saying she just wanted 'an uncomplicated life'.

'It's too late for that,' he said, pushing the money on her. Then he mentioned her daughter, Mary, and the name of the child's probable father, apprising Connolly, 'We know all about your lover's record. Your mother can't cope with a kid. We can have the kid taken into care any time we choose.'

Connolly was sobbing when she whispered, 'Are you the law?'

'Special Branch' borrowed the politicians' artifice and answered the question with another question. 'What do you think?'

Connolly had composed herself by the time she enquired, 'Tell me more about what there's in it for me and what I must do?'

'What's in it for you? – Quite a lot of money, if you do as you're told.'

'How much is a lot?' she pushed.

'Enough,' 'Special Branch' assured her evasively. Still sitting beside Ms Connolly on the bed, he took out his wallet and dealt £100 from a wrinkled bundle of notes. As he deposited the bribe in her lap, he said, 'There's a hundred pounds for you as a taster, just to show good faith. But remember, if you accept it, then you're committed. If you're in any doubt, say so now.'

Maureen Connolly vacillated, but couldn't wrench her eyes from the seductive inducement. As she began fingering the notes, 'Special Branch' turned the screw. 'Think of your daughter. Do what's best for her. Try to imagine her growing up without her mother; without you.'

Connolly stood up, decided. She stuffed the cash into her handbag and began to fasten the buttons of her blouse.

'Tell me it's a deal,' 'Special Branch' pushed. 'You must say it.'

Connolly had not once looked at her client's briefcase since she first approached him. Even if she had, it is unlikely that she would have noticed the minute perforations down its sides, the sensitive earpieces of one of the world's most sophisticated electronic surveillance systems. Inside the briefcase was a custom-built tape-recorder. It was switched on and off by the carrier simply raising or lowering the handle. Almost every word since Ms Connolly accosted 'Special Branch' outside the Piccadilly bus station had been stored in the briefcase's memory.

'I got into the habit of taping almost every conversation I ever had,' 'Special Branch' confided. 'Often, as in this case, the recording would be double-edged. It would incriminate me as much as the other party. But having a precise record of things said on a particular occasion can be incalculable. And if the tape proves a burden, it can always be conveniently lost' – the fate of this recording. He allowed me to read a transcript of that tape, emphasising, 'I can always deny it ever existed. I can always say you made it all up. I'm covered.'

'I don't want to get into trouble,' Connolly told 'Special Branch' warily, just before they parted.

'From this moment, you're protected . . . as long as you don't welsh on the agreement.'

'And all I have to do is make a statement?'

'Nothing more . . . except pointing to this photo and swearing, hand on heart, so to speak, "He's the one. He's the dirty blighter who gave me a fat belly." All we require at this stage is a pact in principle. We'll do all the packaging for you, filling in the gaps, such as dates, times and places.'

'Okay. I'm game,' she said tepidly.

'Good girl. You won't regret it.'

'When do I get the rest of the money?'

'The moment everything's signed and sealed.'

'When will that be?'

'Two weeks at the most.'

'Is it going to hurt him?'

'Embarrass more than hurt.'

'You're sure?'

'Take my word for it.'

'I'm not prepared to lie in court, under oath.'

'That won't arise. We'd never allow it to go that far.'

'How much more money can I expect?'

'We could make it up to a grand.'

'Sounds handy! How do I contact you?'

'You don't. Meet me at the Piccadilly bus station, same place, at eleven o'clock a week from tonight.'

'Are you a private detective?'

'Don't ask questions, then you won't hear any lies.'

'Special Branch' asked Ms Connolly if she wanted a lift back into the city.

'No thanks, I've finished for the night.'

One week later, Connolly failed to keep her appointment. The following day, her mother was questioned. Maureen, apparently, had returned to Belfast to collect her child three days after her brush with 'Special Branch'.

'She only stayed a couple of hours,' 'Special Branch' was informed. 'She didn't say where she was going or what she was going to do. She seemed very agitated. I'm worried about her, but she can look after herself, she's had plenty of practice. I'm more bothered about Mary than Mo.'

Connolly's boyfriend was also missing from his Belfast lodgings. Enquiries during the next 48 hours turned up evidence that pointed to Ms Connolly, her lover and daughter having caught the ferry to Liverpool only a few hours after leaving the house where the child had been staying. Connolly never did return to her Manchester flat.

Of course, the photograph Connolly had been shown was an official police head and shoulders portrait of Stalker.

'Special Branch' was not the least defensive as he detailed the numerous botched attempts to frame or compromise the deputy chief constable of Manchester. There was no truth, of course, in his declaration to Connolly that the man in the photograph had a fetish for women's underwear, that was lurid invention. 'Dirty tricks warfare is just one more weapon in a well-stocked armoury,' he explained frankly when we met for drinks in the Wig and Pen club, directly opposite London's law courts. 'Stalker was becoming a pain to the security agencies, tantamount to a boil on the bum. The general consensus of opinion was that he had to be stopped. The most expedient treatment for a boil is to lance it.

'We held no brief for cowboys, like a few of those who had been involved in some of the shootings, but that wasn't the issue for those who had to look after national security. If it became necessary to sacrifice the career and reputation of one man, then that was no big deal. In war, thousands upon thousands of innocent people go to the wall.

'There were many people in Northern Ireland just waiting to pull the trigger on Stalker. I think Stalker knew, towards the end, that contracts had gone out on him. If he'd returned to Northern Ireland, he could have been dead within a fortnight. Anderton saved his life. Stalker had a gut hunch that he was destined to die in Ulster and he was a mulish fool. He was determined to die a hero, but Anderton deprived him of that grand exit.

'Nobody wanted to frustrate Stalker's murder investigation. Murder is murder. Mitigating circumstances for killing have to be justified in court. We're all on the same side on that subject. But what Stalker couldn't seem to come to terms with was that national security has top priority and rides roughshod – rightfully so – over all other considerations and principles of law enforcement. The Secret Service is a law unto itself and must always remain that way.

'I can't believe that the general public is really unaware that since around 1972, '73, there's been a policy to avoid taking terrorist prisoners, whenever possible. It's not murder, but another form of suicide. Terrorists choose their own fate. You make it clear what will happen if people behave in a certain way and then it's up to them. When you don't take prisoners, you reduce the risk of reprisals; it makes tactical and political sense. Justice is like Utopia: it's a young plant in a neglected garden that gets trampled on every time it tries to grow. I've no doubt that the majority of people in the United Kingdom support wholeheartedly a shoot-to-kill policy against all terrorists, not just in Ireland. They don't want millions of taxpayers' money squandered on showpiece trials. A trial can be a fuse that simply detonates more explosions, more mayhem.'

'Special Branch' may – or may not – have been right in his supposition about the mood of the people, but he was missing the point. Assassinating murderous terrorists was one thing; the random slaughter of unarmed, guiltless people in premeditated acts of revenge, cloaked by the uniform of the crown, was something very different. When we had our meeting, he was no longer in the Force, having retired prematurely due to 'disillusionment' and the 'increasing political interference'. He was in the throes of launching his own 'agency' and was negotiating a tie-up with former FBI agent Gordon Liddy, who was jailed for seven years for his part in the Watergate burglary. Liddy went to prison in preference to revealing all to the Watergate investigation about President Nixon's part in the cover-up conspiracy. After his release from jail, Liddy established the Gordon Liddy Counter-terrorism Academy in Orange County, just south of Los Angeles, California, recruiting 12 full-time 'desperadoes' – all either former British SAS men or ex-Israeli commandos. The fee for any assignment would be $500,000 and they would be specialising in freeing hostages. Liddy once ate a rat for dinner to prove the resilience of the human stomach.

Some people may find it hard to believe that an ex-police officer, whose patch for most of his career had been political security, should be so forthcoming and forthright to someone who was going to chronicle everything he said. I, too, would never have believed it possible to have this sort of interview if it had not been for Nigel West, the military historian who specialises in security matters and is European editor of *Intelligence Quarterly*. Nigel West is the pen-name of Rupert Allason, the Conservative member of Parliament for Torbay, Devon. His father, who was for 19 years the MP for Hemel Hempstead, had been a lieutenant-colonel on Earl Mountbatten's war staff. It was West who named in his book *Molehunt* Graham Mitchell, the former deputy director of MI5, as the mystery Fifth Man in the Burgess, Maclean, Philby, Blunt spy scandal.

We talked in the study of his Victorian home in London's Fulham Road. I was intrigued to discover how a fledgling politician (it was a few weeks before he won his seat in the June 1987 General Election) could possibly

prise such hush-hush information from tight-lipped sea-
soned ex-Secret Service agents. The answer was delivered
with an irreverent guffaw. 'They're always telling stories
to massage their own egos. It's easy, especially when
they're in the company of women. That's when they're
really vulnerable and are eager to show off. They can't
resist boasting. Put a couple of agents together at the bar
or over dinner and they'll be swapping stories all night.
And I'm the fly on the wall.' I tell the story to establish
that, apparently, there is nothing extraordinary about my
experience. Mr West imposes a strict code of conduct on
himself. He never writes about Northern Ireland and his
subject matter has to be at least 20 years old.

Ironically, after the Second World War, Mr West's
father was given the job of preventing the publication of
sensitive military memoirs. 'That's why for a long time I
daren't tell him that I was Nigel West. Once when we
were together as one of my books was being mentioned
on TV, he frowned and said something scathing like,
"That fellow's a bloody awful trouble-maker!" I think, if
he could have had his way, he would have had Nigel West
sent to the Tower!'

A former MI6 officer claims that he was offered
£150,000 to keep quiet about a shoot-to-kill policy has
been 'accepted practice since the mid-Seventies'. The
bribe, to be paid in £30,000 instalments, was to be
laundered through the British subsidiary of an American
MI5 officer, working in counter-espionage with Peter
Wright, author of *Spycatcher*. A Tory Member of Parliament said he may have discussed using the subsidiary to
pass money to the agent who has made the allegation
when they were discussing possible compensation for
early retirement from the army. He had complained to
the MP about an army assassination policy, whereupon
he had been committed to the army hospital at Netley,
diagnosed as 'emotionally unstable'. However, army doctors were forced to admit to the MP that the ex-Secret
Service agent was never medically unfit.

During my evening at the Wig and Pen club with 'Special Branch', he seemed happy to admit that there had been 'at least six attempts' to falsify evidence against Stalker in order to besmirch his reputation.

Why had Connolly been chosen?

'She was one of many under consideration and was ideal because of her vulnerability: an unmarried Catholic mother, on the game, her boyfriend a Loyalist hooligan, her mother an invalid . . . That sort is putty in your hand, usually. The danger is they become scared and do a runner. That's what happened with Connolly. You win some, lose some. It's swings and roundabouts. She was only one of a shortlist of about half a dozen girls.'

Did any of the other girls go through with it and make a statement, sexually incriminating Stalker?

'No, in the end we gave up the idea. It was becoming too complicated, far too iffy. You see, it was not enough for a whore to stand up and say, "Stalker screwed me. I carried Stalker's baby." She would have to be able to state times and places, and describe the warts on his balls, etc. There would also have to be independent back-up; very tricky. Stalker made it difficult for us by rarely being alone. So, we had to look at other options.'

Such as?

'We tried to get him drunk with the idea of engineering a situation in which he had to drive, but he was too smart for that. Whenever he drank, he always had a driver with him and we failed miserably in all our bids to separate them. We slipped LSD in his beer one night, but an off-duty British army corporal picked up the wrong glass by mistake. We also followed him all over Manchester, but he was always clean. We never caught him once being a naughty boy.'

A proposition, similar in nature to the one made to Connolly, was also levied on a British army private who was known to be homosexual. 'He wasn't very keen to co-operate,' said 'Special Branch'. 'Neither did we think that he was made of the right fibre. He could well have snapped under cross-examination; that could have been disastrous for us. You have to know your man.'

What was the carrot dangled in front of the army private?

A long pause as he balanced on the scales of his conscience the advisability of disclosure, then, 'We might have offered him a free supply of drugs, but he wavered and that was enough to put us off. We were reduced to hoping for a miracle . . . and we got one, which just goes to prove the power of prayer! Some people on our side did their best to incite the more notorious Loyalist head-cases and it would have been only a matter of time before one of them took a pop at Stalker.'

13

More Dirty Tricks

The war against Stalker was being waged on two separate fronts: in Northern Ireland and in Manchester. Where did Anderton stand and just how much, if anything, did he know about the plots to discredit his deputy?

There is no doubt that Anderton was still 100 per cent supportive of his bedevilled deputy. He suspected – and indeed hoped – that nothing would deter Stalker. One of the qualities that had swung the vote in Stalker's favour at the time of selecting the investigating officer for Ulster was his strength of character. 'You'll need a broad back,' Anderton had advised him: neither of them could possibly have known at the time just how broad!

The feed-back to Anderton was patchy. After all, he had the largest provincial police force in the country to run without the full-time assistance of an understudy, so there was little opportunity or inclination to suffer other people's headaches.

Stalker tried to spend Monday to Friday in his Manchester office, but he was always liaising with Thorburn and he never knew when he would have to 'drop everything' and fly to Belfast. Even so, it was only human nature for him to counsel his boss and most of Anderton's intelligence came from Stalker and Myers. Of course, it was also impossible for him not to be buffeted by the currents of criticism whipped up by Hermon's insecure acolytes.

Stalker was never forgotten in Anderton's daily prayers. In his office and beside his bed at night, he prayed that Stalker would have the resolve and fortitude to see through his mission safely and with honour. He talked it through with his wife, Joan, and her advice was to 'trust your man; trust others the way *you* would expect to be trusted'.

Naturally, there were conflicting stories. Stalker was complaining that every path he went down was immediately turned into a blind alley, that the RUC and the Security Service were conspiring to obstruct him. Hermon's story was that the man from Manchester was a menace who was hallucinating, seeing demons in every night, ghosts behind every door, skeletons in every cupboard. 'He's read too much detective fiction!' Hermon said dismissively of Stalker. Occupying the uneasy middle ground were Anderton and Myers. Who should they believe? There was the notion that Stalker, quite understandably, was trying to prove he was chief constable material and, therefore, an element of over-zealousness was to be assumed. Against that, there was Hermon, a knight of the realm who, right from the outset, had seen the official inquiry as a needless over-reaction to mischief-mongering and a wanton attack on his authority and personal self-esteem. Conflict was inevitable, Anderton concluded, also believing that Stalker and Hermon were big enough to look after themselves.

Myers was in a different position, with an alternative set of priorities. He was concerned with the smooth running of the forces under his control. Stalker was never quite certain where he stood with Myers and was annoyed by what he interpreted, perhaps unjustly, as fence-straddling.

On the question of how much Anderton knew about the dirty tricks manoeuvres designed to disgrace Stalker and bankrupt his stock of evidence, it is certain that he was *totally* ignorant. So, too, was Stalker. Neither of them has ever been fully aware of the extent of the intrigue. Stalker was conscious of the fact that there were people endeavouring to impede him, but even he would have disbelieved the range of the machinations.

For example, Stalker had been in Belfast only a few weeks when an allegation of corruption against him was levelled in Manchester by a professional police informant, David Bertlestein. This information was passed to Detective Chief Superintendent Peter Topping, who at that time was the head of Y Department, the police internal discipline section. Either just prior or a few days after that event, businessman Gerald Wareing was playing golf with Chief Superintendent Bernard McGourlay, of the regional crime squad. During their round, Wareing happened to mention, almost in passing, that Stalker was a friend of Kevin Taylor, a controversial figure in the northern commercial fraternity and chairman of the Manchester Conservative Association. Superintendent McGourlay was anxious that Stalker should be made aware of the poison talk that was in circulation, especially regarding the nature of his association with Taylor. It was in the belief that he would be helping Stalker that McGourlay tipped off Y Department, hoping that the message would be conveyed by the deputy chief constable. Topping did not see fit to make contact with Stalker on this matter, presumably either because he considered it of insufficient consequence or that Stalker had more pressing problems in Belfast to monopolise his mind. However, two things Topping did do. Firstly, he called for a written report on any connection between Taylor and a syndicate known as the Quality Street Gang. The drugs squad had been following Taylor's BMW car for some time and Topping was informed that this undercover assignment was continuing. Secondly, Topping wrote a confidential report to the chief constable, summarising the information that had percolated through to his department. Topping probably believed that if anyone should alert the deputy chief constable, it should be Anderton and not one of Stalker's own subordinates. Topping did admit in his communiqué that he was 'doubtful about the quality of some of the information'. This document reached Anderton on 17 July 1984, and he read it the same day. For several days he ruminated over what he should do, if anything.

At this point, it is essential to dwell on Bertlestein's background. Basically, he was a parasite conman with a considerable talent for fraud. One of his favourite tricks was to sell someone stolen goods and then tip off the police, so he could later claim the insurance reward; he did that successfully for many years. A judge, when sentencing him in 1973 to six years in prison, even complimented him on his 'plausible manner'. Certainly his most cheeky line of business was eliciting criminal intelligence over a drink from one detective and selling it the next day to another police officer. A Special Branch officer confirmed that Bertlestein was a 'constant pest' who was 'always on the make; never off the phone to his network of police contacts'. But he added, 'He was worth keeping on the payroll because, every now and again, he would strike oil. You could ignore nine of his tips, but the tenth might land you the jackpot. He was always making wild accusations against police officers. He was paranoid and he would literally do and say anything for money. He'd have sold his old mum to the Nazis for a fiver, even less. Anyone wanting to hear lies about Stalker could have bought them from Bertlestein well below the street's going rate.'

It is on record that Bertlestein gave a tip in October 1980 to Detective Sergeant Derek Burgess, of Manchester's fraud squad, about the IRA's blueprints for a new bombing blitz. At the time he contacted Sergeant Burgess, he feared, with good reason, that his arrest was imminent because of his connections with a dubious company, called Cut Price Fancy Goods, which was based in Salford and also had a branch warehouse in Belfast. He told Burgess that the firm's warehouse in Kent Street, Belfast, was high on the IRA's hit list.

Early in 1981, the warehouse went up in flames, after a remote-controlled explosive device was detonated, exactly as Bertlestein had forewarned, decorating him with a reputation that he did not deserve. Inevitably, he tried to trade the information about the new bombings in return for a blind eye being turned to his fraudulent dealings, for which he was about to be charged.

When he came up trumps again, this time about two senior IRA brigade commanders travelling, via Stranraer, to a top-level international terrorist battle briefing in Manchester, he was treated by some detectives as if he had a hotline to every godfather of organised crime in the land.

There had been a high-speed motorcycle chase near Preston, Lancashire, but the criminal top brass managed to escape. Then, in January 1983, Bertlestein was arrested in Bolton, Lancashire, on charges relating to cheque frauds, when immediately he began dropping the names of his police friends. He demanded to make calls to all the various divisions of the Greater Manchester police force. The message to each of his police contacts was, 'You owe me. Now I'm collecting.' Still he was held in custody . . . until he alleged that he had 'shattering proof' of police corruption. Suddenly, Bertlestein was back on the streets.

The fraud squad was being outwitted by the Quality Street Gang because they seemed always to have advance warning of police raids, which pointed to an internal leak high up in the plumbing. Bertlestein promised Detective Superintendent Derek Ankers, of Y Department, that he could finger the mole. It was this boast that prompted Ankers to negotiate a behind-the-scenes bail deal for Bertlestein. The wheeling and dealing culminated in a hearing in chambers, in Manchester, before Judge Prestt.

During that brief sitting in camera, the judge was handed a sealed envelope by Ankers. Inside was a special request for bail with a summary of the reasons.

Apparently, Bertlestein had satisfied Y Department beyond all doubt that he did possess bona fide information that could help to plug the damaging leak, once and for all. The name he gave Ankers was of an officer who was already a suspect. Within a matter of weeks, that officer retired from the force. No charge was ever brought against him, which made political sense, if not exactly promoting a one-law-for-all doctrine. There was not a mention of Stalker. When Sergeant Burgess took exhaustive statements from Bertlestein the following February about the IRA, the informant still, apparently, did not have any dirt to throw Stalker's way. However, as his trial approached, he became desperate. In vain, he pleaded with Chief Inspector Douglas Savage, of the Special Branch, to intervene on his behalf. When that failed, he implored Superintendent McGourlay to prime the court of his value to the police as a 'prized' informant.

Yet it was to be another 18 months before the despairing Bertlestein tossed Stalker's name into the pot. This was approximately during the same period that McGourlay had his gossipy round of golf with Wareing.

While accepting, in principle, that detectives need contacts in the criminal underworld in order to have any chance of keeping up with the game, let alone getting ahead of it, Anderton has always harboured grave misgivings about this area of crime-fighting. It comes back directly to his refusal to tolerate the grey shades of life. There is right and wrong. There are the good people and the bad; the law-abiding and the lawless; heaven and hell. Cross-pollination he sees not only as confusing, but also as a pollutant. Professional informants he despises more than the villains they entrap and abandon. He understands the criminal mind, but not the mentality of the traitor; hence his heightened hostility to the nark. There

182

is something insulting and degrading, he believes, in the soldiers of Christ having to rely on the troops of the devil. To Anderton, this is tantamount to a truce and working arrangement with the Christians' historic sparring partner: the more you play *with* the devil, the harder it becomes to play *against* him.

In every business, there is a squeeze on the middle man. Both manufacturer and retailer traditionally having always begrudged the merchant his percentage. Police overlords and criminals are equally dismissive of the professional informant, their middle man, who is essential for balance, but so often deplored by both sides, the manufacturers of crime and the retailers of the deterrent.

When Anderton received Topping's report on 17 July 1984, he did his homework and tested the strength of the intelligence. He had never heard of Bertlestein; it would have been remarkable if he had. He turned to his trusted lieutenants to sniff around for him. Their report substantiated Anderton's gut reaction. Without hesitation, and to Anderton's credit, the file was committed to the grave, the "No Action" cabinet. On such flimsy evidence, it would have been an insult to have drawn it to the attention of a man of Stalker's professional stature, especially at the most critical crossroad of his career. Every day people make outrageous charges to the police: 'The Metropolitan commissioner of police is in the pay of the KGB . . . the prime minister owns a brothel in Finchley . . . the Queen has donated her corgis for vivisection . . .' Anderton had heard it all before.

That September, Mark Klapish, the proprietor of Cut Price Fancy Goods, went on trial with his associate, Joe 'Swords' Monaghan, who was also a friend of Kevin Taylor. Klapish was originally accused of running a fraudulent firm and making a deal with the IRA. But when the case came to court, there was no mention of the IRA charges. He pleaded guilty to fraud and was sentenced to four years in prison. Amazingly, the court was cleared for

Bertlestein's appearance. After Bertlestein admitted the offence at the secret hearing, Superintendent McGourlay revealed to the judge that the defendant was a police 'grass' of considerable worth.

Superintendent Ankers then followed McGourlay into the witness box, expounding Bertlestein's claims of police profiteering. The outcome was that Bertlestein was sent to prison for two and a half years, a much more lenient sentence than he would have expected for such a conviction, particularly bearing in mind his criminal record.

Monaghan was tried separately at a later date. By that time, Bertlestein had recanted his previous statements and was never called to give evidence. Accordingly, Monaghan walked free from the court.

At a subsequent public bankruptcy hearing, Klapish categorically refuted the insinuation that he had done business with the IRA.

Early in 1985, Bertlestein had a surprise visit in Preston prison from officers of a new police squad, the drugs intelligence unit, which was under the command of Topping. They were eager to discuss with Bertlestein everything he could recall about police racketeering. In this connection, Bertlestein talked extensively about Stalker, bragging that 'this is the chapter and verse that'll see [Stalker] drummed out of the Force'. He was lying his heart out, from beginning to end.

Just a few weeks later, in March 1985, Bertlestein collapsed and died in jail of a heart-attack. Detectives from Topping's unit questioned the Home Office pathologist who performed the post mortem.

'Was the cause of death a straightforward heart-attack?' they wanted to know.

'Definitely.'

'Could it have been induced?'

'By mental stress, maybe; but not through physical pressure or chemical stimulant. Not in this case.'

'There's no possibility that he was murdered?'

'No possibility whatsoever.'

14

Countdown to Crucifixion

In April 1985, Stalker, who was completely oblivious to the calumny being spread about him on the mainland, was threatening to resign from the official inquiry in Northern Ireland because of 'this impossible situation'. He was getting nowhere. Men in high office in the RUC he saw as saboteurs. In return, the RUC hierarchy branded Stalker an IRA pussycat.

Stalker contended that he had been appointed to conduct an 'independent' inquiry, which meant he had to be free from interference and impediment. Conversely, Sir John Hermon argued robustly that 'independence was all very well', but it could not be allowed to over-ride national security.

Stalker let it be known that if he resigned, he would 'go public' on his reasons for doing so. He had no intention, he emphasised, of submitting an official report that was not complete. The threat to 'go public' certainly won him no friends among the Establishment. From that moment, his chances of ever becoming a chief constable had gone forever. Every policeman, especially one as senior and experienced as Stalker, should know that in situations like this, when you hold a gun to someone's head, the odds are that it will backfire.

There was a meeting in Belfast between Sir John Hermon and the Northern Ireland MI5 liaison officer, who wanted 'to avoid a breakdown' with Stalker. He was anxious, if at all possible, that Stalker should be 'kept sweet'. He did not relish the prospect of Stalker 'cutting loose' and, in a fit of pique, 'shooting from the hip'. The MI5 liaison officer intimated that he would seek advice from 'a higher source', making it explicit that he had no wish to impede Stalker's murder investigations. No MI5 agent had ever been implicated in any of the actual shootings, so there was nothing for the Security Service to cover up in that respect. For them, the principle at stake was the secrecy of their work. *What's the point of a Secret Service if its undertakings are made public?* All sides had come to the conclusion that it would need a non-aligned arbiter to resolve the dispute because of the intransigence of the parties.

In June that year, Stalker, Sir John Hermon and a formidable coterie of senior MI5 officers sat down together around a conference table in London to try, one final time, to hammer out a solution that would be acceptable to everybody. By the end of that meeting, Stalker began to sense that the tide was turning his way. MI5 had come round to the view that the hayshed tape-recording should be released to him. There was, however, to be a sting in the tail. The tape would be handed over only on the condition that Stalker solemnly swore not to pursue the question of who gave authority for the bugging. Stalker, like any other policeman, did not like to have any areas of possible investigation declared 'out of bounds'. Even if not totally happy with the proposition on the table, Stalker was prepared to go along with it; after all, he was hunting killers, not snoopers. The meeting ended amicably enough, with handshakes all round.

MI5 were now content for Stalker to have access to the tape. At last, Stalker began to feel that he was making progress. If there was a loser that day, it had to be Hermon, but it did not show.

Stalker returned to Belfast and promptly requested the tape on the terms agreed in London. Hermon informed him that the tape had been destroyed. Apologetically, Hermon said he had no idea how this had happened, but there was definitely a transcript in existence.

A transcript, of course, has nothing like the legal credibility of an original recording. For a start, it has no status in law; it merely helps one to refer to specific points without continually having to re-play a tape while searching for revelant dialogue.

Stalker asked for a copy of the transcript. Hermon stipulated that if Stalker's new request was to be seriously considered, he (Stalker) would have to sign an internal RUC declaration, swearing himself to secrecy. In other words, he could read the transcript, but could never make use of it: his hands were bound yet again by red tape. Hermon told Stalker that he expected the inquiry to be terminated without the inclusion of material from the tape.

Three days after the London meeting, Hermon went over the case with Sir Barry Shaw, the DPP, at one point saying that he was reluctant to let Stalker have any information about the tape and would do so only if ordered in the public interest 'from above'.

A memo arrived on Douglas Hurd's desk, updating the Home Secretary on the latest developments, particularly relating to the current demands and stands being made respectively by Hermon and Stalker. One can only surmise that at ministerial level a decision was taken that the release to Stalker of the MI5 tape transcript would not be in the best interests of the general public. Despite daily pressure from Stalker, it became clear that he was wasting his time. He could see no alternative but to produce an interim report without access to the contents of the tape. The most he could do now was to make a personal appeal, within the report, to the DPP for him to intervene on his behalf. There was another weakness in this line of attack, and Stalker knew it. Hermon considered himself the appointing officer of the inquiry and, therefore, he expected everything to be channelled through him. All other memos from Stalker to the DPP on the tape issue, sent via Hermon's office, had become bogged down in the system.

Through dogged door-to-door, foot-slogging detective work, Stalker and his team reckoned that a prima facie case of murder and/or conspiracy to pervert the course of justice could be levelled against at least 12 members of the RUC. Included in Stalker's dossier was evidence that a document purporting to link Michael Tighe with terrorism had been forged. The bogus report indicated that paid informants within the Ulster Catholic community had fingered Tighe as a 'fringe activist' with the IRA, whatever that was supposed to mean. There were two glaring inconsistencies, which made it essential for Stalker to interrogate the alleged informants, because it was apparent to the Manchester team that a statement had been tampered with and backdated. The RUC flatly refused to allow Stalker near the moles.

Stalker had been profoundly moved by the family of Michael Tighe and he spent many hours with them, not only in the process of synthesis, but also to evince that he really was tracking nothing but the truth, however embarrassing it might prove to his own profession. One of Stalker's detectives made it known that the entire Manchester troupe rated the Tighes 'lovely, decent people'.

The apprehension among the less partisan politicians in Northern Ireland and the Westminster MPs was that the RUC's independent and non-sectarian pretensions could be scuppered. No small matter was the British Government's industrious endeavours to make stick an historic accord with Dublin, which, it was feared, could be imperilled. The Hermon/Stalker pantomine certainly was no hit with those whose job it was to keep Government wheels turning. The Irish Prime Minister, Dr Garrett FitzGerald, publicly expressed his distress at seeing 'the RUC being inexorably distanced from the Belfast Catholics'. A coroner, who had refused to conduct the inquests on some of the victims suspected of having been cold-bloodedly murdered by the RUC, also gave meticulous testimonies to Stalker, which should have been nails in the coffin, but a few key figures were determined to avoid a pubic burial at all costs.

Stalker's interim report was finally delivered to Hermon in September 1985. Stalker was taking no chances; he had it bound like a book, with every page numbered in sequence. Custom was for such a document to be strung together by spiral binding, but Stalker wanted to reduce the chances of anyone doctoring it between it arriving at RUC headquarters and being forwarded to the DPP. Gold embossed lettering on the cover marked it as 'Secret'. Protocol dictated that the DPP's copy should go first to Hermon. Stalker and Thorburn delivered the report to the chief constable at the RUC's Knock headquarters. Hermon was not there to meet them, which slightly irked Stalker. Instead, it was Hermon's deputy, McAtamney, who took charge of the sensitive document. But Hermon – and he alone – would be responsible for seeing that Sir Barry Shaw received his copy.

Although the interim report was only a starter, it was still dynamite. Prosecutions were recommended. Officers to be charged or admonished were named. The RUC and its procedures were condemned. Structural reforms were urged. It was Stalker's belief that, during the expansion of the RUC in the Seventies, many officers had been promoted beyond their ability. Numerous officers of senior rank were underqualified, it was maintained, and this had led to juniors being entrusted with responsibilities beyond their capabilities, leading to gross errors of judgment. When miscalculations had backfired, the elder statesmen had closed ranks in order to protect themselves, as well as the juniors, who had been afforded too much autonomy. Lies had been told in the witness box during major trials in an attempt to keep the RUC's name-plate polished. The report was a scathing indictment of the law enforcement agencies in Northern Ireland.

Hermon was outraged. Stalker's broadsides were as much a censure of Hermon as an appraisal of the imperfections of the organizations. Any criticism of the structure was tantamount to a complaint against Hermon. Everyone close to the chief constable says that he took the stricture very personally, particularly because it came from a mere deputy chief constable, who had no experience of running his own constabulary. Contained in the bulky volume was the formal entreaty to the DPP for a copy of the hayshed tape transcript.

Although the report was framed, generally, in the unemotive, prosaic language of the civil servant, there was no camouflaging the acrid relationship that prevailed between Stalker and Hermon. There was bridled anger, frustration and hostility breathing from every page. Keeping a choke-chain on potentially counter-productive rhetoric cannot have been easy for Stalker, but he is both creative and disciplined with words; to become a journalist was his first ambition and now he is a professional writer, but Hermon did not appreciate Stalker's literary style.

Stalker and his team waited in Belfast, expecting a swift reaction, if only something non-committal and nebulous. After two weeks, when there was still no news from Hermon's office, Stalker pulled out of Ulster, taking his men and woman back to Manchester. Hermon continued to sit on Sir Barry's copy of the report. The weeks passed and marched into months. Stalker complained to Anderton, who pledged to do his utmost to determine what was happening. Stalker feared more chicanery in Ulster, not by Hermon but by those whose careers were on the line if the report was accepted and acted upon. His critics retaliated once more by saying that Stalker could see spooks in his soup; that he had become 'intoxicated by the juice of intrigue' and was 'not living in the real world'.

Anderton, of course, had not seen the report. It was none of his business and it would have been unethical and a breach of confidence for Stalker to have gone into detail with him. Nevertheless, from all the previous rumblings, Anderton was able to make an educated guess as to the drift.

The RUC sat on Stalker's half-term report for five months, during which time ideas designed to rubbish it were tossed about. It was not until February 1986 that the DPP's copy landed on Sir Barry's desk.

The countdown had already begun for the self-demanding perfectionist whose idealism was blighting his job prospects.

15

Watershed

Kevin Taylor, the flamboyant, extrovert social climber in the Manchester establishment and friend of Stalker, was no stranger to the RUC. Stalker may not have remembered, but he had been in the company of Taylor at a Manchester hotel while another police officer, Bill Mooney, was present. A crowd had gathered round Taylor on a staircase, watching him tossing a coin for £50 a flick – not, however, against Stalker or Mooney. This was typical of Taylor; he was a showman who made friends easily, like Stalker – who, by comparison, appeared studious and retiring.

Taylor had taken a liking to Chief Superintendent Mooney, mainly because of his swashbuckling crusade in Northern Ireland against terrorism. John Wayne was his favourite movie star. (In that respect, he also had something in common with Anderton.) Stalker and Mooney were Taylor's local heroes and he liked to surround himself with high octane people. After that evening, Taylor did his best to keep in touch with Mooney, who was based at the RUC's Belfast headquarters, but without much success.

Quite a substantial amount was known by the RUC about Stalker's private life, long before he had finished his interim report; a lot more than he would ever have guessed.

One of the men Stalker had taken with him to Ulster

was Detective Superintendent John Simons. On his return to Manchester, Simons had been appointed acting head of the fraud squad, which started to dig deeply into the enterprises of a number of businesses and their personnel.

Going back even further – to 1983, to be precise – there was a political contretemps that was destined to be a watershed in the Stalker Affair.

Taylor had been voted chairman in 1982 of the city Conservative Association, having demonstrated his flair for fund-raising. He employed a marketing manager by the name of Kim Berry, who worked from the Conservative Association's office in Didsbury, a respectable, net-curtain suburb of southern Manchester. With the job went a car, a Vauxhall Nova. Quite unexpectedly, her salary was stopped and Miss Berry consulted her solicitors, who advised her that she should retain the car as leverage. Shortly afterwards and late one afternoon, Miss Berry's mother happened to look out of the living-room window of the home in the industrial town of Bury, nine miles due north of Manchester's city centre. Two men appeared to be trying to break into the Vauxhall Nova and Mrs Berry alerted her daughter who, after seeing for herself what was going on, summoned the police. That done, the two women hurried into the street to challenge the men who were behaving suspiciously. One of them was a former detective sergeant with Manchester CID. He had been convicted and sent to prison for attempting to bribe a police officer and demanding money with menaces. Before resigning from the force, he had served under Stalker in the drugs squad. At the time of the car incident, the ex-policeman was working as a private detective.

When confronted by the two irate women, he told them that he and his partner had been hired to repossess the car.

Kim Berry demanded to know who had hired the private detectives. According to Miss Berry, the former police officer indicated that he had been commissioned by Taylor. She pleaded with him to 'hold fire' until she had recovered her 'things' from the car. Apparently, he raised no objection and stood back while Miss Berry used her key to unlock the vehicle. But as she leaned inside, she was seized from behind and propelled from the car 'like a rag doll'.

Miss Berry's head struck the doorway and, at one point, her legs were squashed against the steering wheel. Finally, she was thrown to the ground. Kim's father was in the house and he witnessed the scuffle. When he saw his daughter knocked down, he ran into the street and, aided by his wife, tackled the private eyes. Both Mr and Mrs Berry were punched and left dazed, cut and bruised.

Before the PIs had a chance to drive away, the police arrived. The ex-Manchester CID man was escorted to a police van, invited inside and questioned. During the next hour, the two parties tendered their conflicting versions.

'At the outset, the police were very sympathetic,' said Miss Berry. 'They were all very kind and understanding, and seemed genuinely appalled by what had happened. They could see our injuries. The three of us needed medical treatment. A change came over the police, though, after they'd talked with one of the PIs. They seemed to harden towards us.'

Anderton had his own troubles to occupy his mind. His relationship with the Greater Manchester Police Authority was nose-diving to an all-time low. There had never been any love between them and even mutual respect had always been minimal. Now the only common bond was enmity. Anderton and Gabrielle Cox, a former chairman of the Authority, had been in opposite corners since the first day they met, which was at a comprehensive school in Moss Side. Anderton was at the school, where Mrs Cox taught, to talk to pupils about Police Week. Later, he had coffee with staff and that is when Mrs Cox 'tackled' him on the prickly subject of alleged police brutality in Moss

Side – Anderton's own old stamping ground – where Mrs Cox not only taught but lived. Neither of them could possibly have known that Mrs Cox was destined to become chairman of the Police Authority and that their clashes would be likened to heavyweight pugilism, so punishing was the open conflict.

'I already had a view about him from his public announcements,' said Mrs Cox, recalling that first meeting. 'He had an inspector with him and I mentioned that I'd like a word with the chief constable. It was the inspector who then introduced us. I kept pressing the point of police brutality in Moss Side and Anderton followed the usual line of, "Well, of course, we do have our rotten apples, just like anybody else, but only a few, and we do our best to deal with it and weed them out." He told me that he was having talks with black leaders in the community, but I didn't find him very convincing and I kept endeavouring to elicit some further commitment from him. His looks to his inspector screamed, "Save me!" He was finally rescued by the headmaster, who said something light to me like, "I think you've had him to yourself long enough!"'

Mrs Cox was to serve for two years as vice-chairman of the Police Authority, followed by three years as chairman, between 1983 and 1986. 'When a complaint was made about an officer from within the force, then I think Anderton was supportive of any internal investigation. But if the complaint came from outside, from the public, or from the Police Authority, then he would be very defensive and withdrawn; that was my experience. His men could never do any wrong in his eyes if they came in for external criticism. That was fine if you were a policeman; not so fine if you were an ordinary member of the public with a grievance.

'My chairmanship was a very hard-wearing three years. We did not have a relationship at all. We didn't see eye to eye on anything. We met only when we had to, and then it was always a strain. Before anything was discussed, the atmosphere would be thick with resistance. Battle lines were drawn up from Day One. He saw my committee as the enemy, trying to undermine all his plans; subversives contriving among ourselves in an underground plot to overthrow him and everything he stood for. He was Mr Good and I was Mrs Evil, the high priestess of the anti-Anderton movement.

'It developed into a fight for power; I would never try to hide that fact. Neither side would voluntarily sacrifice one inch, hence the pitched battles. Anderton had a strong view that he should be totally independent on every issue, major to minor, whereas we believed that policing could work only by the consent of the electorate, with the Police Authority representing the people. We fought over everything, from plastic bullets to the police band.

'After a disturbance in London, Anderton decided that his force should be equipped with plastic bullets. We said no, but he went ahead and bought them. We argued that although he had bought the bullets, they must be the property of the Authority and we proposed returning them to the manufacturer. We were at each other's throats again. Anderton promptly appealed to the Home Secretary, who ruled that the chief constable could have plastic bullets on loan. Anderton was laughing. He'd won again. We had battles over every conceivable issue. He never made any concession to the view of public representatives. Some Police Authority chairmen are able to work closely with their chief constable, but we didn't get along at all.

'My meetings with Anderton tended to be shouting matches. The more I stood up to him, the more he shouted. He was always shouting at me because, by nature, he's a bully, but I gave as good as I got, without losing my temper. He had an extra problem with me, I believe, because I was a woman. He seemed incapable of treating me as the chairman of his Authority who just happened to be a woman. In his world, no doubt, women are expected to do as they're told and know their place, without dissent. Certainly he never afforded me the courtesy of treating me as an equal. I'm sure he must have been very pleased to see the back of me. It was never the way it should have been. It was not good for the police or the people.'

Mrs Cox has a theory about Anderton's high profile; she believes it is a contrived mechanism for pleading his case through the public. He makes a sensational statement, knowing the media will be unable to resist it, and that becomes the peg on which he hangs a very different argument, usually involving a dispute with some authority, such as the police committee. Because he has always been surrounded in public life by so many enemies, he sees self-generated publicity as the art of self-defence. Against that, it has to be said that he was humming a similar tune long before he had – or needed – a public stage.

There was one member of the Police Authority – not Mrs Cox – who used to secretly tape-record every private and confidential meeting of the committee and would sell the transcripts to a freelance journalist. The main motive was to embarrass Anderton rather than the financial reward. This same member had often discussed with his friends the possibility of tricking Anderton into attending a function that suddenly turned into a 'live' strip show, with a photographer poised in the wings, but Anderton is not that easily duped.

As spiritually Anderton moved towards the Roman Catholic faith, so a part of his daily prayers became the Solemn Novena, something he included each night and morning, describing the words as 'so very beautiful'.

In 1986, he was elected president of the Association of Police Officers, a post that is held for a year and is very time-consuming, which meant that he saw even less of his wife than before. They could go days meeting only to the sound of the alarm-clock and as they kissed goodbye on the doorstep. When he is at home, he has little in common with his public image; he maunders around in jeans, quietly attending to odd jobs, listening to his favourite records, watching Western movies on television – or sport, especially boxing, preferably amateur, and Rugby League – and exchanging gardening tips with his neighbours. 'I have the best neighbours in the world. They're behind me all the way.'

The people Anderton seems most comfortable with are those who have become successful after starting life impoverished. Freddy Pye is a typical example; his father was a bus driver. 'I can remember only too well my old man raiding the piggy bank so that we'd have something – not much – to eat for the rest of the week.' Pye is now the deputy chairman of Manchester City Football Club, a partner in two businesses with one of England's most legendary footballers, Bobby Charlton – a soccer school and a travel company – a Lloyds underwriter, a former chairman of Stockport County Football Club and chairman of one of the north-west's largest metal-producing factories. Pye began his working life as a scap-metal merchant and during the last 25 years has met many policemen socially, usually through his sporting interests. He became a friend of both Anderton and Stalker.

When Pye owned Wigan Athletic Football Club, he invited Anderton to the boardroom to be presented by the club president with a polished miner's lamp, a symbol of Wigan and all that the town had represented for so long. It was a mark of recognition for one of the town's most distinguished 'Old Boys'. 'Anderton and the president stood in tears as they discovered their fathers had worked in the same pitface gang,' said Pye. 'They stood at the window crying as they looked out towards the church where Anderton married Joan, to the streets he walked as a boy and had grown up in. He can be a dewy-eyed sentimentalist, but basically Anderton's very much a man's man.

'If you really want to know what Anderton's like as a private person, you have to try to forget his public image. He's had a bad press, there's no denying that, and as a result he's greatly misunderstood. People tend to think he's a one hundred per cent tub-thumping churchman, but he's nothing like that. He's not forever quoting the Bible and lecturing from the pulpit. He goes to church, yes, but religion's not an obsession with him. It's not something he goes on about during dinner or over a drink.

'In the nicest possible way, Anderton's a real commoner: just like you or me; one of us. But he doesn't tolerate fools gladly: in that sense, he can be very impatient. It's also true that he's a very private individual and has to really know you before he'll open up. When finally he feels he does know you well enough to relax, then he's one of the lads. You'd be surprised!

'There's no escaping the fact that Anderton can be a very hard man: he has to be at times. He soon put down the riots. No messing! He does a good job, most people think. All the policemen I've ever met have respected Anderton, including Stalker. He's a smashing bloke, an interesting companion and never, never dull. The people he tends to fall out with are the leftwingers. He had a superb relationship with Archie Thornhill when he was chairman of the Police Authority.' Thornhill built up a bookmaking chain of shops in the Manchester area and sold out to Ladbrokes, turning himself into a multi-millionaire. He now lives in Bolton.

Anderton's other millionaire friend, Luis Anton, was first employed in Britain as a wine waiter. 'He worked his cobblers off,' said Pye. 'He made his money with sandwich bars, then got into importing and ended up Portuguese consul in Manchester. Anderton met him through the Pope's visit. People who think Anderton's a stuffed-shirt just don't know the fella. You couldn't meet anyone more down-to-earth than me and we have always hit it off. Certainly he's the best policeman we've ever had. When he goes, who will replace him? It'll be impossible.

'I've also known Stalker for twenty years – another good policeman, who was stitched up good and properly . . . a fall guy if ever I saw one. He fell foul of the wrong people in Ireland – not the hardest thing to do in the world – and they made sure he toppled. I know he feels Anderton should have pulled him to one side to warn him about the muck that was in the air, but in the end it's all a matter of personal style. I suppose both men are right in their own minds. It's tragic!

'Certain people have insinuated that Anderton behaved improperly by accepting a gift from me. What they're talking about is the miner's lamp, which was a presentation from Wigan Athletic Football Club. I simply happened to be chairman of the club at the time. Some folk will go to any lengths to try to discredit their enemies, but they're on to a loser over me and Anderton.'

However, back to the Kim Berry saga: statements were taken and it was explained to the Berrys that a report would be 'filed' and they would be 'kept informed'. The outcome was that the official police file on the incident was stamped 'No Further Action'.

When the Berry family learned that the PIs were not to be prosecuted, they were angry. They consulted their own solicitor with a view to instigating a private prosecution. Their legal representative promised to make inquiries. In the end, the prospect of taking on Kevin Taylor and the Conservative Association proved too daunting a proposition for the Berrys, though the reasoning remains a mystery. Any legal action would have concerned the events that occurred outside the Berry's home, of which neither Mr Taylor nor the Conservative Association were a material element. Whatever the merits or misconceptions of their analysis, the Berry family decided to 'forget about it' and to 'keep [their] heads down'.

Instead of pursuing the matter through the courts, Kim Berry went to see Ann Carroll, who was a member of the Conservative Party's national executive. Miss Berry, through her former job, obviously knew her way around the Conservative Party power corridors. She would have known that Mrs Carroll had been gunning for Taylor ever since he first came on to the political map. Mrs Carroll was busily compiling a dossier to present to the party chairman, who at that time was John Selwyn Gummer.

Taylor owned a motor company called Vanland Limited and 15 years earlier, through Vanland, he had sold a number of secondhand Post Office vans. Mrs Carroll claimed to have 'very interesting' information about the mileage recordings at the time of the sale of those vehicles. She had campaigned unsuccessfully against him in 1982 when he first stood for the chairmanship. Six months later, she tabled an emergency resolution of 'no confidence' in the chairman. This attempt to unseat Taylor also failed. After Mrs Carroll's dossier had been delivered to the Conservative Party chairman, Mr Gummer could see no immediate way of intervening. However, early in 1985, the association of which Taylor was chairman was dissolved. During the August of that year, Taylor's sister-in-law, Mrs Margaret Waterhouse, was interviewed by detectives. After they had gone, she telephoned Taylor to advise him, 'They wanted to know everything about you . . . about your past . . . your friends . . . where your money's come from . . .' One of the subjects they had introduced into the catechism was Vanland.

Naturally enough, Taylor was alarmed and he took appropriate measures to try to track down the detectives, hoping to be able to put a few pertinent questions to them. Then, on 29 November, a detective telephoned

Taylor's bank to pump the manager about Propwise, a property company owned by Taylor. The policeman introduced himself to the bank as 'Detective Inspector Stephenson of the fraud squad'.

Taylor was once again tipped off about the police activity and he wasted no time instructing his solicitor, Guy Robson. In accordance with instructions from his client, Robson wrote to the fraud squad, complaining that Taylor's reputation as an honest and respectable businessman was being corroded by unethical scandal-mongering by the police. Several letters were exchanged, until finally a meeting was arranged in Robson's office in Portland Street, Manchester, for 6 January 1986. The police representative who kept that appointment was Detective Superintendent Simons, who had been with Stalker in Northern Ireland. Robson had made sure that Taylor was available, but the detective flatly refused to have any contact with the man he was putting under the microscope. Robson inquired what wrongdoing Taylor was suspected of, but Simons would not answer. It is alleged that Simons retorted, 'I'm the head of the fraud squad. I can make what inquiries I wish.'

Exactly one week later, on 13 January, Robson protested by letter to Anderton. This time, he wanted a meeting with the chief constable. Wisely, Anderton did not allow himself to be drawn into dialogue with the representative of a suspect, which would not only have been unethical, but also an act of treason in the eyes of his lieutenants.

Anderton has been criticised in some quarters for not apprising Stalker of the potential pitfalls of continuing a friendship with a man under investigation. The truth is that Anderton behaved not only properly, but also with impeccable professionalism. Should Anderton have forewarned the friends of every other person under scrutiny by the Greater Manchester police? Of course not. And if Anderton had jeopardised any case through a stray word or a gentle nudge, there would have been a police and public outcry. If it was wrong to warn others, it would have been even more remiss of him to have stepped in on Stalker's behalf.

Most people favour their friends. Anderton sways the other way and practises positive discrimination against them, as an antidote to privilege and partiality. He tramps a lonely road, but he keeps a straight course.

'When you are chief constable, you have to be seen to serve all the people all the time,' he explained. 'The life is wearing and tiring. The understanding of morality has run like a thread throughout my life. I am never economic with the truth.'

It was much to do with Stalker's recommendations that Simons was appointed head of the Operational Support Group, which co-ordinated most of the specialist squads, including Drugs, Fraud, Special Branch, Serious Crimes and Surveillance. Not only was this promotion for Simons, but it revealed that Stalker's assessments and opinions were still strong currency in Anderton country and, so far, none of the flak had done any damage. Simons' immediate superior was to be Chief Superintendent Peter Topping, his own brother-in-law.

Since the Kim Berry episode, more and more pressure to re-open the case had been brought on the police by 'troubled' Conservatives, even though their association had been disbanded and Taylor no longer held office within the party. In his statement to the police, Taylor agreed that he had hired two private detectives to reclaim the Vauxhall Nova, but maintained that the fracas started when Kim and her mother 'began bombarding' the PIs 'with stones'. This was denied strenuously by the Berrys and Kim made at least six statements to the police over a long period, but still the outcome was a decision not to prosecute; this is not unusual when there is direct conflict of evidence and no independent source of verification.

The file on the alleged assault of the Berrys remained

at Bury police station. Meanwhile, the most persistent rumour in Conservative circles in the north-west was that Taylor had not béen prosecuted because of his long-standing alliance with Stalker. The narrative went that one of the PIs had dropped Stalker's name almost immediately he was taken to the police van for questioning outside the Berrys' house. Some disgruntled Tory officials also believed the fact that the PI was an ex-policeman and former colleague of Stalker had influenced the 'no action' decision. The policemen who interviewed the PI were adamant that at no stage during their inquiries was Stalker mentioned, to which not only Mandy Rice-Davis might respond, 'They would say that, wouldn't they?' But I believe them. If you are a friend of the chief constable or his deputy, the last thing you do is mention the fact to a bobby on the beat. Young constables have a nasty, but healthy, habit of turning bloody-minded if they suspect someone of trying to pull rank on them. Many a chief constable, much to the detriment of his blood-pressure and ego, has found a ticket on the windscreen of his stately car, which had been parked for a few chancy minutes on double yellow lines. Name-dropping just does not work, to which anyone can testify who has ever tried to keep his or her name out of a newspaper by saying to a reporter, 'I think you ought to be made aware that I'm a friend of your editor.' The reporter merely gives the editor a blow-by-blow account of what was said. In order to retain his credibility, the editor has to respond, 'At all costs, we publish his name, and be damned!'

It is possible that Taylor simply telephoned Stalker at home, or took him for a drink, and begged a favour, just for old times' sake, but this is yet another specious scenario. The Stalker/Taylor friendship had been an open secret for 17 years. They had been seen together and photographed at public functions, including Conservative balls and dinners, and civic banquets. Stalker had even entertained Taylor in the officers' mess at Manchester police headquarters; on one of those occasions, Anderton was among the company. Therefore, the one person in the world who could not, under any circumstances, obstruct proceedings against Taylor was John Stalker. In any event, the decision not to proceed against the two private detectives was taken at a much lower level, long before it could ever have been an issue for Stalker's judgment. Stalker denies any act of impropriety in this matter and there is no basis on which to doubt his word. If Stalker had established himself as a bulwark against the tide of natural justice in order to screen Taylor and the PIs, there would today be several malcontent policemen hungry to rat on him, now that he is no longer on the Force, but they do not exist.

Nevertheless, the Kim Berry saga probably contributed more to Stalker's plight than any other single incident.

16

Death Wish Comes True

While waiting for an official reaction to his interim report, Stalker was busily working on his final blockbuster. What he did not know was that on 4 March 1986, a few days after Sir Barry Shaw finally received his copy of the interim report, the DPP gave instructions to Sir John Hermon to make available to Stalker everything on record about the hayshed killing tape. Stalker was to be allowed to interview anyone he wished in connection with the shooting of Michael Tighe and Martin McCauley. He was also to be allowed to pursue 'to his complete satisfaction' anything that might substantiate the theory that evidence had been deliberately destroyed.

It was to be several weeks before Stalker learned of Sir Barry's directive to Hermon. In the meantime, Stalker was in constant communication with Sir Philip Myers, who was eager for advance warning of anything explosive that might be detonated by the final report. Stalker disclosed that he was nearing the point where there was nothing remaining to be added to the definitive draft except the trimmings. On hearing that, Sir Philip asked if he may be given an advance copy and Stalker readily obliged. Stalker was advancing recommendations for radical changes in the RUC's structure, especially regarding the accountability of officers.

When Stalker finally heard the news that he had won his battle with the RUC, he took his wife out for a celebration dinner. The following day, he called together his troops and, in an assembly that resembled a War Cabinet meeting, started to prepare for the campaign ahead. They planned to interrogate top personnel in MI5 and the Special Branch, plus a large number of RUC officers, of all ranks, including Michael McAtamney, the deputy chief constable, and even Hermon himself. Sir John would be pressed on the thorny subject of the missing tape and who had given him the information about its destruction. This was the ultimate breakthrough for which Stalker had been poised.

He had his bags packed during the first week of April in readiness to leave home for Ulster at a minute's notice, but the 'all clear' was never sounded. Three times during that month, he called Myers to try to finalise a date for departure. On each occasion, Myers balked him. Finally, as his patience was drained, Stalker made it known to his overlords that it was his intention to fly to Belfast on 3 June, with or without permission.

Anderton was in a dilemma. All his instincts assured him that he could trust his deputy, but he was in a difficult position. Stalker's name kept rising to the surface in a number of undercover workloads. Whitehall was worried, too. There is always a danger in ignoring small bush fires. The wind can change so quickly and turn against you, and suddenly you are having to cope with a raging inferno. At stake was the entire Stalker enquiry. If one muck missile against Stalker stuck, then everything he had achieved in Ulster would be discredited. Anderton agonised for days, weeks. He prayed for guidance while on duty, at home, in the back of his car, during weekend retreats in the hills and, of course, in church on bended knee. He wanted to be fair to Stalker, to the people of Northern Ireland and his profession. There were conflicting interests. He came to the conclusion that he had to allow the natural course of events to unfold.

On Friday 9 May, with Stalker still grounded in Manchester, police raided Wood Mill, the home of Kevin Taylor. A search-warrant had been obtained at 8.15 that morning and was produced on the doorstep of Taylor's luxury home, a converted mill near Bury, where lavish parties were almost part of the fixtures. Guests would often be given a bottle of champagne, not just a glass, as they were received by their high-roller host. Life had not always been that ritzy for Taylor. Before he made his fortune from selling secondhand vehicles, he lived with his wife, Beryl, in a modest semi-detached house in south Manchester.

Taylor and Stalker had first met at a parent/teacher association meeting; their two daughters were pupils at the same convent school. For most of his life, Taylor had been a gambler, loving poker, but prepared to wager £50 or more on the toss of a coin or the chance of snow falling on Christmas Day. He never made any secret of the fact that many of his poker chums had brushed with the law from time to time. Equally, Stalker has been consistent in emphatically denying that he had prior knowledge of Taylor's shady playmates. It was at a boxing dinner at the Piccadilly Hotel in Manchester that Stalker had witnessed Taylor risking £50 on the spin of a coin on a flight of stairs.

Like most gamblers, Taylor felt naked unless a wad of money bulged in his suit. He delighted in taking a bulky roll from his trouser pockets and conspicuously peeling off anything from £300 to £1000 for political or charity funds. When he was not wheeling and dealing, his life centred around casinos, Catholic sporting events and political fund-raising. Most lunchtimes, he could be found at the Film Exchange restaurant, where he had an open-ended charge account.

Taylor applied his gambling impulses to business. He speculated in property and hit a winning streak. Soon he owned the yacht *Diogenes* and even a health and allergy

208

clinic, which he administered from an office in St John's Street, only a few steps from Manchester's Conservative Party headquarters. His property companies included Mistform, Range Lark, MBE and Propwise. His entrepreneurial flair had been responsible for a shopping precinct at Strangeways. One of his companies, Range Lark, had bought a warehouse in Trafford Wharf and the disused Methodist Albert Hall, a listed building, in Peter Street. His idea was to turn the latter into an upmarket 173 – bedroomed hotel. *Diogenes* was usually moored in Marbella, Spain, but the crew would sometimes be ordered to sail to Florida, where Taylor and his family would board, after flying to Miami.

At one Conservative ball, Taylor sat next to Government minister Linda Chalker at the top table, along with Stalker. In November 1985, the guest of honour at the Manchester Conservative Association ball was David Trippier, another Thatcher Government junior minister (Trade and Industry) at the time. On one side of Taylor was Trippier. On the other side was Stalker. There is no disputing that Taylor had a direct line to the highest echelons of power and he liked rubbing shoulders with the rich, famous and influential. If there is such a creature as the orthodox Conservative Party voluntary worker, then Taylor was most definitely atypical – the reason why he made so many bitter enemies in local politics. It was not the fact that he was self-made that turned him into a hate figure, but more his spiv image and ostentatious lifestyle.

During the police raid on 9 May, officers confiscated boxes of documents and photographs. Taylor, who had just stepped from his jacuzzi, shouted at the officers to the effect that 'heads are going to roll for this!' The six detectives had been let in by Beryl Taylor, and it seemed to her and her husband that the chief purpose of the police action was to gather any evidence that might determine the depth of friendship between Stalker and

Taylor. Among the material taken from the house were photographs showing the two men together in 1981 at an extravagant birthday party for Taylor. Detectives went to work trying to identify known criminals in those photographs. There was none. Information reached them that, in 1981, Stalker had also flown to Miami for a holiday on Taylor's yacht. This was verified, but Stalker had paid his own way. At no stage during the entire Stalker Affair was Taylor charged with any offence and his record remained unblemished. He accused the police of 'harassment' and alleged that their 'muck-raking' had pushed him to the brink of ruin.

While the *Diogenes* was moored in Miami, Taylor was offered a million dollars to allow his yacht to be used for drug-smuggling. He was 'appalled' by the proposition and brought his yacht to Britain.

The detectives who seemed to be grubbing around for dirt on Stalker quickly latched on to Frank Minta, another friend of Taylor's among the Conservative activists. During lengthy talks with Minta, they learned about an occasion 18 months previously when Taylor had bought Stalker lunch at the Film Exchange restaurant. Among that lunch party were Taylor's accountant and Minta. Stalker was not even accepting the hospitality while on duty, because it was his day off. From this inquisition the police also established that Taylor might have bought Stalker a drink at a £50-a-head Conservative ball the previous November.

Stalker did get a whiff of the police interest in Taylor back in November 1985, when he picked up from the internal jungle drums that questions were being asked about his old friend. Naturally, he made a few discreet inquiries and was told, 'off the record', that it was 'a trivial matter' and 'of little consequence'; something 'to do with one of Taylor's tenants'. It seems probable that this was a reference to the rumpus outside Kim Berry's house. Stalker saw no reason to guillotine his friendship with Taylor.

Among the wide-ranging accusations by police grass David Bertlestein from Preston prison early in 1985 was that Stalker regularly had free meals at the Kwok Man Chinese restaurant. This information, said Bertlestein, had come from the fraud squad's Detective Sergeant Burgess. The proprietor of the Kwok Man was interviewed and was able to verify that Stalker was a regular customer, but that he always paid for his own meals. Burgess had retired from the Force by the time the investigation began into Stalker, and when he was quizzed on the subject of alleged free meals, he said that he had seen the deputy chief constable at the Kwok Man only once.

At this point, a desperate edge began to take shape in the 'Get Stalker' camp. Detectives toured the city's gay bars, producing photographs of Stalker and asking, 'Have you seen him in here with a man?' When one homosexual replied, 'No, I've never seen him here with a man,' a detective pounced, 'You mean you've seen him here with a woman, right?' 'That's not what I mean,' the young man tried to untangle himself. 'I've never seen him before in my life, here or any place. That's what I mean.'

Undaunted, the same detectives then called on a number of the city's known prostitutes, including those who plied their trade from massage parlours, or as nightclub hostesses and escorts. It seems that they were willing the girls to say, 'Yes, I've slept with that man. He paid me to . . .' But there were no takers. One mother, with three convictions for soliciting, was warned that social workers were planning to take her daughter into care. 'They said they could help me to keep my little girl,' she told me. 'But if they helped me, I'd have to help them. Although it wasn't exactly spelt out, there could be no mistaking the drift. They wanted me to finger Stalker. I didn't know who he was at the time. I do now, of course;

everybody does. I told them to get stuffed. I don't do deals with the Bill. I have my pride, if little else. And I still have my daughter. They were bullshitting, as usual.'

There was no conspiracy including Anderton and other high-ranking officers in Manchester to besmirch Stalker's name. Anderton was after his usual elusive goal, the truth, which can be hard to score when so many fouls are being committed around you. By any standard, it was an extraordinary operation. Certainly Anderton was let down by a number of detectives in the field who were perhaps guilty of over-zealousness.

Unknown to Stalker, he was being followed everywhere he went by plainclothes officers from his own force, young ones whom he had never met. On the evening of Tuesday 27 May, they even occupied a nearby table at the Moss Nook restaurant, where Stalker was dining with Anderton, Colin Cameron, the executive producer of BBC 2's 'Brass Tack', a Manchester-produced programme, and television reporter Peter Taylor. This dinner had been arranged two months previously. Anderton saw no reason for it to be cancelled, which was indicative of his frame of mind and attitude towards his deputy. In his book *Stalker (The Search for The Truth)* Taylor recalled that the chief constable and Stalker were 'both relaxed' and 'Anderton also treated us to an informed dissertation on his favourite wines'. However, the real purpose of the dinner date was for the media men to learn something of the evolving strategy of fighting crime in the inner city jungles. A subsidiary item on the agenda was an informal examination of ways in which to improve relations between the police and the press. Taylor's book suggested that Anderton's relationship with the media left something to be desired. This was probably true and was something Anderton intended working on. Having said that, it is worth noting at this point that few people in history have been so adept at manipulating the media as Anderton, and his tongue is partly in cheek whenever he complains of 'a bad press'. Stalker's Northern Ireland inquiry did not feature in the discussions at the Moss Nook restaurant, but as they walked into the street, Anderton handed Stalker a file which he would need for a meeting at the Home Office the following Friday. Anderton had asked Stalker to deputise for him at that Home Office meeting, a further insight into the chief constable's mood towards his deputy. Ever since Stalker was suspended, the dinner at the Moss Nook has become known as 'The Last Supper', while the file Anderton gave his deputy has been dubbed the 'poisoned chalice'.

Stalker's fate had been determined a few days earlier, following a memo to Anderton from Detective Chief Superintendent Topping. This memo focused on three sensitive issues that could damage Stalker, and was the outcome of a meeting on Thursday 15 May between Topping and Chief Superintendent Arthur Roberts. It said that Taylor was putting stories about that he had paid for Stalker's holiday in Florida and that the deputy chief constable was a regular guest at his exuberant parties; that Taylor intended to incriminate Stalker if the police investigation against him wasn't dropped forthwith; and that Taylor seemed obsessed about his friendship with Stalker and never missed an opportunity to mention the fact whenever he felt threatened. Later, Roberts was to complain that the memo was not an accurate reflection of his conversation with Topping.

Nevertheless, Anderton decided the time had come to end all the speculation. The rumours were going to be substantiated or scuppered – for his sake, for the sake of the Greater Manchester police force and, most importantly of all, for the sake of John Stalker.

There has been much conjecture as to whether Anderton led or followed. True to his style and nature, he led.

The beginning of the spring weekend was only an hour or so away when Anderton telephoned Sir Philip Myers at his headquarters in Colwyn Bay, north Wales. Anderton succinctly briefed Sir Philip, who knew from the chief constable's tone that drastic action was expected, but he alone could not take the responsibility of calling for the suspension of a deputy chief constable, especially the man who was leading one of the most far-reaching police inquiries of modern times, an inquiry that was into its final stage. This was something that would have to be passed to Sir Lawrence Byford, Her Majesty's Chief Inspector of Constabulary at the Home Office. Myers told Anderton as much.

Byford had already left London for his country home in Lincolnshire, where he was to spend the weekend: he is a former chief constable of that county. Myers waited until the Saturday before ringing Byford in Lincolnshire, when they talked at length.

Byford was angry. He was anxious that the Ulster inquiry should not have to be scrapped and re-opened from scratch. Could it be salvaged? he wanted to know. Possibly, they concluded, if they were brisk and pre-emptive. Stalker would have to be removed hastily and distanced from the Ulster package. Byford then spoke with Anderton at home. He wanted to know if Anderton was now prepared to level a formal complaint against Stalker?

Yes, he was, Anderton answered.

Now that the point of no return had been reached, Anderton was ready to be ruthless, for the sake of the Northern Ireland inquiry and to try to prevent fact being overtaken by fiction.

By the Sunday of that weekend, 18 May, the minds of the three men were concentrating on who could be appointed investigating officer, although the final decision would have to be taken by the Greater Manchester Police Authority. The one name that met with unanimous approval was that of Colin Sampson, the chief constable of West Yorkshire.

214

Late that Sunday evening, Myers, as agreed by the others, made a call to Sir John Hermon in Belfast to advise him of a hiccup concerning Stalker. Hermon wanted to know more. Sir Lawrence remained guarded. Nothing was yet offical. The decision to suspend Stalker and the appointment of the investigating officer would have to be made by the Greater Manchester Police Authority.

On the Monday, Byford, Myers and Anderton were due at the Police Federation conference in Scarborough. The three of them arranged to meet in Scarborough for lunch on the Monday at the Royal Hotel. Sampson was also invited, although at that stage he had no idea why he had been included in such an august lunch gathering. His usual chauffeur drove him from Wakefield to the Royal Hotel, arriving just before 12.30 pm, the time they were scheduled to meet in the bar for a pre-lunch drink.

They all shook hands warmly. It was a convivial get-together, reminiscent of a regimental re-union of old comrades; only the medals were missing. A table had been reserved and when they took their seats, the dining room was not busy, though it was soon to be filled with delegates from the police conference.

Sir Lawrence Byford had no doubt assumed, quite rightly, that it would be inappropriate to discuss delicate political police business over lunch in a dining room full of people trained in long-range eavesdropping. Accordingly, before lunch, he had taken aside the hotel manager to negotiate for a small room to be put at their disposal during the afternoon.

During lunch, a few veiled hints amounted to nothing more than a meagre starter and gave Sampson no real clue as to the main course. Sampson was even ignorant of Stalker's Northern Ireland inquiry.

Before leaving home that morning, Anderton had made it clear that he did not expect his wife to socialise with Stella Stalker, until further notice. Although Anderton and Stalker had never been real friends, their wives had become quite close, going shopping together and enjoying each other's company. That was over, at least for the time being.

As soon as the 'gang of four' adjourned to their committee room at the Royal Hotel, it was down to the business of burying a brother. Anderton formally made the charge that: Between 1 January 1971 and 31 December 1985, John Stalker, an officer in the Greater Manchester Police, associated with Kevin Taylor and known criminals in a manner likely to bring discredit upon the Greater Manchester police.

Sampson was stunned. He did not know Stalker personally, but he knew of his reputation. Sir Lawrence asked Sampson if he was prepared to be named investigating officer into the affairs of John Stalker. It was an offer that no one in Sampson's position could afford to refuse, however distasteful he found the prospect, dependent, of course, on his acceptability to the sanctioning body.

It was a long, debilitating day. Anderton was convinced that he was taking the honourable course of action, but not without misgivings. 'Of course I take my work home with me; I'm saturated in it. The job doesn't get hung up in the wardrobe with the uniform; never has done. It's in my skin, in my hair, seeping from every pore, a part of every tear. Joan can't really share the burden, although she tries. It goes to bed with me, shapes my dreams, fuels the nightmares. I'm on duty 24 hours a day, literally. Sleep is no escape because my mind works through the night. Solutions are often worked out in my absence, so to speak, while I'm asleep, and they're waiting for me on the tip of my tongue when I wake up. Some of my most inventive answers to problems have come to me in dreams. I trust my subconscious: it's a constant source of ingenuity.'

By the end of the meeting in the Royal Hotel, Sampson's mandate had been expanded to include the Northern

Ireland inquiry. Although there was no question of Stalker continuing in Ulster, there had been an assumption that the investigating officer could not be expected to undertake both jobs. However, as the discussion developed, the more feasible it became, and Sampson expressed his willingness to replace Stalker in Belfast while also investigating him.

On that same Monday, while Anderton, Myers, Byford and Sampson were discussing Stalker's future, Stalker made a telephone call to Hermon, pushing for an appointment, refusing to be delayed any longer. Hermon checked his diary. Like all chief constables, he was a very busy man. But Stalker was not going to hang up until he had a date confirmed. Stalker's name went into Hermon's business diary for Monday 2 June. Stalker felt happier.

That evening, Myers placed a call to Hermon from the hotel in Scarborough, but the RUC chief constable could not be reached: he had already left police headquarters and was not going home. The message Myers dictated for Hermon made it clear that Stalker would not be keeping his 2 June appointment. He did not elaborate.

The removal of Stalker from the Northern Ireland inquiry could not be achieved in London, Manchester or Scarborough, but only in Belfast, where the commission originated. Much of the meeting in Scarborough focused on tactics. The upshot was that Myers should fly to Ulster to confer with the DPP, Sir Barry Shaw. No obstacles were anticipated at the Northern Ireland end, where there would be much rejoicing.

Anderton was saddled with the dirty jobs. He was expected to liaise with Roger Rees, the clerk to the Greater Manchester Police Authority, and to talk in private with the Authority's chairman, Norman Briggs. The suspension of Stalker could not be assumed a formality. The political factor was crucial. The Manchester Police Authority was dominated by members of the Labour Party. Few of them had any love for Anderton.

217

To them, he was a reactionary and represented the rightwing, repressive philosophy of law enforcement.

Since the abolition of Metropolitan boroughs and local government reorganization, numerous members of the Police Authority had suffered bruising, head-on collisions with their strong-willed chief constable. Many of the Labour group resented his power; among that number was Tony McCardell, one of five members of Manchester city council, flag-bearer of the hard Left, and also chairman of the rather toothless city police monitoring unit. McCardell and his supporters wanted Anderton to be totally accountable to the Authority. Not merely as regards overall policy, but in the day-to-day running of the police force. McCardell explained, 'I go much further than the official Labour Party line. I believe it should be up to the Authority to decide if an individual policeman should be armed or whether the police should be on duty outside a factory, where striking pickets are protesting. It's my opinion that the Authority should legislate to the chief constable on all these matters. Chief constables are equivalent to old-fashioned warlords with their own private armies. They're an anachronism in this day and age. Their power-bubble has to be pricked.'

McCardell, who was brought up a Roman Catholic but became a non-believer in the wake of the Aberfan disaster – 'I can't believe a God would allow something like that to happen to little children' – never tried to conceal his hopes of winkling out Anderton. It was McCardell who suggested Anderton needed psychiatric therapy after the chief constable was reported, incorrectly, as believing he had a personal hotline to God. And on 25 January 1987, McCardell was quoted in the *Sunday Express*, alongside an article of mine on Anderton, as saying, 'I believe Mr Anderton has lost the respect of the people of Manchester. If he was the chief executive of a firm, you would be asking him to seek medical help. I have no personal

218

dislike of Mr Anderton. In a perfect world, however, I would like to see Mr Stalker replace him.'

McCardell and his followers could identify with Stalker, who was not only approachable and always affable, but seemed to have retained his Socialist roots, whereas Anderton, to them, had reneged on his heritage.

There is nothing machiavellian about Stalker. You could hold diametrically opposed views to Stalker on virtually any issue – morality, religion or politics – and it would not automatically preclude a sociable relationship with him, which cannot be said of Anderton. Tolerance is Stalker's trademark.

This is John Stalker talking at his bungalow home – part of the smallholding with five acres of land – at Warburton, Cheshire, just a 15-minute drive from the end of the main Manchester airport runway: 'From the moment I joined the police, it was the detectives who were special people to me. They were my idols. I admired their capacity to enjoy themselves. They never took life too seriously. However grim their lot, they were always able to laugh . . . at themselves, as well as at others. Unconsciously, I was modelling myself on them.'

He became a detective while a 22-year-old and at 25 was the youngest detective sergeant in Manchester in 150 years. 'I think I was a natural detective. I had the ability to put people at their ease. I've always been a fluent talker. I've never had to browbeat people. I genuinely like people and I'm a good listener, which is important for a policeman, especially a detective. You have to really care for the truth. To succeed in the police Force, there are three things you cannot do without: a sense of humour, an understanding wife and a *desire* to work long hours. I stress deliberately the word desire. It's not sufficient just to be willing to put in a 16-hour day . . . day after day; you have to be begging for it, which demands a special kind of man and an extra-special kind of woman supporting him. You cannot get by with just

219

two out of those three requirements. You must have the lot. I did. I certainly have the very special kind of woman.' He turned to acknowledge his wife, at the same time running the back of a hand across two misty eyes. Emotion still lumps in his throat whenever he reflects on Stella's unselfish loyalty.

He remembered the time when he was first conscious of fear. It was during the 1970s, while he was number two in the bomb squad and the IRA were hitting Manchester. 'Part of my job was to examine all suspicious devices found in public places. I didn't know much about explosives, but I was the police expert! You didn't call out the army until you had confirmed that it was a bomb, which, in all probability, would be achieved by blowing yourself up. If it went bang, it was a bomb! Most of the time we relied on the law of luck and the science of hunch. I was armed a lot, with the type of gun you now see in the hand of James Bond.

'When I led raids, I fully expected to find armed men on the other side of the door. I was afraid, not just for myself, but also for all those people for whom I was responsible. Religion was no help at all. My outlook was much more secular. If I was going to be shot, I wanted to be killed – not injured, not crippled for the rest of my life. But it was essential that I left home happy, knowing that my family respected and loved me, as a dad and a husband. I had to be at peace with myself and then I could collect my gun and say to myself, "I don't want to die today, but if it happens, I'm ready." Once or twice I went on armed raids after a row in the morning with Stella and without having made up. Those were the days on which I wanted to die least of all.

'I still prefer this country's firearm's policy to that of the United States, but I fear we're on the inevitable slide. I once thought I was going to be killed by an old man in America. I went into a shopping mall with my brother, who wanted to buy a handbag for his wife. As we came out of the shop, a senile security guard stopped us and asked to look in the plastic shopping bag I was carrying. I put my hand in the carrier and pulled out the handbag which my brother had just bought, only to find myself looking down the end of a shaking revolver. The old man couldn't stop trembling, an arthritic finger on the trigger. He was as terrified as I was. I shouldn't have been so quick reaching into my bag, but what an indictment it is against society when you are likely to be shot dead in the street for the offence of making a quick movement.'

Anderton knew that it would be fatal – for him – to allow the Manchester Police Authority to debate his request for Stalker to be investigated. There would have been an uproar and all the dirty washing would have been hung out to dry in front of the press. Councillor Norman Briggs was chairman of the Authority and he became the protagonist. As chairman, Briggs was entrusted with executive powers. In other words, in an emergency, he could take action without first seeking approval from the other members of the committee.

If McCardell had been chairman, for example, Anderton would have been stymied. But Briggs, a retired electrical engineer and a staunch Labour Party traditionalist, was as much at war with the Left as was Anderton. In this respect, there was an affinity between the two men. Briggs knew only too well that McCardell wanted his job, a fact never disputed by McCardell. It was a case, said McCardell, not of seeking power for its own sake, but in order to establish the sort of police force in which he and his like-minded allies believed. The Authority had become yet another boxing ring for a Left *v.* Right punchup within the Labour Party, something Anderton was prepared to exploit.

Briggs believed in supporting the chief constable; that was the first and foremost function of the Authority, he argued. The crime rate was soaring, resources were falling, so the least the paymasters could do was lash out on morale-boosting, which cost nothing. McCardell maintained that propping up something that was fundamentally wrong was immoral. Briggs and McCardell could not have been greater antagonists if they had been in different political parties. Anderton was confident that he could handle Briggs.

Roger Rees, the clerk to the Authority, made the telephone call for Anderton at 10.00 am, telling Briggs that a 'police problem' had 'cropped up'. Naturally, Briggs immediately wanted to know 'what's up?' Rees intimated that the matter was 'too delicate to elaborate on' over the telephone and he wondered whether Briggs would mind going to Swinton town hall, where the Police Authority held their meetings. An appointment was made for the same day, which was the morning after 'the Last Supper' at the Moss Nook restaurant.

When Briggs arrived at the clerk's office, Rees was not alone. Anderton was already there and it was he who did most of the talking, quickly identifying Stalker as 'the problem'. He explained that during the investigation of a businessman, Stalker's name kept coming to the fore. There was a yacht involved, which was under observation by the United States' coast guards, the FBI and the US National Narcotics Border Interdiction System, which is responsible for co-ordinating efforts to intercept drugs entering North America. Finally, the businessman's solicitor had indicated that Stalker might be called as a defence witness should his client be charged with any offence.

'Potentially very embarrassing,' Anderton commented. He emphasised that there was no witch-hunt and no question of prejudging his deputy. It was in everyone's favour, though, to resolve 'this problem' without delay. 'If it be rumour, let it be rubbed out, but there's only one way to find out.'

There was also the matter of five photographs which had been confiscated during the raid of Kevin Taylor's home. All the photographs had been taken during Taylor's fiftieth birthday party. Stalker appeared in only one of them, but his wife could be seen in the others. Several other people in the photographs had been identified and they would constitute a part of the case against Stalker, Briggs was told. Stalker's holiday in Florida was mentioned by Anderton, saying that the question of who paid would be something that needed resolving.

Briggs wanted to know what Anderton had in mind. Anderton told him. The chairman of the Authority saw no alternative, though he too was determined that it should be done in such a way as to avoid preconceptions – which was a noble sentiment and might even have seemed feasible in theory, but not in practice. At least Anderton was realistic enough to appreciate that there were no means of minimising the impact. Anderton's will became Briggs' way: Stalker would be sent home on indefinite leave, as opposed to suspension, and Colin Sampson would be appointed investigating officer. The Northern Ireland factor was none of Briggs' business and, therefore, did not figure in the considerations of that meeting.

Official notification to the relevant authorities in Northern Ireland of these dramatic developments was delegated to Sir Philip Myers, who flew to Belfast and negotiated through the DPP, Sir Barry Shaw. In view of the overt enmity between Stalker and Hermon, one would have imagined this to be the easiest of all the loose ends to tie. After all, on the question of Stalker's interim report, Hermon had demanded the right of 'first look' as the appointing officer. Now, however, he disclaimed that title, contending Sir Philip had appointed Stalker and, therefore, it was he who should take responsibility for the sacking. Like Anderton, Hermon is no mean politician. He could visualise the 'conspiracy' headlines if he was officially the one to relieve Stalker of his Ulster assignment. There were many people who would be made very happy by the announcement, but it had to come from the mainland. Publicly, Hermon took the line that he was dismayed by Sir Philip's promulgation, because it could only delay the final chapter of the Northern Ireland 'cover-up' inquiry. Myers was left to do his own dirty work.

On the afternoon of the same day that Briggs had his emergency meeting at Swinton town hall – Wednesday 28 July – Rees telephoned Stalker, who was attending to his farmyard animals on his smallholding when Stella summoned him with words like, 'It's for you. Something urgent.'

'Who is it?' he asked, not keen to be disturbed on his day off.

'It's Rees. He sounds funny.'

'Funny?'

'Uptight. Perhaps it's just me. I don't know.'

Stalker, dressed for farm chores in wellies, padded into his capacious living room.

The message from Rees was curt and not very sweet. Stalker was *not* to report for work as usual the following day. Instead of being in his office at 8.00 am, he should not arrive until 10.00.

'What's going on?' Stalker wanted to know.

Rees apologised for not being able to illuminate Stalker further. All would be revealed in the morning. On that mysterious note, Rees hung up, leaving Stalker in frustrated suspension.

Rees was followed on the hotline by Anderton, who was equally vague and terse. 'I'm sorry, but I can't say any more,' having already said nothing.

'What was that all about?' Stella asked.

'I've no idea,' Stalker murmured, confused.

All evening they tried to fathom what could be happening. 'It can't be anything *too* serious,' Stalker reasoned. After all, only the night before he'd been out to dinner with the chief constable at the Moss Nook restaurant and there hadn't been a hint of conflict. Anderton had also given him a confidential file – the 'poisoned chalice' – for reference at a Home Office meeting on the coming Friday, when Stalker would be deputising for his chief, or so he understood. It had been Anderton's sparkling form at the Tuesday evening dinner that persuaded Stalker that the reason for the 'unnerving' call from Rees and Anderton's 'remoteness' could not possibly indicate a rift between himself and his boss.

Stella could tell that her husband was frantic with worry. They discussed little else that evening. He came to the conclusion that it must have something to do with Northern Ireland, probably another manoeuvre to defer his return. Stella agreed. Neither of them could think of an alternative. Still Stalker did not sleep that night.

Anderton rejects suggestions that there was anything reprehensible about his conduct at the Moss Nook restaurant. Should he have been rude and have ignored Stalker? Life had to continue as normal, until it ceased to be that way. Briggs might not have co-operated. The complaint could have been placed before the full Police Authority committee, locked for weeks in dispute. In such an event, Stalker would have continued in office, attending the Home Office meeting as planned. The 'poisoned chalice' was not an artifice to placate Stalker, just in case any ripples of rumour lapped his way. The file had been passed to Stalker for him to have time to prepare himself adequately for a meeting that he might well be attending. Even Anderton was surprised by the momentum. He believed also that he would still be working with Stalker after the investigation had been completed. Anderton's friendliness at the Moss Nook restaurant was an honest mirror of his feelings towards John Stalker. It would also have been a breach of procedure if Anderton had discussed anything with Stalker the night before the confrontation with Sampson. The chief constable of West

Yorkshire had specifically requested that he – and he alone – should lay the charges against Stalker.

On the Thursday, Colin Sampson was on the road early. Alongside him was Assistant Chief Constable Donald Shaw. The 40-mile drive from Wakefield to Manchester was expected to take them 75 minutes at that busy time of the morning. The commuter traffic into Manchester was exceptionally heavy and it was later than 9.30 am before they were on their way up to Anderton's office on the eleventh floor of Greater Manchester police headquarters. Briggs was already there, drinking coffee with Anderton. Two more coffees were fetched by one of Anderton's factotums. The format for the meeting with Stalker was finalised. It would be chaired by Sampson. They all nodded their agreement, then at 10.00 am precisely they made their way, in single file, next door to Stalker's office, in the mourning manner of a hanging procession.

Apprehension and strain furrowed Stalker's face as he greeted them, trying to be informal. Handshakes over, Sampson assumed command forthwith, his approach brisk and matter-of-fact. Rumours were doing the rounds, he said, alleging injudicious associations. This had to be looked into thoroughly and it was best that Stalker went home 'on leave of absence', still drawing full pay.

Stalker was brimful with questions, but Sampson stopped him in his tracks. Sampson was not prepared to elaborate. The questions would be answered in the outcome of his inquiries.

To begin with, Stalker did not realise that his connection with the Northern Ireland inquiry was being severed irrevocably. He did not relish the idea of being sent home on 'leave of absence' and instead opted to take his annual holiday. It sounded better. He had his pride to preserve, without being an obsessively proud man. His meeting the following day at the Home Office was cancelled. So, too, were all his other official engagements. At no time was it

226

a rancorous meeting. Voices were never raised. In just a few minutes, it was all over. Stalker was then left alone to tidy his office, gather up his personal belongings, and depart. He had no idea how long it might be before he would be back – if ever – although Sampson had estimated that the examination of Stalker's affairs would 'take about a month'. The others, rather funereally, returned through the adjoining door into Anderton's office. Briggs excused himself and went to the chief constable's lavatory, where he vomited. 'I now know what it's like to have to be witness at an execution,' he was later to say to a council colleague. 'In a way, I was more than a witness; I was the executioner. I pulled the lever. I could have said "no" and referred it to a jury [the full Police Authority]. But I'm satisfied I did the right thing. I wasn't pressured. I'd do it again, the same way. Being sure I did right doesn't make it any easier. It was a bloody awful day; the worst of my life. I looked into his face and I felt ashamed. He looked as if he was just being told that his wife had been killed in an accident. I said to myself, "What a bastard you are, Norman!" Civilised life can be very brutal.'

That was a bad day for Anderton, too. He prayed more than usual. He locked himself in his private praying room before the arrival of Briggs and the others from Wakefield. He asked God to take over. He talked to God and laid bare his intimate ferment. Throughout the build-up to this crisis, he had consulted God at every stage. By the time he emerged from his prayer room, he felt safe that he had God on his side. Not that Stalker was in the wrong and Anderton was in the right, but that God approved of what was being done. Throughout the day his stomach was knotted the way it had been before leading his men against rioters. By the time he arrived home that evening, he was ready for a glass of his favourite malt whisky, but he could not take his mind off Stalker.

Together, Anderton and his wife prayed: this time for the Stalker family, for Stella and the two children. They prayed for the Stalkers to have the strength to see it through with dignity. Anderton also prayed for Sampson to unearth the whole truth. An appendage to his prayers was that he hoped the truth would vindicate his deputy. Sleep did not come easily for either Anderton or his wife.

John and Stella Stalker did not sleep at all.

That evening, Briggs complained of chest pains, which he dismissed as stress. He could not sleep either, his mind in turmoil as he contemplated the reaction of his Police Authority colleagues at the next day's meeting.

Briggs came to the conclusion that no item on Stalker should be included in the agenda for the meeting: it was too late for that, anyhow. It was not until the 'private and confidential' section of the meeting that Briggs boldly told members, 'It is with regret that I have seen fit to suspend John Stalker from duty.'

A statement, drafted by Rees the previous day in anticipation of the outcome of the Authority meeting, was issued to the media, stating:

'1. Information had been received in relation to the conduct of a senior police officer which discloses the possibility of a disciplinary offence.

2. To maintain public confidence, the chairman of the Police Authority, Councillor Norman Briggs, JP, has requested the chief constable of West Yorkshire, C. Sampson, Esq., QPM, to investigate this matter under the appropriate provisions and the Complaints Authority, an independent statutory body, has agreed to supervise the investigation through its deputy chairman, Roland Moyle, Esq., who has approved the appointment of Mr Sampson.

3. The deputy chief constable is on temporary leave of absence whilst the matter is being investigated.'

The two other statements – from Anderton and the RUC – followed the Police Authority communiqué. Anderton said, 'I find it very regrettable indeed that this situation has arisen and I am obviously upset by what has happened. It is my hope that this matter will be cleared up as quickly as possible.'

The RUC observed simply, 'The chief constable (Hermon), in consultation with Her Majesty's Inspector of Constabulary, is considering the implications of this development.'

Stalker, distraught and confused, telephoned Anderton, but the chief constable was not available. Stalker left a message, asking Anderton to return his call. When they did eventually speak, the conversation was notable only for its brevity. It ended with Anderton saying solicitously, 'Mr Stalker (note, not "John"), you must look after yourself now.' Stalker would not know that Anderton was emotionally drained as he put down the receiver.

Publicly, the Police Authority backed Briggs. Privately, they pilloried him. He told a close friend, 'The knives are out for me. They're making my life hell.' He complained of anonymous hate telephone calls during the night. They would start at midnight and be repeated every hour until four or five o'clock. All attempts to trace them failed because they were made from local pay-phones and the caller would stay on the line no longer than half a minute. After a life devoted to the community, it was mortally wounding for him to end up the target of such malevolence. 'I've had to leave my phone off the hook, but no councillor and magistrate should have to do that. How can I help people in need, if they can never get through to me?'

Some leftwingers in the north-west spawned the speculation that Stalker had been 'set up' by Freemasons in the RUC and in Manchester. Briggs, an active Freemason for many years, was accused of having been 'got at' by his brethren friends in the Manchester police force, something he denied categorically. His health deteriorated so acutely that his doctor recommended he go away on holiday and keep his destination a secret. When he returned, he confided in another councillor, 'They're still after me. The abuse is unbearable. There are those who even wish me dead.'

He died of a heart attack on 1 August.

17

'The Day My Life was Saved'

Stalker was at the wheel of his red, four-door BMW, driving me from his home to Altrincham railway station, after we had spent a day together analysing his past, pondering his future, evaluating the present.

A bus driver hooted and shook a fist at him for not giving way. Stalker quietly acknowledged the bus, but not its driver, slipping his BMW through the tangled traffic with the relaxed indifference of a man weaned on hairy car chases.

'I never thought I'd be saying this; never in my life.' The preamble was aired in the tone of a man coming to terms with a fait accompli not of his own making. 'Probably the luckiest day of my life was the one on which I was removed from the Northern Ireland inquiry. If I'd been allowed to go back, I doubt whether I'd be alive today. Everyone there knew what I intended doing. It would have been very different from the first time round, when no one knew what I would find, let alone recommend. But if I'd returned, the whole of Ulster would have known that I was head-hunting, and I'd have been a marked man. It doesn't take a fortune to hire a hitman in Belfast. The price of a pint of Guinness would have been enough. That's all my life would have been worth. You have to be philosophical, especially when there's no alternative!' He did not mean that he was pleased to have been removed from the Northern Ireland inquiry, simply that the decision, as terrible as it was at the time, probably saved his life. By 'head-hunting' he meant that he would be naming names and levelling accusations.

Earlier, at his bungalow, he had started to reminisce about the Moors Murders, saying, 'I must be about the only serving policeman who was actively involved in that – ' At that point, he cut himself off with a hand over his mouth. 'But I'm *not* a policeman, am I?' The Sampson report into Stalker's conduct had been completed and received. Stalker had been reinstated as Greater Manchester's deputy chief constable, only to resign to become general manager of the Channel 4 television series 'Brookside', which he had left amicably after just three months to write his autobiography and to be groomed as a television presenter for a new BBC current affairs programme.

'I still think I'm a policeman. Sometimes I jump out of bed in the morning and hurry to the bathroom, thinking I've overslept and will be late in my office at police headquarters. I pull myself up in midstride and say to myself, "John, wake up! That's all over. The uniform's gone. You're free." But I'm not free, not really. The past won't let go, not completely. It's as if I'm on a leash. I can go only so far, then it pulls me up with a jolt, tightening around my throat, choking me. Yes, I'm still choked! The past year is still a surrealistic dream. At times I find it hard to come to terms with the fact that it has happened. There were occasions when I was very near to total despair because of the unfairness of it all.

'What I shall never forgive the police for is the killing of my family's pride in what I'd done for all those years. My daughters were immensely proud of their dad and the work he did, but not any more. They loathe the police. So does Stella, but not me. I'm not bitter, not even with Anderton. He behaved honourably within his own code. In his shoes, I should have gone about things differently, but that's a matter of style.

'I do believe that my 30 years with the police were not wasted. It's a job worth doing. I hope that the pain will die one day. My dearest wish is for my family to come to terms with what has happened.'

Stella shook her head resolutely. 'Never!' she vowed. 'I've seen too much. I've had to watch while my husband was kicked in the teeth. I'll never forget, never forgive. No loving wife could.'

Stalker's daughters Colette and Francine had grown up knowing Anderton as their Uncle Jim. Suddenly, he had become their Wicked Uncle. 'It's beyond their comprehension – and mine,' said Stella. 'They don't understand why he hasn't talked to us, why he hasn't explained. The silence is an insult. My husband deserves better than that, when you consider his service to the public and the fact that his children have had to grow up almost entirely without a father.'

'It hasn't been *quite* that bad,' Stalker countered, redressing the balance. 'Whenever I had any time off, I would make my daughters the most important people in my day. I would try to take them somewhere special, so that it would be a day to remember. I don't think I failed them as a father, despite being a 24-hour-a-day policeman.'

Often when he reads in the newspapers about people who appear to have suffered an injustice, he writes to them sympathising. 'I would never have done anything like that before my own experience, but I now know its power. The public backing kept me alive – six thousand letters, little gifts, treasured mementoes, bouquets of flowers for the wife. I've learned the enormous capacity of ordinary people to respond in a positive way. I was never a cynical policeman. I always believed in the innate goodness of human nature and my faith, in that respect, was not let down when it was put to the severest test. Six thousand letters of support came through my letter-box to keep pushing up my chin. Every day, without a break,

233

bouquets of flowers were delivered for Stella. Old ladies sent cakes which they'd baked specially for us. Clotted cream came from pensioners in Devon and Cornwall. Very poor people posted me books they'd won as prizes at school 50 years ago. I received a crucifix which had been brought back from a pilgrimage to Lourdes. People, in their own way, were saying, "We're with you. Don't snap. We know what you're going through. We've been there ourselves. You're not alone. The sun will shine again, you see."

'People are precious. My £22,000 legal bill was paid by public donations. One star of a television series, William Tarmey, Jack Duckworth in "Coronation Street", delayed going into hospital for his fifth heart by-pass operation just in order to appear at a benefit concert in my honour. When someone like that is prepared to risk his own life for you, then you are made to feel very humble – not sorry for yourself, but proud to have such friends, proud to be part of the human race.'

When we had arrived at his smallholding, Barns Lane Farm, Stella, looking every bit a farmer's wife, had come to meet us at the rustic gate, two Lassie lookalikes hacking at her heels. A sign alerted strangers that they were in a Neighbourhood Watch area. Breathlessly, Stella had recounted an earlier panic. Their pony and one of the pigs had been let out by a prankster. Suddenly the policeman's pulse was beating again. 'It's all right, I've got them back,' Stella reassured.

Emergency over, John Stalker relaxed into the novel role of country squire. They had 20 pigs, three horses – the largest a fine hunter which belonged to the children – chickens, geese, ducks and the inevitable vegetable patch. A field had been put aside for the riding members of the family to prepare for gymkhanas. 'You'd never believe that we're both deeply-rooted city folk,' he mused, leading me to a cottage on the opposite side of the grounds from the bungalow. It was in the loft, a refuge from the telephone and domestic tremors, where Stalker did all his private work. There was even a bed, 'but there'll never be a phone'. Self-consciously, he straightened his sweater, remarking, 'I've never been dressed like this before at this time of day.' He fingered his open-neck collar and drew attention to his casual trousers. 'A new life, a new uniform. Now I'm with the BBC, I must look the part.'

Unlike Anderton, Stalker had no passion for the police when he was a boy. 'I drifted into the Force, very much as an afterthought,' he recalled. 'My first job was with an insurance company – British Engine, Boiler and Electrical – but after nine or ten months, I realised that routine office work wasn't for me.' He happened to be sheltering from the rain one afternoon when, across the road, he saw an advertisement for police recruits. The poster was outside Newton Street police station. 'The bus didn't come, so I crossed the road and joined the Force instead!' He became a police cadet on 2 May 1956. 'What appealed to me about the police was the outlet for sport. I was good at all sports, but especially athletics, boxing, cricket and football.' In 1952, he was named 'Sportsman of the Week' in the comic *Rover*, winning a £2 postal order prize, which he returned, explaining to the publishers that he would be endangering his amateur status if he accepted money; an early example of Stalker's probity. The editor of the comic 'fully understood' and substituted a wrist-watch for the postal order.

Two pounds were equivalent to a week's wages for Stalker. 'I'd been at school with a few lads who'd joined the police. I was amazed that they'd been accepted. I couldn't see them displaying personal courage, being brave enough to put their lives on the line. I said to myself, "If they're good enough, I'm damned sure I am." No one in my family had even been a policeman.'

He had been born into a cramped two-up, two-down terraced house in Ash Street, part of the blot of the landscape in northern Manchester. His parents were paying a weekly rent of nine shillings. Stalker's grand-father, on his mother's side, had been a stationmaster and a devout Catholic. In contrast, Stalker's own father, Jack, came from a long line of Orangemen, who had crossed the Irish Sea to Liverpool in search of work, finally settling in Manchester. Jack Stalker took an apprentice-ship in engineering, devoting his entire working life to Metro Vickers, based in Trafford Park. He was also active in politics, having joined the Young Socialist League in 1930.

'We were so poor when I was a small boy that the breath of life was a luxury,' John Stalker said, rather melodramatically. 'We had nothing except our family, which always seemed enough. My plan, when I joined the police, was to serve a few years, during which time I would enjoy myself and hopefully become equipped for some kind of managerial career. I did not see myself as a 30-year man. My interview was conducted by Robert Mark – he was a superintendent at the time in the old Manchester City Police. Mark also recruited Anderton. He made his reputation as a talent-spotter. I think he was consciously searching for a new breed of policeman. During a two-year period, he recruited a future genera-tion of chief constables and deputies. He was a truly great man.' At least this was something about which Anderton and Stalker could agree.

There are certain criminals for whom Stalker has a sneaking admiration. Anderton would never make such an admission. 'For me, the juice of detective work was the intellectual challenge.'

If you are to become a master detective, you have to be able to make a meal out of minutiae. Synthesis is a science. Stalker had all the necessary qualities and he knows he did. Only the cream are chosen to protect royalty and other VIPs, including the prime minister and members of the Cabinet. Stalker was one of the chosen few. 'There have been criminals I've respected. I'm not talking about thugs and rapists. I mean villains with brilliant minds who were virtually saying to me, "Come on, let's see how good you are at chess. It's my brain against yours. Have you a kipper brain to match your kipper feet? Let's see what you have inside that head of yours." That kind of cerebal contest can be stimulating and invigorating.' The dénouement was reward enough.

In contrast, Anderton has said, 'I would have vicious criminals flogged until they begged for mercy.' He told Lesley Garner, of the *Sunday Telegraph*, that certain people should be 'cast aside and forgotten, they are so criminal, so unconcerned, so lacking in any moral sense of their own or feeling for the community'. His rhetoric has described crime as 'a bursting boil on the skin of life'.

Anderton's language is foreign to Stalker.

'But it's wrong to believe that the chief constable and his deputy have to be alike in order to make an effective partnership,' said Stalker. 'Some of the best partnerships have been between men who couldn't agree on the time of day, but in public they were always in step, presenting a united front. They fought their battles behind closed doors, never out in the open, and they always respected each other.'

In three sentences, he had revealed everything about his relationship with Anderton.

Has he any regrets? 'Only that I don't have any sons. I should have loved a couple of boys. I'm proud of my daughters and I treasure them, but I also wanted lads as well. Yes, I'm sad about that.'

How does he wish to be remembered? 'Not just as an ex-policeman from Manchester to whom something rather unsavoury and extraordinary happened. I hope to be as successful and respected in my new world as I was in the last.'

Sampson's report on Stalker, running to 1500 pages (including statements from 154 witnesses, 64 photographs,

50 exhibits and 156 miscellaneous documents) was delivered on 6 August 1986 to the Police Complaints Authority. The investigation had taken nine weeks, at a cost to the taxpayer of £200,000. Stalker was cleared of any serious offence, but he was indicted on what amounted to 10 alleged misdemeanours, eight of them concerning the purported misuse of police vehicles. The other two counts revolved around his attendance at Conservative Party functions, and associating with Kevin Taylor and known criminals 'in a manner likely to bring discredit upon the Greater Manchester Police'. On the issue of Stalker's holiday in Florida with Taylor, Sampson had this to say, 'There is no evidence to prove that Deputy Chief Constable Stalker accepted a gift or undue hospitality from Mr Taylor. Nor has any evidence been found to show their relationship was corrupt or could be the basis of a criminal charge.' Sampson reiterated that there was 'no allegation made of any criminal offence', pointing out, 'Indeed, if there were so, the papers would be submitted to an entirely different authority. What is alleged is a series of disciplinary offences clearly demonstrating a less than excellent standard of professional performance. The standard of excellence is that which is set by the service itself and expected of it by the public. In consequence, therefore, I have given the most careful consideration to the whole of the circumstances of this case, and having regard to the considerable amount of public speculation and interest it has generated, I am of the opinion that the evidence supports, indeed demands, that it be ventilated before an independent tribunal.'

The fate of Stalker was to be decided on Friday 22 August by the Manchester Police Authority. Following the death of Briggs, Councillor David Moffat had been appointed acting chairman. Arrangements were made for the Authority members (24 Socialists, three Tories, three Liberals and 15 magistrates) to receive a summary of the report, some 144 pages, on the morning of Wednesday 20 August.

Stalker made two final requests: condemned men, by tradition, are allowed only one. Stalker was permitted none. He had hoped to be able to plead his case personally to the Authority, but that was ruled out of order. He had also asked Anderton for permission to park his car at Bootle Street police station, just a few yards from the office of Stalker's solicitor in the city centre. 'No,' decreed Anderton.

'Bastard!' Stalker erupted to his wife. And so the die was cast.

At the meeting, starting promptly at 3.30 pm in Swinton town hall, Sampson presented his report and was questioned for at least two hours. Then it was Anderton's turn. For more than an hour he was on the defence, refusing to be drawn on his behind-the-scenes involvement if, indeed, there had been any. Throughout, he maintained that his actions had been dictated by the circumstances and that there had been no conspiracy against Stalker, of which he was aware.

After an adjournment at 7.30 pm, the Labour group constructed a motion that Stalker should be reinstated forthwith, but that he must be 'more circumspect in his political and criminal associations in future in view of his high office'. The Labour group voted en bloc for the motion, supported by 11 magistrates and two Conservatives. Opposing the proposition were the three Liberals, two magistrates and a Tory.

McCardell said later, 'I was watching Anderton's face as the verdict became apparent. His head dropped. He seemed to slump, to deflate. He couldn't believe it. If looks could kill, I wouldn't be alive today. He was shattered.'

McCardell was not wrong in his assessment. Anderton had expected the Authority to back Sampson's demand for the case against Stalker to be adjudicated by an independent tribunal. However the Authority voted, in Anderton's eyes the Sampson inquiry had not cleared Stalker. For the chief constable, there could be no eschewing the conclusion in Sampson's summary: 'What is alleged is a series of disciplinary offences clearly demonstrating a less than excellent standard of professional performance'. As the deputy, Stalker was responsible for the discipline of the 7000 officers under him in the Greater Manchester force. How could he ever again reprimand others if his own discipline was questionable? He judged Stalker exactly the same way that he would expect to be judged himself. He considered Stalker's position untenable. Stalker had risen to the top because of his brilliance, therefore he could not be given the benefit of stupidity or ignorance. How could a man who had been virtually peerless as a detective, have a friend for 17 years and apparently know so little about the company he kept? Anderton could not live with what he was being asked to believe.

Stalker, not unnaturally, saw things somewhat differently. On hearing the news, he told the press, 'I have been exonerated completely. I think that's the important thing. I always said that my good name was all that mattered to me. My life has been ripped apart, dissected and put together again. The Police Authority has decided that I am a suitable person to be their deputy chief constable.'

Anderton did not see it that way at all. He felt that the Labour members of the Authority had used Stalker as an instrument with which to beat him over the head. He believed they were not so much on Stalker's side as against him. The Stalker issue was a convenience for them. They wanted a parcel of conspiracy, accommodating all their usual bogies – Freemasons, the Establishment, MI5, the RUC and the military – and packaged by Anderton. Whatever the truth of Anderton's vision, there is no escaping the fact that Stalker was caught in the crossfire. By winning with the Authority, he had to lose with Anderton.

Stalker was back at work the day after the special Authority meeting – Saturday 23 August, 1986 – but Anderton was not there to greet him. It was the Bank Holiday weekend and Anderton had gone with Joan to their Lake District retreat, where he spent much of the time contemplating his future relationship with his born-again deputy. They would have to try to live together, for the sake of the force, but it would never be quite the same again. He equated it with a marriage that had gone through a three-month separation. It might survive, but the odds were against it thriving. Nevertheless, on his return to Manchester on the Monday, Anderton was able to state publicly, 'It may be thought that personal relationships at senior command level in the Greater Manchester police force could be affected by the traumas of the past few months, but John Stalker and I have always worked very well together in the public interest and to the good of the force, and there is no reason why we cannot do so again. A police force without a deputy chief constable is not fully effective, and I am glad to have John Stalker back on duty.'

Off stage, however, all was not bright lights and sweet harmony. During Stalker's extended leave, certain news-papers had seemed uncannily well-informed about every-thing that was happening in Stalker's life. Intimate details of his Northern Ireland saga were colouring the headlines. The background information and minutiae of the political in-fighting had been incredibly precise and accurate. Anderton assumed that the mole must have been very close to Stalker. He instinctively disliked the idea of Stalker waging guerrilla warfare through the press, with what appeared to be well-orchestrated leaks. The chief constable seemed to think that Stalker had been sucked into what he saw as an anti-Anderton conspiracy.

McCardell did not help matters by openly declaring

that he wanted Stalker as chief constable. Stalker suspected that McCardell and his hard Left confederates wanted anyone other than Anderton, and Stalker was a convenient alternative, a supposition which was probably not far from the thruth. Certainly Anderton felt uneasy working alongside a man who had become a cause célèbre with his most clamorous adversaries in politics and the press.

Consequently, the door between them was closed – literally. No longer did Stalker have casual, free access to Anderton's suite. Until the morning that Sampson triggered the guillotine, the connecting door between the offices of the chief constable and his deputy had always been left open, allowing the daily business to ebb and flow unimpeded. Now it was locked on Anderton's side. Stalker felt cut off. And he was, of course. Many of his old allies at Chester House had become wary of him. How could a pillar of the Establishment be a martyr of the revolutionary Left?

There were whispers in the Mess. Although the press had not been admitted to the Greater Manchester Police Authority meeting to consider Stalker's future, everyone in the city seemed to have heard the story of one of McCardell's pack advocating that Stalker should not merely be sent back to work, but be paraded to Chester House behind a marching band and American drum majorettes. In view of his past experience with the Authority, Anderton had no doubt that Stalker had become the new vehicle through which they hoped to injure and humiliate him.

McCardell had this to say after Stalker had resigned from the police, 'Despite Sampson's assurances to the contrary, the feeling persisted among the majority of the members of the Authority that Stalker had been sabotaged, knifed in the back, because he had been so successful in Ulster.

Until conclusively proven to the contrary, I'll always believe that Stalker was the victim of a conspiracy.'

There was, indeed, a conspiracy against Stalker, which I have uncovered, but not by the people McCardell and his fraternity would like to see incriminated, namely Anderton and Hermon. Neither of them was a party to the 'Irish Connection' to defame Stalker. The duplicity came from Secret Service cowboys and lower-ranking police officers, including those in the Special Branch, who were motivated by self-preservation.

In the early winter of 1986, when Myra Hindley offered to help locate the buried bodies of Pauline Reade and Keith Bennett, Chief Superintendent Peter Topping discussed with Anderton the possibility of returning to the moors with a search party. Stalker was not excluded from those talks, although some newspapers reported that he had been 'snubbed' by Anderton, suggesting this alleged new rift was Stalker's reason for resigning. The truth is that, in effect, Stalker eliminated himself by his lack of enthusiasm for the moors mission. Stalker opposed Topping's proposals on the following five accounts: 1. The chances of finding bodies in winter were remote. 2. Failure would only distress further the grieving parents. 3. It smacked of a publicity exercise. 4. Manpower could be better deployed elsewhere, on active cases in which the perpetrators were still free and a danger to the public. 5. The Moors Murders were ancient history and no useful purpose could be served titillating the public or tormenting the relatives of the victims with futile gestures.

Stalker was right and wrong. Right in as much that it was not the ideal season for grave-hunting on Saddleworth Moor. Wrong in everything else. For the people of the north-west, the Moors Murders will never be history, never forgotten. It is something they do not want to forget. Anderton is very often a public echo, illustrated by his statement on 6 July 1987, after the body of Pauline Reade had at last been unearthed: 'I hope this will be the closing chapter, that the final story is being told and that the book can be closed on what can only be described as one of the most horrendous, seediest of crimes involving children ever to have taken place. We all hope and pray that happens, because we regard it as our basic fundamental duty to find and identify the missing children and see they are properly laid to rest where their families can visit their graves and pay their respects in the way that has been denied them so long.'

At a political level, Stalker will never be a match for Anderton, whose utterances have always tended to monitor the heartbeat of the hoi polloi. Searching for the bodies of missing children would never be out-of-season for Anderton.

Stalker cares just as passionately as anyone else, shown by his comments a few days before the body of Pauline Reade was dug from its unholy place of unrest. 'The victims of Hindley and Brady are frozen forever in time as children. If they were alive today, they would be approaching middle-age, but to everyone they remain timeless and ageless. While Brady and Hindley survive, so too do the memories of those they killed. The dead, in this case, are more alive than the living, and quite rightly so. I'm not saying that I believe Brady and Hindley should have been executed. I have to be consistent with myself. If I advocate the death sentence for them, I have to wish a similar fate for all the other cold-blooded murderers, and I don't. All my instincts are against capital punishment, not on religious grounds, but because of the mistakes that can be made, that *have* been made. I cannot leave out Hindley and Brady from the equation. They are part of the sum principle.

'No policeman ever becomes hardened to cases in which children are the victims. Whenever a child was reported missing, the chill would come in as night came down. I made a point of always keeping in touch with the desperate parents. The negative phone call is just as important as the positive one. You say, "No news so far, I'm afraid, but we're still looking. I'll call you again in an hour, whatever." No news, you see, is good news compared to bad news. The parents of missing children are comforted and helped by involvement. They like to know that we haven't all gone home to bed. I have never been involved in this type of case without thinking: *It could be my daughters. How would I be feeling at this moment? What would I want – and expect – from the police? If I don't catch this man, one of my daughters could indeed be next.* That was always a compelling incentive to solve a crime.'

Stalker resigned from the police, not because he had been omitted from the fresh developments on Saddleworth Moor, but as the result of a conversation with senior Home Office officials, during which he posed the question, in response to a comment, 'Are you saying that I shall now never make chief constable?'

The unequivocal reply was, 'That is a correct interpretation.'

'If I couldn't reach the top, I didn't want to carry on,' Stalker explained. 'When your whole life has been one of climbing, you cannot settle for standing still, even if it's on the next ledge to the summit.'

The two protagonists of the Stalker Affair both saw themselves as the hapless casualties of prejudiced persecution. Both were destined to be denied their passionate ambitions. Anderton reluctantly accepted that, because of his high profile, he would never become the commissioner of the Metropolitan police. Stalker had been told that for him the rank of chief constable would always be a tantalising, elusive target.

18

The Final Solution

On Thursday 9 January 1986, Sean O'Callaghan – wanted by Scotland Yard since 1983 for questioning in connection with plots to assassinate British politicians – flew from Shannon in the Republic of Ireland to New York. His passport was a sufficiently plausible forgery to fool the immigration authorities at JFK airport, or so he believed. The bogus name he had assumed for the purpose of his clandestine international manoeuvres was Sean Brennan. His occupation was listed in the passport as funeral director. He had taken a year off his age, making himself 32. Birthplace: Dublin. Distinguishing marks: a beard. Police photographs showed him with a moustache. The US visa, purporting to have been issued legitimately in Dublin, certainly seemed to pass the acid test at JFK's point of entry.

When he emerged from customs, where he had nothing to declare, he was met by Michael O'Malley, a Catholic born in Boston who moved to New York with his parents when he was nine. His parents, staunch supporters of the Irish Republican movement, had emigrated in 1939 to the United States from Dublin. O'Malley, senior, became a New York street cop. His wife served in the local deli. Michael O'Malley did not share his father's partiality for law and order. He was hardly ever at school from the age of 13 and he ran in Queen's with a teenage gang known as the Irish Rat Pack, the plague of the neighbourhood.

The police response to arson, gang rape, mugging and vandalism in the poorest area of Queen's was to round up the Irish Rat Pack for questioning. By the time Michael was 17, he had 13 convictions, all for relatively minor offences, though potentially dangerous, such as throwing fireworks into cars. Not surprisingly, his father disowned him; but not before Michael had disowned his dad. Having a cop for a father was not the ideal credential for an aspiring hoodlum.

After leaving home, Michael's first job was as a runner in Queen's for an illegal bookmaker. Next step down the ladder saw him running errands for a debt collector. By the time he was 24, he had his own loan sharking business, employing four shake-down collectors. He moved into Manhattan, renting a spacious apartment between First and Second Avenue on the fashionable East Side. At the same time, he opened an office in Eighth Avenue, on the less salubrious West Side, above a massage parlour and sandwiched between a gun shop and a drug store. Already he was mixing socially with the hierarchy of the New York IRA Connection. He dabbled in managing prostitutes, who came across friends and clients who were looking for drugs, mainly cocaine and heroin. Michael O'Malley found ways of supplying the market as a middle man. In a short time, he had become a merchant of many vices. In his passport, he called himself an entrepreneur. He paid his dues regularly to certain police officers, insuring himself against the risk of prosecution. As time went on, he found himself dining regularly with IRA fund-raisers. Visiting terrorists were given the VIP treatment, often in the presence of New York policemen.

After meeting O'Callaghan (alias Brennan) at Kennedy airport, they drove to O'Malley's apartment, where immediately they began drinking beer.

During the 747 flight from Dublin, O'Malley, in row 35, seat C, had watched the movie, eaten two meals and drunk several miniature bottles of whisky. Everything he did, in fact, was noted by two male passengers three rows behind him in economy class. The inquisitive passengers in seats D and E, row 38, were an MI5 agent and an officer in the Special Branch. The MI5 agent was disguised as a priest.

The British officers were collected at the airport by an FBI agent, whose field code name was Benson. They were taken to a safe house in Queen's, no more than a 15-minute drive from JFK. Inside the safe house were two more agents – one attached to the CIA and the other with the Drug Enforcement Administration. The DEA man had been based in Florida for three years, before being switched to New York the previous month because his face had become too well-known in Miami. Both Benson and the CIA agent were on their own respective Washington agency establishments and were working undercover in New York, without alerting the local police.

For the past three months, O'Malley's office and apartment had been bugged, including his telephones, by the CIA. Copies of all transcripts had been shared with the FBI and the DEA. In that period, they had accumulated detailed information about all of O'Malley's nefarious activities. With the assistance of MI5, they had also identified his Irish connections. The bugs at O'Malley's office had been installed by a CIA operative posing, with all the authentic back-up data, as a fire safety officer from city hall. The bugging of O'Malley's apartment had been a straightforward lock-picking exercise while he was out.

They had learned of Sean O'Callaghan's impending trip to New York from a trans-Atlantic conversation between the two men. O'Callaghan had made the call to O'Malley's apartment at 5.00 pm (US East Coast time) the previous Sunday, 5 January.

The FBI in Washington had struck a deal with immigration to ensure that O'Malley had a safe passage into the USA at JFK. Neither the FBI nor MI5, at that stage, knew what false name O'Malley would be using. Another

Special Branch officer, who was not travelling on the flight, stood behind O'Malley in the check-in queue at Shannon. As soon as he heard the airline checker refer to O'Callaghan as 'Mr Brennan', he abandoned the line and passed a message to his colleague and the MI5 agent who were waiting, further back in the queue, to board the same flight. This information was also signalled to Benson on an unlisted Queen's number, which was a military field phone inside the safe house.

The FBI had also taken over an apartment in O'Malley's block. It was from this address that all O'Malley's personal calls and home conversations were monitored.

Very shortly after O'Malley returned to his apartment from the airport with O'Callaghan, agents heard the American say, 'I've made reservations for tomorrow with KLM.'

Benson knew all about the two seats reserved for O'Malley on the KLM direct flight to Amsterdam. O'Malley's booking had been for two return tickets.

'Why didn't they simply arrange to meet in Amsterdam?' the MI5 agent asked Benson. O'Malley gave the answer a little later, when he told O'Callaghan, 'You'll be meeting useful people tonight. We're going to a party. You'll meet people who can make anything happen for you. Whatever you need, they can provide. They're very sympathetic towards your cause, Sean. You can trust them. Every drop of blood in that house tonight will be Irish. I exaggerate a little. American/Irish. Same thing! In return, you'll have to help them to get snow white into Ireland.'

'Snow, what?' O'Callaghan exclaimed.

'Snow white. Hot snow! You know!'

O'Callaghan was alluding to drugs, heroin and cocaine.

A few seconds later, the conversation is alleged to have continued thus, 'There's no market for it back home.'

'You're kidding!'

'There isn't the money.'

'People find money. My friends are looking for new frontiers.'

O'Callaghan promised to do what he could. 'Whatever's asked, within reason.'

The two men were heard to open cans of beer. Later, O'Callaghan asked, 'How much does your man in Amsterdam know?'

O'Malley answered, 'Enough, which is nothing!'

Both laughed.

At 7.30 pm, they drove from the apartment in O'Malley's black Continental, followed all the way by the surveillance team to a large, imposing residence in extensive grounds near Coney Beach. The licence numbers of other arriving cars were also noted. Most of the guests at that party were already known to the FBI. The party had been impossible to infiltrate, so the FBI had no record of what occurred inside.

O'Malley and O'Callaghan were the first to depart the party at eleven o'clock, heading back to Manhattan, where they parked outside a singles bar in Second Avenue. They stayed in the bar for 53 minutes, emerging with two women, both believed to be hookers. From the singles bar, they returned to O'Malley's apartment, a drive which took no longer the five minutes. Very little was recorded from the apartment during the final hours of the night. The bedroom had not been bugged. The girls exited the apartment block separately, going their own ways by taxi – the first at 4.09 am, the second at 4.31.

By eight o'clock, O'Malley and O'Callaghan were on their way to JFK. A taxi had been called to the apartment. Both men were travelling light, carrying only overnight bags.

The FBI, negotiating with the Dutch police and Amsterdam Immigration, massaged the way for the unchallenged passage into Holland of the two undesirables. O'Malley's US passport was bona fide. The MI5 and Special Branch agents, accompanied by Benson, also joined the flight to Holland.

From the international Schiphol airport, they were taken by taxi past the Royal Palace, through Dam Square, to the Pulitzer Hotel, beside the canal in old Amsterdam. From the hotel, an impressive, traditional establishment, O'Malley made a local telephone call. Half an hour later, they were on the move again, with their luggage, heading by taxi towards the renowned nightlife. They were dropped off at one of the city's spartan 'brown bars', which are popular for their stark sparseness and potent Heineken brew. In the bar they met, by appointment, a man who was later identified by Amsterdam detectives as 35-year-old Bent Timman. They did not stay many minutes in the bar – just long enough to effect introductions and to drink one glass of beer each.

They walked purposefully through the bustling, labyrinthine entertainment area to the canal, where they boarded a glass-domed pleasure cruiser. Everywhere they went, they were followed by local undercover detectives, while the representatives of MI5, FBI and the Special Branch waited for news at the waterside Amstel Hotel.

After disembarking from the illuminated canal cruiser, O'Malley, Timman and O'Callaghan went on foot to the Dutchman's attic flat, just two blocks from the inimitable Skinny Bridge landmark, stopping at several bars on the way. They were not off the streets until 5.00 am. Later the same day, O'Malley and O'Callaghan flew back to New York.

For the next 48 hours, O'Callaghan remained inside O'Malley's apartment. During that time, he made numerous telephone calls. One was to Pan American Airways to book a flight back to Shannon. Another call was to a Seamus on a Dublin number, the quintessence of which went, 'Mick's man in Amsterdam will do the job for us.'

'On what terms?'

'Attractive.'

'Translate.'

'Five grand, plus beer and fag money.'

'We'll need to blow a bank to pay for that!'

Two-way laughter.

'We don't pay a cent, Seamus.'

Long pause, then, 'Who the fuck does?'

'We have sponsors.'

Another pause. 'What's the fucking catch?'

'Not now . . .'

'You haven't given a commitment?'

'Jesus, no!'

The following day, O'Callaghan flew back to Shannon.

The MI5 agent and the Special Branch officer decided not to catch the same flight as O'Callaghan, to avoid the possibility of being recognised because their faces might have become familiar to the Republican terrorist. Instead, they travelled by British Airways to London, where they transferred to an Aer Lingus flight to complete the flight to Shannon.

A few days later, an IRA war council assembled at a farm near Dundalk. O'Callaghan was one of the principals at that conclave. So, too, was Evelyn Glenholmes, who was still wanted for questioning by Scotland Yard in connection with the bombings in London during the autumn and winter of 1981.

Two people died on 10 October 1981 when a nail bomb exploded outside army barracks in Ebury Road, Chelsea. Another 35 people were badly hurt. A week later, a bomb was planted under the car of Sir Stuart Pringle, the former commandant general of the Marines. Sir Stuart was seriously wounded. On 26 October 1981 bomb disposal officer Ken Howarth was killed by an IRA booby-trap in the Oxford Street Wimpy Bar. Another explosive device was defused in Debenhams. The attorney general in 1981, Sir Michael Havers, was lucky to be away from home on 13 November: a time-bomb devastated his bedroom.

Another IRA terrorist high on Scotland Yard's wanted

list, who was present at the war council summit outside Dundalk in January 1986 was Patrick Murray. He was suspected of having conspired with Patrick Magee in the attempt to assassinate Prime Minister Margaret Thatcher and other senior members of her Government. Magee was jailed in 1984 for the bombing outrage at the Grand Hotel, Brighton. He was also believed to be a ringleader of the 1983 blitz on London. *On 10 December a time-bomb outside Woolwich Barracks injured three members of the military staff. Three days later, a time-bomb was discovered in Phillimore Gardens and made safe. The police had reason to believe that a Member of Parliament was the target. Eight days before Christmas, a car bomb outside Harrods killed six people. Three of the dead were police officers. The number of people injured totalled 92.*

O'Callaghan had to report on his American and Dutch expeditions. He informed the meeting that for £5000, plus costs, Bent Timman would murder John Stalker in Manchester. O'Malley had introduced O'Callaghan to Timman as an Orangeman. Timman was a professional killer, with no allegiances and no interest in politics. It was important that Timman understood O'Callaghan (Brennan) to be a Protestant. The plot was for the murder of Stalker to be blamed on the Belfast Protestant extremists, or even the RUC itself, providing a propaganda extravaganza for the IRA and its Republican fanatics. The killing would have to coincide with Stalker's planned return to Belfast, ideally the day of his departure. The job had to be subcontracted because O'Malley, Glenholmes and Murray were not prepared to chance a trip to England. None of them was confident of being able to slip into England undetected, whatever their disguise and however credible their papers. It was not a job that could be done in a day. Stalker's movements, habits and routine would have to be documented. O'Callaghan estimated that Timman would need to be in Britain at least a fortnight. An essential element of the plot was to distance

253

the IRA from the assassination. Word on the grapevine pointed to Stalker having reached a decision that a number of IRA suspects had been cold-bloodedly murdered by the RUC's special task force. Would the IRA kill a senior British policeman who was in the process of embarrassing the Protestant-orientated RUC? Of course not. How neat, therefore, the wile.

There was an argument over whether the IRA should be instrumental in establishing a drugs market in Ireland, both sides of the border, for American traffickers. Some felt that it would be counter-productive. O'Callaghan asked, 'How else do we pay for the hardware? We have to pay in the only currency we can afford.' After a sometimes barbed debate, tacit approval was given.

Not everyone at that meeting was who they seemed. One IRA lieutenant had been a Special Branch mole for more than two years, probably the most precarious tight-rope-walking act on earth. Before noon the next day, a Special Branch officer had a comprehensive report of the previous night's meeting.

O'Malley was never picked up for questioning by the FBI or any of the other US law enforcement agencies, such as the DEA. Presumably, they did not want to scare off bigger fish, also hoping that O'Malley would lead them to racketeers not yet known to the crime-fighters.

On 17 February the same year, O'Malley flew from New York to Miami. After staying two nights at a hotel in Biscayne Bay, he caught a plane to Nassau in the Bahamas. He has never been seen since, his tracks going cold at Nassau's international airport. No one knows where and with whom – if anybody – he stayed. Neither is there a record of his re-entering the United States at any sea or air port. He could, of course, have returned with a false identity.

Almost simultaneously, Evelyn Glenholmes and Patrick Murray disappeared from circulation in the Republic of Ireland.

254

Stalker was never told about the IRA threat to his life. My information is that Stalker was not tipped off nor offered extra protection because 'he was only in danger if he resumed his role in Ulster'; a specious contention. Unless there was an official conspiracy to subjugate Stalker, there could have been no reason for anyone to doubt that he would be returning to Belfast to complete his assignment. Cynics could be forgiven for wondering whether or not the British Secret Service might have judged the sacrifice of Stalker an acceptable gambit. Even a blessing.

Neither did the Special Branch feel disposed to warn Anderton of an IRA death plot, substituting the Greater Manchester chief constable for his deputy, still employing Timman, after it was announced publicly that Stalker had been grounded.

By then, Anderton had talked about his conversion to Catholicism. The Special Branch mole within the IRA reported that if the assassination bid proved successful, a call claiming responsibility would be made to the Manchester police, purporting to come from the Loyalists.

Proof of a planned IRA initiative in Manchester was provided in June 1988 at an Old Bailey trial, when a Scotland Yard explosives expert revealed how he unearthed a deadly arsenal beneath a layer of soil and pine needles in a forest near Manchester. Two Irishmen had been followed by an undercover team of detectives as they buried nearly 200lbs of explosives. The cache, the prosecution claimed, could have been used to make 25 bombs and 'to sustain a prolonged campaign of terrorist violence'. With the explosives, which were buried in five plastic dustbins, were a ready-made radio-controlled bomb and three AK assault rifles and two pistols.

'A few people have been trying to harm me for many years now,' said Anderton. 'I have to be very careful. I'm more concerned for my wife than for myself. There's no way of establishing an infallible personal security screen

255

and also doing properly the job of chief constable. There are times when I have to be exposed. All I can do is reduce the risk to a tolerable minimum. For the rest of the time, I have to rely on luck.'

In April 1987 Anderton made clear his position on drugs. Speaking at the national Drugs Conference of the Association of Chief Police Officers, he said that a 'softly-softly' approach in cities where rival drugs gangs were fighting for territory was 'clearly a recipe for disaster'. The conference, attended by foreign police chiefs as well as those from Britain, heard Anderton plead for a re-think of attitudes towards the enforcement of drugs laws. 'There are demands from many sides, particularly among some intellectual elite, for the more frequent exercise of substantial police discretion towards persons apparently guilty of the unlawful use of drugs and for their compassionate treatment and care – the victims of the system as they are called. Experience shows, however, that so long as the market prevails, and so enormous are the profits to be made, there will always be new drugs barons waiting eagerly to step into the shoes of those who are taken out of circulation by the law enforcement agencies.'

Anderton argued that there was a good reason for not relaxing attitudes towards the drug-user, including those who preferred soft drugs. The condoned use of drugs, such as cannabis, created a developing indifference and a social climate in which the use of hard drugs was more likely. He feared gang warfare in a climate in which even the police felt intimidated. 'As in all the many facets of policing, a proper balance has to be struck between the need for strict law enforcement on the one hand and appropriate compassion, care and rehabilitation on the other. At the end of the day, however, somebody has to convince offenders that they are wrong and that, surely, is a perfectly legitimate job for the police to do.'

On 26 March 1986, Bent Timman flew to Libya for a *business* assignation with the masterminds of Gadaffi's international terrorist squads. The movements of Timman since that date have remained a mystery. Since then, however, the flow of arms to the IRA from Libya has become common knowledge.

19

New Climax

The campaign to have Anderton removed from office, either by shaming him into retirement or forcing the Home Secretary to act, reached a new climax at the end of 1987, triggered by two media interviews, one in a woman's magazine and the other on radio. In *Woman's Own*, Anderton was reported as saying that he discussed with his wife thugs who used gratuitious violence and that he had come to the conclusion that 'Corporal punishment should be administered so that they actually beg for mercy. They should be punished until they repent of their sins. I'd thrash some criminals myself, most surely. I could punish people quite easily.' Nothing new in that: for years Anderton has been trotting out those sentiments and they appear in an earlier chapter of this book. However, attributed to him in minor headline status within the magazine article, was the phrase, 'I'd be happy to thrash some criminals myself', which was pounced upon by his hawkish opponents on the Police Authority. Renewed demands for his resignation were derisively dismissed by Anderton and his camp. 'The game goes on,' said a source very close to Anderton. 'They know they won't get him out over this, but they're trying to wear him down and make him tire of the hassle. Fat chance! The more they lean, the more he'll push back. They never learn. Mr Anderton will go when *he's* ready . . . and not a minute before. In fact, the longer they hound him, the longer he's likely to stay, just to spite them.'

Meanwhile, Anderton was taking the magazine to task, pointing out that he had never used the word 'happy' and he had a tape-recording of the interview as proof. The word *happy* was certainly not in the text and he hoped that those critics who had been so quick to condemn would be equally prompt to apologise. He also commented that there was nothing new in the *Woman's Own* story, which is not strictly true. Deep in the second column of type was a reference to his Home Office meeting, when the formula for a truce was drawn up between himself and his Police Authority. He was quoted as saying – it is not something that is disputed and it is also on tape, 'I listened to their advice and then carried on as I always have done and always will.' That, more than his reaffirmed commitment to corporal punishment, precipitated the fresh round of huffing and puffing. The Police Authority felt slighted.

The second interview which was responsible for raising temperatures was given by Anderton to an Irish radio station, during which he described gay sex as 'an abomination that should never have been legalized', prompting a prominent member of his Police Authority to declare, 'Enough is enough. This man has to go. He has become a legend in his own mind.'

During the programme, Anderton had elaborated, referring to the legislation on homosexuality, 'I think it was one of the worst changes in legislation ever enacted in this country, and those who were instrumental in changing the law, if they are still alive, will surely live to regret it. It is an abomination. How anyone could say it is not sinful or against the law to engage in practices of that kind is beyond my comprehension. I abhor it.' Of AIDS patients, he said, 'I do not think anyone deserves to get it. The fact that they have got it is a consequence of their own malpractice. They had a choice and they chose to ignore the risks and, therefore, suffered the consequences. That is part of the natural order of things in God's creation. To that extent, it is a judgment of God because what they did was inevitable and they chose to ignore it, so they must accept the consequences.'

Most of Anderton's speeches these days are recycled: this one was no exception. The fact that the Police Authority decided that Anderton should face a special disciplinary committee hearing was not because the Chief Constable's speeches were becoming more rabid, but merely indicated a re-charged resolve to try to unseat him, however remote the prospects.

So it was that Anderton was informed that he would have to defend himself on 29 January before the committee. The committee comprised six Labour Party members, one Conservative, a Liberal, and three magistrates. A statement from the Authority said that the committee would be consulting 'top barristers', and that the investigation would concentrate on Anderton's 'lastest outbursts', which 'contravened the agreement with the Home Office', something Anderton disputed.

The tripartite understanding negotiated between the Home Office, Anderton and the Greater Manchester Police Authority fell considerably short of constituting a binding contract. It was generally understood that Anderton would *endeavour* to clear with the Authority any *new* opinion which he planned to make public, if it could *reasonably* be *interpreted* as contentious or divisive. 'How could a repeat speech possibly be seen as a new opinion?' chuckled a senior member of Anderton's camp. Suddenly semantics had become the name of the game.

A day later, it was announced that the special disciplinary committee would also examine 'other statements' made by Anderton, including claims that AIDS victims were 'swirling around in a cesspool of their own making', a speech which dated back to the previous Christmas. 'Seems like they believe in trying a man over and over again for the same offence until they get a jury that convicts,' observed one senior policeman on Anderton's private staff.

A few days later, the Police Authority changed its mind and decided that its disciplinary committee would meet in private, which suited Anderton. He had already made other arrangements for that day: he would be at St Dunstan's Church, Moston, in the city of Manchester, where he was to be received into the Roman Catholic Church. It was a very private service: Joan was there, but not Gillian, who was at work. There was no question of Joan converting to Roman Catholicism, once again scuppering the myth that Anderton manipulates his wife.

Friday 29 January had become billed as the day on which Anderton's fate would be decided, a preposterous notion. The Police Authority would have no more power on 29 January 1988 than they had on all the previous dates when they had tried, with spectacular failure, to rid themselves of the cross on their back. It was nothing more than another bout of shadow-boxing. 'They couldn't get their act together if they hired a Hollywood director!' was an example of the scorn which poured forth from Chester House. A more considered opinion from the eleventh floor of police headquarters was, 'It appears that their lawyers are having a hard time assembling a case. They're now talking about a private hearing at the end of March, when a decision will be taken whether or not to instigate a full inquiry. In the meantime, business as normal.'

An uncompromising warning to those people who were eager to oust Anderton came at the end of the *Woman's Own* piece, when he said, 'But if there was a whisper that I was leaving because of that [meaning outside pressure], I would serve until I was 65 – just to confound them.'

Many people are puzzled by the monotonous regularity of Anderton's press interviews, bearing in mind the equal regularity of his protests that he has been misinterpreted. Why does he persist in baring himself for the lash of the tabloid headlines and the cruel cut of the cartoonists' imagination? There is no mystery, nothing Freudian. The truth is that he trusts the public more than he does his peers and politicians. Dealing direct with the public is his concept of genuine democratic accountability. 'Live' television and radio are his favourite media, because the risk of biased editing is eliminated. Newspapers, he knows, will always lampoon him, but he would rather be misquoted than ignored, something he has in common with the politicians he distrusts.

Many people feel duty-bound to dislike Anderton, but find that hard to sustain when in his company. He even 'charmed' John Mortimer, that devout and delightful sceptic and master of courtroom cross-examination. Like myself, Mortimer was influenced by Anderton's 'ever-charming smile', genial soft voice, and humour. They are yet more puzzles and contradictions. 'The charm of his company, which is undoubted, lies in the constant element of surprise,' wrote Mortimer, in his book *The Character*.

Anderton's radical roots constantly become tangled with his conservative reputation, so that it is impossible to separate them. Of young black people in *his* city, he has said, 'My family didn't live in Manchester, theirs did. They have more right to be here than I have. And what are we offering them? No jobs. No future. Nothing.' He confounded Mortimer by opining that 'half the people in prison should never be there', his sense of timing impeccable as he stretched the pause, before unleashing the sting in the scorpion's tail, 'although the other half should never be let out.' Neither is it an insignificant boast that he has sacked more officers than any other chief constable, but he is on record as being opposed to a suspect's right to silence. 'Everyone is accountable to God and his fellow men. So a man's silence should be some evidence against him. We owe God an explanation. He calls on us to explain our conduct, once it's questioned.' Neither does he favour the use of tape-recorders for interrogation purposes, yet feels justified in using them when conversing on his office telephone.

In his autobiography, John Stalker portrays Anderton as cold and heartless. Stalker bitterly describes a four-day silence after his reinstatement, during which time Anderton made no contact. 'He knew I was going to be back at my desk that day, but he did not telephone. I can say that his four-day silence after my reinstatement seemed to me another indication of childish discourtesy. But much worse, in my view, it was unprofessional and showed a disregard for the efficiency of the Force.' Stalker, of course, must qualify in courtroom parlance as a hostile witness. Anderton may have faults, but a lack of emotion is not one of them. If anything, he is over-demonstrative: so many of his watersheds have been flooded by tears. Although Anderton rates himself progressive, I sense that he trusts the past more than the future. Scarcely a day goes by without him nibbling at nostalgia for sustenance. He remains thankful for his hard military days, when he spent most of his nights tackling brawling drunks in some of Europe's toughest and most bawdy neighbourhoods. 'I suppose it was the moment of truth, a time for coming to terms with the harsher realities of life.'

The streets of Manchester would have been daunting, perhaps overwhelming, he says, if he had not been initiated in the ghettoes north of the border. He reflects thus on his bobby-on-the-beat days, 'I certainly saw something of the tragedy, the heartache, the humour, the joy and the courage that go to make up the daily lot of the majority of people. Like all policemen, I came into contact with every level of society and learned what it was to try to be all things to all men. And that, if you can succeed, is a good lesson. I think it is fair to say that the pavements of Manchester were the best possible training ground for an aspiring young bobby like myself. Without the aid of a personal radio and a fast car, one had to meet the needs of the public on their own ground and in such a thriving, cosmopolitan city that could be a testing experience.'

Anderton flinches if anyone makes reference to his *subordinates*. 'The men who serve with me are not subordinates. I don't like that word and never have. Senior officers should look upon their juniors as serving with them, rather than under them.' His attitude to others, he says, is a legacy of his youth. 'I learnt quickly that people matter most of all and that inessential material gains were simply a bonus. And I honestly believe that my life was immeasurably enriched by true values and the insights impressed on me by them. As my life and career have progressed, I have, as a result of that early experience, been better able to understand and appreciate human failings. And I also hope that I have been able to exercise a better judgment of problems facing the community and often caused by the conditions in which people have to live.' He sees a great similarity between the preacher in the pulpit, the prisoner in the dock, and the policeman in the witness box: each, in his own way, required to account for himself to his conscience, his fellow men, and his Maker.

There is never any conflict for Anderton between celestial and terrestrial law. 'Personally, I feel as much at home in church as I do in a charge office, in a cathedral or a court of law. They are places where the determination of truth and justice, and a concern for human welfare should be the paramount considerations for all who pass through them. It is not enough to correct what has gone wrong. We must discover why it went wrong in the first place and then try to prevent it happening again.

'Christianity can only be right for me if it allows me to see the non-Christian point of view. It can only make sense if the door to understanding remains open. It grows in strength only if I allow it to face and withstand the arguments and the criticisms of those who would claim that its doctrines are false. If my proclamation has any substance at all, I have to recognise that non-Christians and atheists are all children of God. A practising Christian can, however, be an extremely unpopular chap, not because of the restrictions he puts on himself, but for the demands he makes on other people. A Christian who takes his stand, who declares his love of God, is throwing down the gauntlet and must be prepared to meet, and even at times suffer, the consequences.'

The *misuse* of leisure continues to trouble Anderton. 'I am not for a moment suggesting that pleasure, as such, is necessarily sinful, nor do I wish to give the impression that I am a killjoy. Nothing could be further from the truth. But I am becoming increasingly alarmed that pleasure is fast developing into something which is regarded as a justifiable end in itself, with no proper thought being given to its real effect on the individual engaged in it or on the society in which it takes place. Pleasure should be like a piece of a jigsaw puzzle which, properly fixed into the whole picture of life, makes it complete and recognisable and sensible. A piece of a puzzle intentionally kept separate, deliberately put on one side, is useless and meaningless, and that which it is designed to complement remains incomplete. The true purpose of the piece only becomes apparent when it fills the gap and when it is seen in relation to all the other pieces. And so it is with our lives. Pleasure has no place on its own. Its purpose is, or should be, to refresh our minds, bodies and spirits, so that the whole of our lives may be purposeful. Far too many of us today are living selfish lives with personal pleasure and self-satisfaction operating as both the mainspring and the goal.'

Stalker's autobiography, published in February 1988, caused a furore in Parliament and renewed demands for charges to be levelled against officers in the Royal Ulster Constabulary who were deemed to have been guilty of conspiring to pervert the course of justice. In Parliament, the Attorney General, Sir Patrick Mayhew, reported that prosecutions would be against the public interest. During his speech, Sir Patrick said that the inquiry, concluded by Colin Sampson who replaced Stalker, had been unable to substantiate accusations of more serious offences, a reference to the conspiracy to murder allegations. During the heated debate, Ken Livingstone, the MP for Brent East, was suspended for five days, when he accused Sir Patrick of being 'an accomplice to murder'. When called upon by the Speaker of the House, Bernard Weatherill, to withdraw or rephrase his remark, Livingstone refused and the Members voted 166 – 16 to suspend him. Kevin McNamara, Labour's Ulster spokesman, detected 'a government gag . . . incredible beyond belief.' The House echoed to the cries of 'cover-up'.

Anderton was considerably dismayed by some of Stalker's recollections and interpretations. Stalker wrote of returning to work on a Saturday – his first day back after the Sampson inquiry into him – and being on his own; no Anderton, no reception committee, no red carpet. 'The staff of the chief constable's office never work on a Saturday,' a senior member of it explained. 'Of course there was no one there: Stalker should have been surprised if there had been. It was a contrived situation.' Staged to evoke more anti-Anderton publicity? Anderton's supporters see it that way.

Stalker seems particularly distressed by the 'Last Supper' working dinner party on Tuesday, 27 May 1985 at the Moss Nook restaurant in Manchester, an issue described more fully in a previous chapter. Outside the restaurant, Anderton gave Stalker a file for a meeting on the Friday at the Home Office: that much is mutually agreed. The following day, Stalker received a telephone call from Roger Rees, the Clerk to the Greater Manchester Police Authority, who said that certain allegations had been made against the deputy chief constable and that he should be in his office at ten o'clock the next morning to speak to Colin Sampson, chief constable of

West Yorkshire, who would be investigating them. Stalker accuses Anderton of hypocrisy. He believes that the presentation of the papers for the Friday conference was a charade, because the chief constable must have known that the guillotine was about to drop. Anderton, on the other hand, denies any suggestion that he was sporting with his deputy. He admits he was aware that something was going to happen very soon but, even at that late stage, claims he was not privy to the forthcoming timetable of events.

In the meantime, everything had to go on as normal. The file given to Stalker was a genuine one, and at the time it was entrusted to him, there was every chance that he would be attending the meeting on the Friday. Still Stalker cannot fathom why Anderton did not give him some warning, just a word even, of what to expect. The answer is no more devious than Anderton's uncompromising commitment to impartiality. We are back to Anderton's revulsion at double standards. If it was right for him to tip off his deputy, why should every suspect in the land not be forewarned? Why should a senior police officer expect privileged treatment? Anderton does not subscribe to the Old Pals' Act. 'It would have been easy for Mr Anderton to have said something, but it would also have been wrong,' asserted one of the chief constable's senior aides. 'Mr Anderton took the hard way, but he has a clear conscience. He played it by the book.'

Anderton is on record as saying, 'In my opinion, a man who joins the service cannot escape the increased constraints placed on him by virtue of his new office. A policeman should not simply please himself what he does or how he behaves off duty, regardless of his position. However much they like to believe they are ordinary members of the public in uniform, the truth is that the public expect from them and, indeed, from anyone in public life, a standard of irreproachable behaviour which the public may not themselves be prepared to emulate. It

267

is an old-age conflict between what society would have a police officer do and what they hope he will permit them to do. It is not good enough to lay claim to the belief that people in authority are merely representatives of those they command. Since all police officers are leaders in society, they must set their standards above the norm. They must be beyond reproach or criticism. They must accept the highest possible ideals and if they cannot uphold them, they should relinquish their station and step down.' He has since stood by this view.

Strenuously repudiated are claims that there was a conspiracy at the highest level, of which Anderton was a part, to bankrupt Stalker's findings and to have him sacked from the Northern Ireland inquiry. 'If there was such a conspiracy, why would the inquiry have been allowed to continue with virtually the same team?' is the point made by Manchester police headquarters. 'Why was the final report almost identical to the one Stalker prepared? The arithmetic's all wrong.'

Stalker was also peeved because he had not been included in the plans to re-open the Moors Murders case, with renewed digging at Saddleworth. 'That was an operational matter which isn't the business of a deputy chief constable,' said Anderton's aide. 'It's the concern of the investigating officer. In any case, Stalker was off duty when all the decisions were made. It was not a snub, just a matter of normal procedure. Everything had to be kept under wraps because it was so secret. The fewer people who knew, the better, but no slight was intended. There was life at stake.'

There is a theory that Stalker became over-sensitive, almost paranoid, after his return to duty. He writes of being frozen out by Anderton, but there is another version. 'Mr Anderton tried to involve Mr Stalker as much as possible, but he didn't want to know. He wouldn't join in, not even when he was in the Mess.' The gregarious mixer had become a loner. Was Stalker, in the end, a victim of his own bitterness?

It is worth remembering that it was Anderton who offered his hand on their first meeting after Stalker's reinstatement. And it was Stalker who refused it.

In February 1988, the Attorney General, Sir Patrick Mayhew, announced in the Commons that as a result of the Sampson/Stalker Report, certain officers would face disciplinary hearings in Northern Ireland, as opposed to criminal proceedings. The hearings were to be conducted by Charles Kelly, the chief constable of Staffordshire.

Meanwhile, Hermon dismissed Stalker's book as 'The Gospel according to St John'. On BBC television, he said, 'John Stalker was considered to be the most proficient detective investigator in the United Kingdom. I don't want to say too much about this. I believe there are many people who are more mature and more experienced who could have done it. I have got the proverbial duck's back. It runs off me. We can make mistakes. With what we have to do, there are bound to be mistakes. But they will be honest mistakes.'

Later, Sir John announced his intention to retire in 1989, stressing that his decision was not influenced by Stalker's allegations. 'A maximum of 10 years for any chief constable is quite enough.'

The task of filling Stalker's £35,000 a year post was a long and tedious one. The job had to be advertised twice in the *Police Review*. None of the first batch of applicants was considered suitable: there was a woman/from the Metropolitan Police and two of Anderton's men, one of them black-balling himself the moment he admitted being a Freemason. Peter Grimshaw, chairman of the Manchester Police Authority's personnel committee, said no officer should apply unless he had a sufficiently strong personality to hold his own with Anderton. 'You don't want a fellow who doesn't think he could work with a chief constable because he is frightened of him, but someone able to fight his corner.' In the end, David Wilmot, the deputy chief constable of West Yorkshire, was chosen. Anderton said he was 'delighted' with the appointment.

On Friday, February 20 1988, Anderton and his Police Authority announced yet another reconciliation, both partners promising to try harder to make the marriage work. Anderton agreed that if he was uncertain about the likely reaction to anything he might say, he would first consult Her Majesty's Inspectorate of Constabulary. As he left the meeting in Swinton town hall, he said, 'Today is the first day of the rest of my police career. I am very happy.'

Bibliography

Newspapers:

Sunday Times:

'Doubts and fears behind the Stalker investigation' by Chris Ryder and David Connett (22 June, 1986)

'Stalker: car snatch probe started investigation' (10 August 1986)

'Hot money link in Stalker report' by Barrie Penrose and David Connett (17 August 1986)

'A fair cop' by David Connett and Barrie Penrose (24 August 1986)

'Telling the truth, the whole truth, so help him God' (25 January 1987)

Sunday Times Magazine:

'Chief Constable James Anderton, a Profile' by Joan Bakewell (April 1979)

'A Life in the Day Of' by Alison Coles (26 July 1987)

Times:

'A Cromwell for the pure blue army' by Peter Davenport (11 September 1986)

271

Sunday Telegraph:

'Britain's toughest policeman' by David Rosenberg (7 January 1979)

'Trials of the long distance copper' by Alan Cochrane and Christopher Elliott (29 June 1986)

Sunday Telegraph Magazine:

'God's Policeman' by Lesley Garner (1 February 1987)

Post and Chronicle, Wigan:

The Donald Hanson Interview (10, 11, 12 March 1976)

Daily Telegraph:

'James Anderton: the puritan policeman' by John Gapper (11 September 1986)

Observer:

'The Stalking of Stalker' by David Leigh and Paul Lashmar (22 June 1986)

'Nosy police chief who refused to give up' by David Leigh, Paul Lashmar and Jonathan Foster (20 July 1986)

'RUC faked report on shot boy, Stalker found' by David Leigh and Jonathan Foster (27 July 1986)

'Lying pest behind the Stalker probe' by David Leigh, Paul Lashmar and Jonathan Foster (28 September 1986)

'Prophet on the thin blue line' (25 January 1987)

Observer Magazine:

'Chief Constable James Anderton', profile by Joan Bakewell (22 July 1978)

Guardian:

'The Terry Coleman Interview' (3 June 1978)

'Stalker's RUC inquiry' by Peter Murtagh and Paul Johnson (16 June 1986)

'The day they eavesdropped on a death' by Peter Murtagh (7 October 1986)

Independent:

'Police feeling mounts that Anderton must go' by Terry Kirby (13 January 1987)

Sunday Express:

'Why is it thought so strange that I pray every day?' by Michael Prince (25 January 1987)

'If I'd gone back to Ulster I'd be dead by now' by Michael Prince (20 December 1987)

Books:

Those Dark Satanic Mills (A. D. Gillies, Archivist, Wigan Record Office, 1981)

In Character by John Mortimer (Penguin, 1984)

Stalker – The Search for the Truth by Peter Taylor (Faber and Faber, 1987)

Stalker by John Stalker (Harrap, 1988)

Index